Allan Ashworth

M.Sc., A.R.I.C.S.

Formerly a lecturer in quantity
surveying, University of Salford

Contractual procedures in the construction industry

Second edition

Longman
Scientific &
Technical

Longman Scientific & Technical,
Longman Group UK Limited,
Longman House, Burnt Mill, Harlow,
Essex CM20 2JE, England
and Associated Companies throughout the world.

First published 1991

British Library Cataloguing in Publication Data
Ashworth, Allan
    Contractural procedures in the construction
    industry. — 2nd ed. — (Longman technician series)
    I. Title   II. Series
    346.41

ISBN 0-582-07617-X

Set in Times 10 on 11pt
Produced by Longman Group (FE) Limited
Printed in Hong Kong

To Margaret, Amanda, and Caroline

To Margaret, Amanda, and Christine

Contents

Preface to the second edition

The new edition of this book endeavours to reflect the changes which have occurred in the contractual procedures which are used in the construction industry. The process of change, whilst evolutionary and gradual, has gathered pace as we move towards the end of the twentieth century. There is also a sense in that nothing is new, that history is repeating itself and that the pendulum continues to swing to and fro. In contractual terms this is to some extent due to the influences from other countries, the dissatisfaction of present arrangements and to changes within the social and business aspects of society. In many cases it is also the result of a lack of a real understanding of human relations; since in essence that is what contractual arrangements are all about.

The industry has faced major changes in recent years due partially to changes in government legislation but also in response to a call for improved efficiency, effectiveness and economy. Subcontracting arrangements, the continued move towards different forms of contractor-designed projects and the response by the professions are all helping to reshape the construction industry and the methods which are used to link the employer or client with a completed construction project.

In preparing the second edition of this book I have tried to incorporate the changes which have occurred since the publication of the first edition. I have chosen to include a chapter on the *Joint Contracts Tribunal Intermediate Form of Building Contract*, since this is now being used more extensively in place of its competitors. I have also considerably enlarged the section dealing with procurement, largely in response to an absence of this material in other textbooks. I have added two chapters here. One is largely a scene setter with the other identifying those factors which should be considered prior to choosing a method of procurement. A major part of the book still, however, concentrates on a review of the *Joint Contracts Tribunal Standard Form of Building Contract* (known as JCT80) and this has been updated and amended where necessary.

The construction industry continues to be in a state of flux, enjoying rapid development, expansion and good fortunes for a season and then a period of decline. The construction tap acts as a regulator of government performance and this factor needs to be borne in mind during the selection and recommendation of procurement patterns and the application of contract types.

I would like to continue to express my appreciation to those from whom I have sought advice during the preparation of this second edition. I also wish to acknowledge the very real support of my wife and family who continue to show me their patience during such times.

Allan Ashworth,
York 1991

Preface to the first edition

The aim of this book is to provide a knowledge of the nature, purpose and legal requirements of a construction contract, and its application to the various types of project encountered in this industry. Although the book has been prepared largely with the needs of the higher technician in mind, it provides a good basis for anyone wishing to gain an understanding of contractual procedures within the construction industry.

The contents of the book have been divided into eight convenient sections, the largest of which includes a commentary on the *JCT Standard Form of Building Contract* (1980 edition). This commentary has grouped the clauses on the basis of common-theme chapters for easy reference purposes. A further section covers the contractual arrangements and conditions which are appropriate to subcontract works, both of a nominated and domestic type. The JCT group of forms are likely to be the most important conditions of contract with which builders, surveyors and architects need to be familiar.

The first section of the book provides for a brief introduction to the principles of contract law. Discerning students will, however, wish to read more widely. They should therefore be prepared to make reference from time to time to one or more of the standard textbooks dealing with the principles of law. It is anticipated, however, that students may have already a good understanding of that subject or are studying it concurrently with a study of contractual procedures.

Other sections of the book provide for a detailed description of the contractual methods and documents which can be used in the construction industry, and the parties normally encountered on a construction project.

A brief examination of the other forms of contract in common use is also included. The final sections describe arbitration procedures and some of the more common legal case law which is of interest and relevance when examining contract conditions.

In preparing this book I would like to express my thanks to my colleagues who have offered their advice, and to Mrs Frances Dewar who typed the manuscript in her usual, efficient manner.

Finally, I would like to express my very real appreciation of the support of my wife and family who have helped me in innumerable ways.

Allan Ashworth, 1985

Acknowledgements

We are indebted to the copyright holder RIBA Publications Ltd. for their kind permission in allowing us to reproduce extracts from the JCT Standard Form of Building Contract.

Part 1

Contract law

Chapter 1

The English legal system

There are many individuals within the construction industry who will, at some time in their careers, become professionally involved in either litigation or arbitration. The laws which are applied in the construction industry are both of a general and a specialist nature. They are general in the sense that they embrace the tenets of law appropriate to all legal decisions; and are special since the interpretation of construction contracts and documents requires a particular knowledge and understanding of the construction industry. It should be noted, however, that the interpretation and application of law will not be contrary to or in opposition to the established legal principles and precedents found elsewhere. It is appropriate at this stage to consider briefly the framework of the English legal system.

The nature of law

Law, in its legal sense, may be distinguished from scientific law or the law of nature and from the rules of morality. In the first case, scientific laws are not man-made and are not therefore subject to change. In the case of morality it is less easy to draw a distinction between legal rules and moral precepts. It may be argued, for example, that the legal rules follow naturally from a correct moral concept. The difference between the two is, perhaps, that obedience to law is enforced by the State whereas morals are largely a matter of conscience and conduct. The laws of a country are, however, to some extent an expression of its current morality, since laws can generally only be enforced by a common consensus. Law, therefore, may be appropriately defined as a body of rules for the guidance of human conduct but which may be enforced by the authorities concerned.

Classification of law

Law is an enormous subject and some specialization is therefore essential. A complete classification system would require a very detailed chart. Essentially the basic division in the English legal system is the distinction between criminal and civil law. Usually, the distinction will be obvious. It is the difference between being prosecuted for a criminal offence and being sued for a civil wrong. If the aim of the person bringing the case is to punish the defendant then it will probably be a criminal case. However, if the aim is to obtain some form of compensation or other benefit then it will generally be a civil case.

Alternative methods of classification are to subdivide the offences that are committed against persons, property or the state under these headings. Laws may also be classified as either public or private. Public law is primarily concerned with the state itself. Private law is that part of the English legal system which is concerned with the rights and obligations of the individuals.

Sources of English law

Every legal system has its roots, the original sources from which authority is drawn. The sources of English law can be categorized in the following ways:

Custom

In the development of the English legal system the common law was derived from the different laws associated with the different parts of the country. These were adapted to form a national law common to the whole country. Since the difference between the regions stemmed from their different customary laws, it is no exaggeration to say that custom was the principal original source of the common law. The term 'custom' has three generally accepted meanings:

1. General custom — accepted by the country at large.
2. Mercantile custom — principles established on an international basis.

3. Local custom — applicable only to certain areas within a country. The following conditions must be complied with before a local custom will be recognized as law:

(a) The custom must have existed from 'time-immemorial'. The date for this has been fixed as 1189.
(b) The custom must be limited to a particular locality.
(c) The custom must have existed continuously.
(d) The custom must be a reasonable condition in the eyes of the law.
(e) The custom must have been exercised openly.
(f) The custom must be consistent with, and not in conflict with, existing laws.

In some countries the writings of legal authors can form an important source of law. In England, however, because of tradition, such writings have in the past been treated with comparatively little respect. They are, therefore, rarely cited in the courts. This general rule has always been subject to certain exceptions and there are therefore 'books of authority' which are almost treated as equal to precedents. Many of these books are very old, and in some cases date back to the twelfth century.

Legislation

The majority of new laws are made in a documentary form by way of an Act of Parliament. Statute has always been a source of English law and by the nineteenth century it rivalled decided cases as a source. If statute and common law clash, then the former will always prevail, since the courts cannot question the validity of any Act. The acceptance by the courts of Parliament's supremacy is entirely a matter for history. Today it is the most important new source of law because:

(a) the complex nature of commercial and industrial life has necessitated legislation to create the appropriate organizations and legal framework;
(b) modern developments such as drugs and the motor car have necessitated legislation to prevent their abuse;
(c) there are frequent changes in the attitudes of modern society, such as that relating to females, and the law must thus keep in step with society.

Before a legislative measure can become law it must undergo an extensive process.

1. The measure is first drafted by civil servants who present it to the House of Commons or the House of Lords as a 'Bill'.
2. The various clauses of the Bill will already have been accepted and agreed by the appropriate government department prior to its presentation.

3. Before the Bill can become an Act of Parliament it must undergo five stages in each house.
    First reading — the Bill is introduced to the House.
    Second reading — a general debate takes place upon the general principles of the measure.
    Committee stage — each clause of the Bill is examined in detail.
    Report stage — the House is brought up to date with the changes that have been made.
    Third reading — only matters of detail are allowed to be made at this stage.

The length of time which is necessary for the Bill to pass through these various stages depends upon the nature and length of the Bill and how politically controversial it is. Once the bill has been approved and accepted by each House, it then needs the Royal Assent for it to become law.

A Public Bill is legislation which affects the public at large and applies throughout England and Wales. It should be noted at this point that Scottish law, although similar, is different from English law. A Private Bill is legislation affecting only a limited section of the population, for example, in a particular locality. A Private Member's Bill is a Public Bill introduced by a back-bench Member of Parliament as distinct from a Public Bill which is introduced by the government in power.

Delegated legislation arises when a subordinate body makes laws under specific powers from Parliament. These can take the form of:

(a) Orders in Council;
(b) Statutory Instruments;
(c) By-laws.

Whilst these are essential to the smooth running of the nation, the growth of delegated legislation can be criticized, because law making is transferred from the elected representatives to the minister, which is in effect the civil servants. The validity of delegated legislation can be challenged in the courts as being *ultra vires*, i.e., beyond the powers of the party making it, and thus making it void. The judicial safeguard depends on the parent legislation, i.e., the Act giving the powers. Often this is extremely wide and such a restraint may therefore be almost ineffectual.

All legislation requires interpreting. The object of interpretation is to ascertain Parliament's will as expressed in the Act. The courts are thus at least in theory concerned with what is stated and not with what it believes Parliament intended. A large proportion of cases reported to the House of Lords and the High Court involve questions of statutory interpretation and in many of these the legislature's intention is impossible to ascertain because it never considered the question before the court. The judge must then do what he thinks Parliament would have done had they considered the question.

Since Britain's entry into the European Community on 1 January 1973 it has been bound by Community Law. All existing and future community law which is self-executing is immediately incorporated into English law. A self-executing law therefore takes immediate effect and does not require action by the United Kingdom legislature.

Case law

Case law is often referred to as judicial precedent. It is the result of the decisions made by judges who have laid down legal principles derived from circumstances of the particular disputes coming before them. Importance is attached to this form of law in order that some form of consistency in application in practice can be achieved. The doctrine of judicial precedent is known as *stare decisis*, which literally means 'to stand upon decisions'. In practice, therefore, a judge, when trying a case must always look back to see how previous judges dealt with similar cases. In looking back the judge will expect to discover those principles of law which are relevant to the case he now has to decide. The decision he makes will therefore seek to be in accordance with the already established principles of law and may in turn develop those principles further. One fact which should be noted is that the importance of case law is governed by the status of the court which decided the case. The cases decided in a higher court will take precedence over the judgments in a lower court.

The main advantages claimed for judicial precedent are:

1. Certainty — because judges must follow previous decisions, a barrister can usually advise a client on the outcome of a case.
2. Flexibility — it is claimed that case law can be extended to meet new situations thereby allowing the law to adjust to new social conditions.

A direct result of the application of case law is that these matters must be properly reported and published and should be readily available for all future users. Consequently there is now available within the English legal system an enormous collection of law reports stretching back over many centuries. Within the construction professions a number of different firms and organizations now collate and publish law reports which are relevant to this industry. Computerized systems are also available to allow for rapid access and retrieval from such reports.

Examples

The following are some examples of how the above sources of English law are appropriate to the construction industry:

Custom   — Right to light
                 — Right of way

Legislation — Highways Act 1959
— Town and Country Planning Act 1971
— Local Government Act 1972
— Control of Pollution Act 1974

Cases — *Hadley* v. *Baxendale* 1854
— *Sutcliffe* v. *Thackrah and Others* 1974
— *Dawber Williamson Roofing* v. *Humberside County Council* 1979

The courts

There are a number of different courts in which civil actions may be tried. Cases are first heard in either the High Court or the County Court, and should an appeal be necessary, then the matter is brought to the Court of Appeal. Where the matter is still not resolved then it is brought to the House of Lords. Technical cases may be heard in the official referee's court. A further alternative is to allow the dispute to be settled through arbitration.

County Court

There are approximately 340 districts in England and Wales in which a County Court is held at least once a month. These are divided into 60 circuits, each with its own judge. A County Court can hear almost all types of civil cases. Its jurisdiction is limited to actions in contract and tort up to sums of £5,000; actions for the recovery of land where the net annual value for rating does not exceed £1,000; equity proceedings where the sum involved does not exceed £30,000 and some bankruptcy claims. These sums are kept under review. The main advantages claimed for County Courts are their lower costs and shorter delays before coming to trial. These are also the two similar reasons claimed for arbitration. The court comprises a circuit judge assisted by a registrar who is a solicitor of seven years' standing. The latter mainly performs administrative tasks but, with the leave of the judge, he may hear actions in which the defendant does not appear, admits liability or where the claim does not exceed £2,000.

In order to reduce litigation coming before the County Court, and enable those with very small claims to bring an action without fear of excessive court costs, a 'small claims' procedure is now available.

The High Court

The High Court hears all the more important civil cases. It is the lower half of the Supreme Court of Judicature and was brought into being under the Judicature Acts 1873—1875. It comprises three divisions which all have equal competence to try any actions, according to the pressure of work, although certain specific matters are reserved for each of them.

1. The Queen's Bench Division (known as QBD) deals with all types of common law work, such as contract and tort. This is the busiest division. Matters concerning the construction industry usually come to this High Court. The division is headed by the Lord Chief Justice and there are about 40—50 lesser judges. These are known as puisne (pronounced 'puny') judges. There are two specialist courts within QBD. The Commercial Court hears major commercial disputes, usually in private, with the judge hearing the case in the more informal role of an arbitrator. The Admiralty Court hears maritime disputes.
2. The Chancery Division deals with such matters as trusts, mortgages, deeds, and land, taxation and partnership disputes. The division, whilst nominally headed by the Lord Chancellor and the Master of the Rolls, is actually run by a Vice-Chancellor, with the help of about 10—12 lesser judges.
3. The Family Division deals with matters of family disputes such as probate and divorce. This Division is headed by a President and three lesser judges.

The High Court normally sits at the Strand in London but there are fifteen other towns to which judges of the High Court travel to hear common law claims.

The Court of Appeal

Once a case has been heard either party may consider an appeal. This means that the case is transferred to the Court of Appeal where three judges usually sit to form a court. The High Court has the right to refuse an appeal. In civil appeals the appellant has six weeks from the date of judgment in which to give the Court of Appeal formal notice of appeal. The appellant must specify the exact grounds on which the appeal is based and on which the lower court reached an 'incorrect' decision.

The civil division hears appeals on questions of law and of fact, rehearsing the whole of the evidence presented to the court below relying on the notes made at the trial. If the appeal is allowed the court may reverse the decision of the lower court, or amend it, or order a retrial. It can hear appeals about the exercise of discretion; for example, discretion as to costs.

Most appeals are heard by three judges, although some (e.g., appeals from County Court decisions) can be heard by only two judges. Decisions need not be unanimous. The head of the court is the Master of the Rolls, perhaps the most influential appointment in our legal system.

The House of Lords

Appeals from decisions of the Court of Appeal are made to the House of Lords, although leave must first be obtained to do so and this is sparingly given. Permission is only given if the appeal is of general legal importance. The Court used to sit in the Chamber of the House of Lords but since 1948 it has usually sat as an Appellate Committee in a committee room in the Palace of Westminster. The normal rule is that a case can only go to the House of Lords after it has been heard by the Court of Appeal, so the case progresses slowly up the judicial hierarchy. In exceptional circumstances it is possible to leap-frog over the Court of Appeal, but this is rarely done. There must be at least three judges for a committee to be quorate, although in practice appeals are heard by five judges.

All of the courts must apply statute law in reaching their decisions and, in general, the lower courts are bound by the decisions of the higher courts. In practice, the law resulting from a case to the House of Lords can only be changed by an Act of Parliament.

Arbitration

Arbitration is an alternative to litigation in the courts, and is widely used for the settlement of disputes which involve technical or commercial elements. The tribunal is chosen by the parties concerned, and the powers of the arbitrator largely depend upon agreement between these parties. Arbitration is more fully explained in Chapter 20.

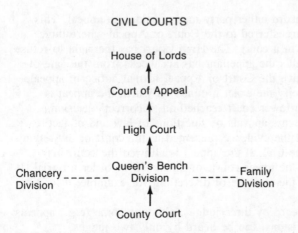

CIVIL COURTS

House of Lords

↑

Court of Appeal

↑

High Court

↑

Chancery Division — — — — — — Queen's Bench Division — — — — — — Family Division

↑

County Court

Fig. 1.1 The court system

The lawyers

Solicitors

There are around 60,000 solicitors in England and Wales. They are the lawyers that the public most frequently meets and as such are the general practitioners of the legal profession. A solicitor's work falls into two main categories of court work and non-court work. The latter accounts for about three-quarters of their business. A solicitor operates in many ways like a businessman, with an office to run, clients to see and correspondence to be answered. Traditionally, property (conveyancing and probate) has been the main fee earner.

The Solicitors Act 1974 gave solicitors three monopolies: of conveyancing; probate; and suing and starting court proceedings. The conveyancing monopoly was, however, significantly eroded by the Administration and Justice Act 1985. This allowed for licensed conveyancers to do this work.

The Law Society is the solicitor's professional body and as such it has two roles. Firstly to act as the representative body of solicitors and secondly to ensure that proper professional standards are maintained and that defaulting solicitors are disciplined. It lays down the rules on professional conduct, the most important of which prohibits touting for business or unfair attraction of business. Advertising of solicitors' services is now allowed in the press and on the radio, but they must be very careful what they say about themselves. They cannot claim, for example, that they do a better job than another firm of solicitors.

Barristers

There are about 4,000 barristers in England and Wales. They are specialist advocates and the specialist advisors of the legal profession. About 10 per cent of the Bar is made up of Queen's Counsel. Whilst solicitors may appear in the lower courts, barristers have a monopoly over appearing in the higher courts. Some of their work is non-court work, such as advising on difficult points of law or on how a particular case should be conducted.

Barristers cannot form partnerships with other barristers; several barristers will, however, share a set of rooms, known as chambers, and employ clerical staff and a clerk between them. They will not, however, share their earnings in the way that a firm of solicitors would.

Some legal jargon

ad valorem   According to the value. For example, stamp duty on sale of land is charged according to the price paid.

affidavit	A written statement to be used as evidence in court proceedings.
attestation	The signature of a witness to the signing of a document by another person.
caveat emptor	Let the buyer beware.
certiorari	An order of the High Court to review and quash the decision of the lower court which was based on an irregular procedure.
chattels	All property other than freehold real estate.
consideration	Where a person promises to do something for another it can only be enforced if the other person gave or promised to give something of value in return. Every contract requires consideration.
counterclaim	When a defendant is sued he can include in his defence any claim that he may have against the plaintiff, even if it arises from a different matter.
custom	An unwritten law dating back to time immemorial.
defendant	A person who is sued or prosecuted, or who has any court proceedings brought against him.
enactment	An Act of Parliament, or part of an Act.
ex-parte	An application to the court by one party to the proceedings without the other party being present.
expert witness	One who is able to give an opinion on a subject. This is an exception to the rule that a witness must only tell the facts.
fieri facias	A court order to the sheriff requiring him to seize a debtor's goods to pay off a creditor's judgment.
frustration	A contract is frustrated if it becomes impossible to perform because of a reason that is beyond the control of the parties. The contract is then cancelled.
good faith	Honestly.
goodwill	The whole advantage, wherever it may be, of the reputation and connection of the firm.
in camera	When evidence is not heard in open court.
injunction	A court order requiring someone to do, or to refrain from doing something.
judicial review	An application made to the Divisional Court when a lower court or tribunal has behaved incorrectly.
limitation	Court proceedings must begin within a limitation period. Different periods exist for different types of claim.
liquidated sum	A specific sum, or a sum that can be worked out as a matter of arithmetic.
liquidator	A person who winds up a company.
moiety	One-half.
official referee	A layman appointed by the High Court to try complex matters in which he is a specialist.

plaintiff	Person who sues.
plc	A public limited company. Most used to call themselves 'Ltd' but changed this when UK company law was brought into line with EC law in 1981.
pleadings	Formal written documents in a civil action. The plaintiff submits a statement of claim and the defendant a defence.
pre-trial review	Preliminary meeting of parties in a County Court action to consider administrative matters and what agreement can be reached prior to the trial.
quantum meruit	As much as he has earned.
res ipsa loquitor	The matter speaks for itself.
retrospective legislation	An Act that applies to a period before the Act was passed.
seal	This used to be an impression of a piece of wax to a document. Now a small red sticky label is used instead. The absence of the seal will not invalidate the document, since to constitute a sealing neither wax, wafer, a piece of paper or even an impression is necessary.
sine die	Indefinitely.
special damage	Financial loss that can be proved.
specific performance	When a party to a contract is ordered to carry out his part of the bargain. Only ordered where monetary damages would be an inadequate remedy.
statute	An Act of Parliament.
statutory instrument	Subordinate legislation made by the Queen in Council or a minister, in exercise of a power granted by statute.
stay of proceedings	When a court action is stopped by the court.
subpoena	A court order that a person attends court, either to give evidence or to produce documents.
uberrimae fidei	Of utmost good faith.
unenforceable	A contract or other right that cannot be enforced because of a technical defect.
vicarious liability	When one person is responsible for the actions of another because of their relationship.
void	Of no legal effect.
voidable	Capable of being set aside.
with costs	The winner's cost will be paid by the loser.
writ	The document that commences many High Court actions.

Chapter 2

Legal aspects of contracts

A number of Acts of Parliament affect construction contracts, although it is only during this present century that they have begun to play any significant part. Historically the law of contract has evolved by judicial decisions, so that there now exists a body of principles which apply generally to all types of construction contract. These principles have been accepted on the basis of proven cases that have been brought before the courts.

Construction contracts are usually made in writing, using one of the standard forms available. The use of a standard form provides many advantages, and although standard forms are not mandatory in practice their use should be encouraged in all possible circumstances. It is important to remember, however, that the making of a contract does not require any special formality. A binding contract could be made by an exchange of letters between the parties, rather than signing an elaborate printed document. On some occasions a binding contract could be made by a gentlemen's agreement, i.e., by word of mouth. There are, however, many practical reasons why construction contracts for all but the simplest projects should be made using an approved and accepted form of contract.

Definition of a contract

A contract has been defined by Sir William Anson as 'a legally binding agreement made between two or more parties, by which rights are acquired by one or more to acts or forbearances on the part of the other or others'. The essential elements of this definition are as follows:

1. Legally binding. Not all agreements are legally binding. In particular there are social or domestic arrangements which are made without any intention of creating legal arrangements.
2. Two or more parties. In order to have an agreement there must be at least two parties. In law one cannot make bargains with oneself.
3. Rights are acquired. An essential feature of a contract is that legal rights are acquired. One person agrees to complete part of a deal and the other person agrees to do something else in return.
4. Forbearances. To forbear is to refrain from doing something. There may thus be a benefit to one party to have the other party promise not to do something.

Agreement

The whole basis of the law of contract is agreement. Specifically, a contract is an agreement bringing with it obligations which are able to be enforced in the courts if this becomes necessary. Most of the principles of modern contract date from the eighteenth and nineteenth centuries. The concept of a contract at that time was of equals coming together to bargain and reach agreement, which they would wish to be upheld by the courts. Whilst it is still true that individuals come together to form agreements, it should be recognized that many contracts are formed between parties who are not equals in any way, even where the law may pretend that they are. A major criticism of contract law in recent years has been that the wealthy, experienced and legally advised corporations have been able to make bargains with many people who are themselves of limited resources and poorly legally represented. Because of this the law of contract has gradually moved away from a total commitment to enforce, without qualification, any agreement which has the basic elements of a contract. In particular, Parliament has introduced statutes which are often designed to protect relatively weak consumers from businessmen having greater bargaining power. Despite this, the courts are still reluctant to set aside an agreement having all of the elements of a contract and in this respect follow their nineteenth-century predecessors.

The elements of a contract

Capacity

In general every person has full legal powers to enter into whatever contracts they might choose. There are, however, some broad exceptions to this general rule. Infants and minors, that is anyone under the age of eighteen years as set out in the Family Law Reform Act 1969, cannot contract other than in certain circumstances, such as, for example, for necessaries or benefits. Persons of an unsound mind, as defined in the Mental Health Act 1959, can never make a valid contract. Other persons of an unsound mind, and those unbalanced by intoxication are treated alike. Their contracts are divided into two types, those for necessary goods (the situation with minors above) and other contracts where the presumption is one of validity. Corporations are legal entities created by a process of law. A company can only contract on matters falling within its objects clause, and since the records of companies are matters of public record available for inspection at Companies House it used to be the case that a company could not have a contract enforced against it if it lay outside its object clause. The presumption was that those entering into contracts with a company knew or ought to have known the contents of the objects clause. Consequently anyone making an *ultra-vires* (outside-the-powers) contract with a company only had themselves to blame. On entry into the European Community in 1973 this *ultra-vires* doctrine had to be revised, since it is not followed in the other countries of the Community.

Intention to create legal relations

As mentioned earlier, merely because there is an agreement, it cannot be assumed that an enforceable contract exists. English law requires that the parties to a contract actually intended to enter into legal relations. These are relations actionable and enforceable in the courts. If it can be demonstrated that no such intention existed then the courts will not intervene, despite the presence of both agreement and consideration. In commercial agreements the courts presume that the parties do intend to enter into legal relations. (This is different from social, family and other domestic agreements, where the general rule is that the courts presume

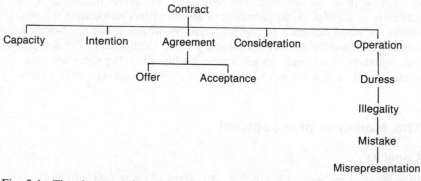

Fig. 2.1 The elements of a contract

that there is no intention to enter into legal relations.) These are the general rules and it is also possible to demonstrate the opposite intention.

In contract law we need to know what we have agreed. It is possible for two parties to use words which are susceptible to interpretation in different ways, so that they do not have the same idea in mind when they agree. It is important that both parties have agreement to the same idea (*consensus ad idem*). The classic case to which students should refer is *Raffles* v. *Wichelhaus* (1864).

Offer and acceptance

The basis of the contract is agreement and this is composed of two parts: offer and acceptance. In addition, conditions are generally required by law (in all but the simplest of contracts) to make the offer and acceptance legally binding.

The offer

An offer must be distinguished from a mere attempt to negotiate. An offer, if it is accepted, will become a binding contract. An invitation for contractors to submit tenders is inviting firms to submit offers for doing the work. The invitation often states that the employer is not bound to accept the lowest or any tender or to be responsible for the costs incurred.

An offer may be revoked by the person who made it, at any time before it is accepted. Thus a contractor may submit a successful tender in terms of winning the contract. He may, however, choose to revoke this offer prior to formal acceptance.

Tenders for building works do not remain on offer indefinitely. If they are not accepted within a reasonable time the offer may lapse, or be subject to some monetary adjustment should it later be accepted. The building owner may stipulate in his invitation to the tenderers that the offer should remain open for a prescribed period of time.

Offers concerned with building projects are generally made on the basis of detailed terms and conditions. The parties to the contract will be bound by these conditions, as long as they know that such conditions were incorporated in the offer, even though they may never have read them or acquainted themselves with the details.

In many instances with building contracts the offer must follow a stipulated procedure. Such procedures often incorporate delivery of the offer by a certain date and time, in writing, on a special form, and in a particular envelope, and stipulate that the offer must not be disclosed to a third party. Failure to comply with these procedures will result in the offer being rejected.

The acceptance

Once an agreeable offer has been made, there must be an acceptance of it before a contract can be established. The acceptance of the offer must be unconditional and it must be communicated to the person who made the offer. The unconditional terms of acceptance must correspond precisely with the terms of the offer. In practice, of course, the parties may choose to negotiate on the basis of the offer. For example, the building owner may require the project to be completed one month earlier and they may result in the tenderer revising his tender sum. A fresh offer made in this way is known as a counter-offer, and is subject to the conditions now applied.

An offer or acceptance is sometimes made on the basis of 'subject to contract'. In practice the courts tend to view such an expression of no legal effect. No binding contract will come into effect until the formal contract has been agreed.

Form

'Form' means some peculiar solemnity or procedure accompanying the expression of agreement. It is this formality which gives to the agreement its binding character. The formal contract in English law is the contract under seal — that is, one made by deed. The contract is executed — that is, it is made effective by being signed, sealed and delivered.

1. *Signature.* Doubts have been expressed regarding the necessity for a signature. Some statutes make a signature a necessity.
2. *Sealing.* Today this consists of affixing an adhesive wafer, or in the case of a corporate body an impression in the paper, and the party signs against this and acknowledges it as his seal.
3. *Delivery.* This is not now necessary for legal effectiveness. As soon as the party acknowledges the document as his deed, it is immediately effective.
4. *Witnesses.* These attest by signing the document. They are not usually a legal necessity.

Consideration

Another essential feature of a binding contract, other than a contract made under seal, is that the agreement must be supported by consideration. The most common forms of consideration are payment of money, provision of goods and the performance of work. Consideration has been judicially defined as 'some right, forbearance, detriment, loss or responsibility given, suffered or undertaken by the other in respect of the promise'. In building contracts the consideration of the contractor to carry out the works in accordance with the contract documents is matched by that of the building owner to pay the price. The following rules concerning consideration should be adhered to:

1. Every simple contract requires consideration to make it valid.
2. The consideration must be worth something in the eyes of the law. The courts are not concerned whether the bargain is a good one, but simply that there is a bargain.
3. Each party must get something in return for his promise, other than something he is already entitled to, otherwise there is no consideration.
4. The consideration must not be such that it conflicts with the established law.
5. The consideration must not relate to some event in the past.

Duress and undue influence

Duress is actual or threatened violence to, or restraint of the person of, a contracting party. If a contract is made under duress it is at once suspect, because consent has not been freely given to the bargain supposedly made. The contract is voidable at the option of the party concerned. Duress is a common law doctrine which relates entirely to the person and has no relation to that person's goods. As such it is a very limited doctrine and is one where cases are rare.

Unenforceable contracts

Contracts may be described as void, or voidable or unenforceable. A void contract creates no legal rights and cannot therefore be sued upon. It may occur because of a mistake as to the nature of the contract, or because it involves the performance of something illegal that is prohibited by a statute. A void contract will also result because of the incapacity of the parties, as in the case of infants. Corporations cannot make contracts beyond their stated powers which are said to be *ultra vires* — 'beyond one's powers'.

A contract is said to be voidable when only one of the parties may take advantage. In cases involving misrepresentation, only the party who has been misled has the right to a void in one of the ways previously described.

Unenforceable contracts are those that are valid, but owing to the neglect of the formalities involved a party seeking to enforce it will be denied a remedy.

Mistake

The law recognizes that, in some circumstances, although a contract has been formed, one or both of the parties are unable to enforce the agreement. The parties are at variance with one another and this precludes the possibility of any agreement. Mistake may be classified as follows:

1. *Identity of subject matter.* This occurs where one party intends to contract with regard to one thing and the other party with regard to another. The parties in this situation cannot be of the same mind and no contract is formed.
2. *Identity of party.* If the identity of either party enters into consideration, this will negate the contract.
3. *Basis of contract.* If two parties enter into a contract on the basis that certain facts exist, and they do not, then the contract is void.
4. *Expressing the contract.* If a written contract fails to express the agreed intentions of the two parties, then it is not enforceable. Courts may, however, express the true intention of the parties and enforce it as amended.

Misrepresentation

Misrepresentation consists in the making of an untrue statement which induces the other party to enter into a contract. The statement must relate to fact rather than opinion. Furthermore, the injured party must have relied on the statement and it must have been a material cause of his entering into the contract. Where such a contract is voidable it may be renounced by the injured party, but until such time it is valid. Misrepresentation may be classified as:

1. *Innocent misrepresentation* — where an untrue statement is made in the belief that it is true.
2. *Fraudulent misrepresentation* — which consists of an untrue statement made with the knowledge that it is untrue or made recklessly without attempting to assess its validity.
3. *Negligent misrepresentation* — is a statement made honestly, but without reasonable grounds for belief that it is true. It is really a special case of innocent misrepresentation, for, although the statement is made in the belief that it is true, insufficient care has been taken to check it.

Where misrepresentation occurs the injured party has several options open to him.

1. He can affirm the contract, when it will then continue for both parties.

2. He can repudiate the contract and set up misrepresentation as a defence.
3. An action can be brought for rescission and restitution. Rescission involves cancelling the contract and the restoration of the parties to the state that they were in before the contract was made. Restitution is the return of any money paid or transferred under the terms of the contract.
4. He can bring an action for damages. The claim for damages is only possible in circumstances of fraudulent misrepresentation.

Disclosure of information

When entering into a contract it is not always necessary to disclose all the facts that are available. A party may observe silence in regard to certain facts, even though it may know that such facts would influence the other party. This is summed up in the maxim, *caveat emptor* — 'let the buyer beware'.

There are, however, circumstances where the non-disclosure of relevant information may affect the validity of the contract. This can occur where the relevant facts surrounding the contract are almost entirely within the knowledge of one of the parties, and the other has no means of discerning the facts. These contracts are said to be *uberrimae fidei*, which interpreted means 'of the utmost good faith'.

Privity of contract

A contract creates something special for the parties who enter into it. The common law rule of privity is that only the persons who are party to the contract can be affected by it. A contract can neither impose obligations nor confer rights upon others who are not privy to it. For example, the clause in the *Standard Form of Building Contract* which allows the employer to pay money direct to the subcontractor may be used by the employer. It cannot be enforced by the subcontractor, however, since he is not a party to the main contract. He may seek to persuade the employer to adopt this course of action but he cannot enforce him to do so in a court of law.

Express and implied terms

The terms of contract can be classified as either express or implied. Those terms which are written into the contract documents or expressed orally by the parties are described as express terms. Those terms which were not mentioned by the parties at the time that they made the contract are implied terms, so long as they were in the minds of both parties. The courts will, where it becomes necessary, imply into building and engineering contracts a number of implied terms. Although the implied term is one which the parties probably never contemplated when making the contract, the courts justify this by saying that the implication is necessary in order to give business efficacy to the contract. This does not mean, however, that the courts will make a contract more workable or sensible. The courts, for example, will generally imply into a building contract the following terms:

1. The contractor will be given possession of the site within a reasonable time, should nothing be stated in the contract documentation.
2. The employer will not unreasonably prevent the contractor from completing the work.
3. The contractor will carry out the work in a workmanlike manner.

Implied terms which have evolved from decided cases often act as precedents for future events. In the majority of the standard forms of building contract all of these matters are normally express terms, since the contracts themselves are very comprehensive and hope to cover every eventuality.

There are some notable terms which are not normally to be implied into building and engineering contracts, such as, for example, the practicability of the design. However, there will be express or implied terms that the work will comply with the appropriate statutes.

Express terms

An express term is a clear stipulation in the contract which the parties intend should be binding upon them. Traditionally, the common law has divided terms into two categories of conditions and warranties.

1. Conditions. These are terms which go to the root of the contract, and for breadth of which the remedies of repudiation or rescission of the contract and damages are allowed.
2. Warranties. These are minor terms of the contract, for breach of which the only remedy is damages.

Implied terms

Implied terms are those which, although not expressly stated by the parties by words or conduct, are by law deemed to be part of the contract. Terms may be implied into contracts by custom, statute or the courts.

1. *By custom.* In law this means an established practice or usage in a trade, locality, type of transaction or between parties. If two or more people enter into a contract against a common background of business, it is considered that they intend the trade usage of that business to prevail unless they expressly exclude it.
2. *By statute.* There are many areas in the civil law where Parliament has interfered with the right of parties to regulate their own affairs. This interference mainly occurs where one party has used a dominant bargaining position to abuse this freedom. Thus in the sale of goods, the general principle *caveat emptor* (let the buyer beware) has been greatly modified, particularly in favour of the consumer by the provisions in the Sale of Goods Act 1979. In addition there have been important changes in relation to exemption clauses brought about by the Unfair Contract Terms Act 1977.
3. *By the courts.* The court will imply a term into a contract under the doctrine of the implied term, if it was the presumed intention of the parties that there should have been a particular term, but they have omitted to expressly state it.

Limitations of actions

Generally speaking, litigation is a costly and time-consuming process which becomes more difficult as the time between the disputed events and the litigation increases. Also rights of action cannot be allowed to endure for ever. Parties to a contract must be made to prosecute their causes within a reasonable time. For this reason Parliament has enacted limitation acts which set a time limit on the commencement of litigation. The rules and procedures in respect of limitation of actions are contained in the Limitation Act 1980. The right to bring an action can be discharged in three ways:

1. The parties to a contract might decide to discharge their rights.
2. Through the judgment of a court.
3. Through lapse of time.

If an action is not commenced within a certain time the right to sue is extinguished. Actions in a simple contract (not under seal) and tort become statute barred after six years. In the case of contracts under seal, then this period is extended to twelve years. The Act does permit certain extensions to these time limits in very special circumstances, for example, where a person may be unconscious as the result of an accident. If damage is suffered at a later date then this will not affect the limitation period, although an action for negligence may be pursued. The period of limitation can be renewed if the debtor acknowledges the claim or makes a part payment at some time during this period. A number of international conventions, particularly with respect to the law of carriage, lay down shorter limitation periods for action than those specified in the Act. For example, in carriage by air under the Warsaw Rules the period is two years.

The Unfair Contract Terms Act 1977

Contractual clauses designed to exonerate a party wholly or partly from liability from breaches of express or implied terms, first appeared in the nineteenth century. The common law did not interfere but took the view that parties forming a contractual relationship were free to make a bargain within the limits of the law. This is still largely the rule today although the growth of large trading organizations has led to an increase in both excluding and restricting clauses to the severe detriment of other parties.

The efforts of the courts to mitigate against the worst effects of objectionable exclusion clauses have been reinforced by the Unfair Contract Terms Act 1977. This Act restricts the extent to which liability can be avoided for breach of contract and negligence. The Act relates only to business liability and transactions between private individuals are not therefore covered. The reasonableness is further extended to situations where parties attempt to exclude liability for a fundamental breach, i.e., where performance is substantially different from that reasonably expected or there is no performance at all of the whole, or any part, of the contractual obligations. The following are subject to the Act's provisions:

1. Making liability or its enforcement subject to restrictive or onerous conditions.
2. Excluding or restricting any right or remedy.
3. Excluding or restricting rules of evidence or procedure.
4. Evasion of the provisions of the Act by a secondary contract is prohibited.

Contra proferentem

Any ambiguity in a clause in a contract will be interpreted against the party who put it forward. It is a general rule of construction of any document that it will be interpreted *contra proferentem*, that is, against the person who prepared the document. As an exclusion clause is invariably drafted by the imposer of it, this is an extremely useful weapon against exclusion clauses. The effect of the rule is to give the party who proposed the ambiguous clause only the lesser of the protections possible. The one who draws up the contract has the choice of words and must choose them to show clearly the intention he had in mind.

Agency

Agency is a special relationship whereby one person (the agent) agrees on behalf of another (the principal) to conclude a contract between the principal and a third party. Providing that the agent acts only within the scope of the authority conferred upon him, those acts become those of the principal, and he must therefore accept the responsibility for them. The majority of contractual relationships involve some form of agency. For example, the architect in ordering extra work is acting in the capacity of the employer's agent. The contractor may presume, unless anything is known to the contrary, that the carrying out of these extras will result in future payment by the client.

A contract of agency may be established by:

1. *Express authority* — that is, authority that has been directly given to an agent by his principal.
2. *Implied authority* — where because a person is engaged in a particular capacity, others dealing with him are entitled, perhaps because of trade custom, to infer that he has the necessary authority to contract within the limits usually associated with that capacity.
3. *Ratification* — that is, where a principal subsequently accepts an act done by his agent, even where this exceeds the agent's authority. This becomes as effective as if he originally authorized it.

In contracts of agency a principal cannot delegate to an agent powers which he himself does not possess. The capacity of the agent is therefore determined by the capacity of his principal.

Chapter 3

Discharge of contracts

A contract is said to be discharged when the parties become released from their general contractual obligations. The discharge of a contract may be brought about in several ways.

Discharge by performance

In these circumstances the party has undertaken to do a certain task and nothing further remains to be done. In general, only the complete and exact performance of the contractual obligations can discharge the contract. In practice, where a contract has been substantially performed, payment can be made with an adjustment for the work that is incomplete.

A building contract is discharged by performance once the contractor has completed all the work, including the making good of defects under the terms of the contract. The architect must have issued all the appropriate certificates and the building owner paid the requisite sums. If, however, undisclosed defects occur beyond this period the building owner can still sue for damages under the statute of limitations. The contract has not been properly performed if there are hidden defects.

Thus, A undertakes to sell to B 1,000 roof tiles. A will be discharged from the contract when he has delivered the tiles, and B when he has paid the price. A question sometimes arises whether performance by another party will discharge the contract. The general rule is that where personal qualifications are a factor of consideration, then that person must perform the contract. Where, however, personal considerations are unimportant it would not matter who supplied the goods.

Discharge under condition

Contracts consist of a large number of stipulations or terms. In many types of contract there are conditions which, although not expressed, are intended because the parties must have contracted with these conditions in mind. It will, however, be obvious that the terms and conditions of a building contract are not of equal importance. Some of the terms are fundamental to the contract, and are so essential that if they are broken the whole purpose of the contract is defeated.

Thus, if a contractor agreed to design and build a building for a specific use, and it is incapable of such a use, the building owner would be able to reject the project and recover the costs from the contractor.

Building contracts frequently contain a number of terms forming a specification. The builder agrees to construct the project in accordance with this specification. If the builder deviates from this in some small way then this will give rise to an action for damages and the contract will not be discharged.

It is, however, well established that subject to an express or implied agreement to the contrary, a party who has received substantial benefit under a contract cannot repudiate it for breach of condition.

Discharge by renunciation

This is effected when one of the parties refuses to perform his obligation. Thus, *A* employs an architect to design and supervise a proposed building project. On completion of the design, *A* decides not to continue with the project. This is renunciation of the contract and the architect can sue for his fees on a *quantum meruit* basis — that is, for as much as he has earned.

Discharge by fresh agreement

A contract can be discharged by a fresh agreement being made between the parties, which is both subsequent to and independent of the original contract. Such a contract may, however, discharge the parties altogether. This is known as a rescission of the original contract. Where one party to a contract is released by a third party undertaking his obligations, then the original contract discharged is termed 'novation'. Any alteration to a contract made with the consent of the parties concerned has the effect of making a new contract.

Frustration

A contract formed between two parties will expressly or impliedly be subject to the condition that it will be capable of performance. If the contract becomes incapable of performance then the parties will be discharged from it. Impossibility of performance is usually called frustration of contract. It occurs whenever the law recognizes that, without default of either party, a contractual obligation has become incapable of execution.

For example, the event causing the impossibility may be due to a natural catastrophe. A agrees to carry out a contract for the repair of a road surface, but prior to starting the work the road subsides to such an extent that it disappears completely down the side of a hill. Impossibility may also occur because a government may introduce a law that makes the contract illegal. For example, A contracts to carry out some insulation work using asbestos. The Government subsequently introduce legislation forbidding the use of this material in buildings, thus making the contract impossible to carry out. A contractor cannot, however, claim that a contract is frustrated if he deliberately causes a delay to avoid completion. For example, a contract for the building of a sea wall must be completed prior to winter weather setting in, otherwise practical performance will become impossible. The knowledge that this predictable event will occur, coupled with a deliberate delay, does not result in a frustration of the contract.

Examples of building contracts being frustrated are extremely rare. It should be noted that hardship, inconvenience or loss do not decide whether an occurrence frustrates the contract, because these are accepted risks. The legal effect of frustration is that the contract is discharged and money prepaid in anticipation of performance should be returned. A party receiving benefit from a partly executed contract should reimburse the other party to the value of that benefit.

Determination of contract

There are provisions in all the common forms of contract that allow either party to terminate the contract. There must, of course, be good reasons to support any party who decides to determine, otherwise a breach of contract can occur. Clause 27 of the Standard Form of Building Contract provides circumstances which allow the employer to terminate the contract with the contractor. In one sense they are fairly exceptional happenings, and so they should be, since they provide a final option to the employer. The decision to determine must be taken very carefully and reasonably. It generally occurs because the contractor is failing to take notice of instructions from the architect to remedy an already existing breach of contract. Clause 28 provides for determination because of either a refusal or interference with payments due to the contractor. It may also occur where the works are suspended for an unreasonable length of time. Again the action to determine must be carefully taken, and is a last-resort decision on the part of the contractor. He takes this decision when he feels that he can no longer continue, perhaps after a number of delays in payment, to work with the employer. Determination of contract by either party results in two losers and no winners. Although there are provisions in the contract for financial recompense to the aggrieved party, these rarely suffice.

Assignment

It sometimes happens that one party to a contract wishes to dispose of its obligations under it, but the extent to which this is permitted is limited. The other party may have valid reasons why it prefers the obligations to be performed by the original contractor. The rule is that liabilities can only be assigned by novation. This is the formation of a new contract between the party who wishes performance and the new contractor, who is accepted as adequately qualified to perform as the original contractor. Liabilities can only be assigned by consent. By contrast, rights under a contract can usually be assigned without consent of the other party, except where the subject matter involves a personal service. Even, however, in those circumstances where the contract does not involve personal service, but specifically restricts the right to assign the contract or any interest in it to a third party then the assignment of rights will not be permitted.

Chapter 4

Remedies for breach of contract

A breach of contract occurs when one party fails to perform an obligation under the terms of the contract. For example, a breach of contract of the JCT 80 conditions of contract occurs if:

(a) the contractor refuses to obey an architect's instruction (clause 4);
(b) the employer fails to honour an architect's certificate (clause 28);
(c) the contractor refuses to hand over certain antiquities found on the site (clause 34);
(d) the contractor fails to proceed regularly and diligently with the works (clause 23).

Defective work is not necessarily in breach of contract, as long as the contractor rectifies it in accordance with an architect's instruction. A breach will occur where the contractor either refuses to remove the defective work or ignores the remedial work required.

A breach of contract may have two principal consequences:

1. Damages.
2. If the breach is sufficiently serious, then determination by the aggrieved party under the terms of the contract. The aggrieved party may decide to terminate the contract with the other, and also sue for damages, or alternatively take only one of these courses of action.

Damages may include both the loss resulting from the breach, the loss flowing from the termination and the additional costs of completing the contract.

Damages

There is, with few exceptions, the rule that no one who is not a party to the contract can sue or be sued in respect of it. There may be other remedies, for instance in tort, but these are beyond the scope of this book.

The legal remedy for breach of contract is damages. This consists of the award of a sum of money to the injured party, designed to compensate for the loss sustained. The basis of the award of damages is by way of compensation. The damages awarded are made in an attempt to recompense the actual loss sustained by reason of the breach of contract. The injured party is to be placed, as far as money can do it, in the same situation as if the contract had been performed. It should be clearly understood that not every breach automatically results in damages. In order for damages to be paid, the injured party must be able to prove that a loss resulted from the breach. Furthermore, the innocent party must take all reasonable steps to mitigate any loss. Damages may be classified as follows.

Nominal damages

Where a party can show a breach of contract, but cannot prove any sustained loss as a result, then nominal damages may be awarded. These comprise merely a small sum in recognition that a contractual right has been infringed.

Substantial damages

These damages represent the measure of loss sustained by the injured party. Despite their name they might be quite small.

Remoteness of damage

A breach of contract can, in some circumstances, create a chain of events resulting in considerable damage, and the question may arise whether the injured party or parties can claim for the whole of the damage sustained. In ordinary circumstances, the only damages that can be claimed are those which arise immediately because of the breach. Damage is not considered too remote if the parties at the time the contract was entered into contemplated that it could occur. If the contract specifies the extent of the liability, then no question of consequential damages arise. Defects liability clauses, which require the builder to rectify defects, do not limit the extent of the remedial work, but may also require other work to be put right that has resulted from these defects.

Special damage

Damages resulting from special circumstances are recoverable if they flow from a breach of contract, and that the special circumstances were known to both parties at the time of making the agreement.

Liquidated damages

Each of the standard forms of contract provide for payment of agreed damages by the contractor when completion of work is not within the stipulated time. These payments are known as liquidated damages, and their amount should be recorded on the appendix to the form of a contract. The sum stated should be a genuine estimate of the damage that the building owner may suffer. If, however, the sum stated is excessive and bears no relation to the actual damage, then it may be regarded as a penalty. In these circumstances the courts will not enforce the amount stated in the contract but will assess the damage incurred on an unliquidated basis. Liquidated damages may be estimated on the basis of loss of profit in the case of commercial projects, but they are much more difficult to determine in the case of public works projects such as roads.

In some circumstances a building owner may seek the occupation of a project even though it remains incomplete. This would normally deprive him of the right to enforce a claim for liquidated damages.

Unliquidated damages

When no liquidated damages have been detailed in the contract, the employer can still recover damages should the contractor fail to complete on time. The sum awarded in this case is that regarded as compensation for the loss actually sustained by the breach.

Specific performance

Specific performance was introduced by the courts for use in those cases where damages would not be an adequate remedy. In building contracts this remedy is only really available in exceptional circumstances. The courts will enforce a party to do what it has contracted to do, in preference to awarding damages to the aggrieved party. A decree of specific performance will not be granted where the court cannot effectively supervise or enforce the performance.

Injunction

Injunction is a remedy for the enforcement of a negative undertaking. A party is prohibited from carrying out a certain action. It is often awarded by the courts as an effective remedy against nuisance.

Quantum meruit

A claim for damages is a claim for compensation for loss. Where, under the terms of the contract, one party undertakes its duty for the other, and the other party breaks the contract, the former can sue upon a *quantum meruit* basis — that is, to claim a reasonable price for the work carried out. It is payment for work that has been earned. If the two parties cannot agree, the question of what sum is reasonable is decided by the court. A claim on a *quantum meruit* basis is appropriate where there is an express agreement to pay a reasonable sum upon the completion of some work. In assessing a *quantum meruit* claim the parties may choose to use the various means that are available. For example, it may be based upon the costs of labour and materials plus profit, or the measurement of the work using reasonable rates.

Part 2

Procurement

Chapter 5

Standard forms of contract

Introduction

There are a variety of standard forms of contract in use in the construction industry. The choice of a particular form will depend upon the circumstances surrounding the project. The forms are often more suited to either building or civil engineering, although forms are available that are appropriate to both these sectors of the construction industry. The status of the designer will also affect this choice. Local authorities, and particularly central government departments, have devised their own forms of contract. Although the central government form is considerably different, local authorities will often use a version of a form that is also used in the private sector. The size of the project will also determine the form used, since the erection of small works need not embrace the complete conditions necessary on major contracts.

A major advantage of using a standard document is that those who use it regularly become familiar with its contents. They thus become aware of both its strengths and its weaknesses, and the suitability for their own specific purposes. The widespread use of standard forms within the construction industry are also partly accounted for by the practical impossibility of writing new conditions for every contract. As long ago as 1964 the Banwell Report recommended that a single form of contract for the whole of the construction industry was both desirable and practicable. Unfortunately this good suggestion has not been acted upon, and there has since this time been an introduction of a plethora of types of standard forms. Although the general layout and content of the various forms appear somewhat similar, the details can vary considerably.

The majority of the standard forms that are in use have been prepared by interested groups who together represent the interests of all sides of the industry.

JCT 80 is the most frequently used form for building contracts, although it has experienced considerable resistance from all quarters of the construction industry. This resulted in a 'final' reprint of the previous 1963 form for use in the transitional period. The later ACA form was developed largely because of the dissatisfaction with JCT 80. It should be clearly understood, however, that the outdated 1963 form now has a very limited life-span and any reproduction of the form will be illegal when the form is made obsolete. It is in everyone's interest in the longer term to ensure that JCT 80 gets widespread usage.

Central government departments will most likely continue to use their own form GC/Works/1, together with any subsequent revisions necessitated by good practice. The ICE conditions of contract are also likely to remain the major form for civil engineering projects.

The standard forms in general use are:

1. *Joint Contracts Tribunal Standard Form of Building Contract* — known as JCT 80. There are a variety of choices available (Fig. 5.1), depending upon whether the client is a public or private body. There are versions available for each of these two types of client to allow for; with quantities, without quantities, or with approximate quantities. The six different versions are, however, very similar in content. JCT 80 is used almost exclusively on building contracts. Since its introduction in 1980 there have been eight amendments as follows:

1 January 1984	— Clause 19.4 Sub-letting; determination of employment of domestic subcontractor.
2 November 1986	— Insurance and related liability provisions.
3 March 1987	— Incorporation of 'Schedules of Work', 'Contract Sum Analysis', 'Formulae for Fluctuations' and other amendments.
4 July 1987	— Miscellaneous amendments.
5 January 1988	— Part 1, new clauses 1.4 and 8.2.2. Part 2, revised clause 8.4
6 July 1988	— 1. Part 4: amendments to clause 41 'Settlement of disputes — arbitration'. 2. Local Authorities versions only: omission of clause 19A 'Fair Wages'.
7 July 1988	— Standard Method of Measurement 7th Edition: Bills of Quantities prepared in accordance with SMM 7.
8 April 1989	— Amendments to VAT provisions.

In addition there are a number of supplements for JCT 80 to cover, i.e. Fluctuations, Sectional completion, and Contractor's designed portion. The latter should not be confused with design and build which is something completely different.

2. *JCT Intermediate Form of Contract* — known as IFC 84. This form was introduced in the mid-1980s in response to the over-complexity of some of the provisions and procedures of JCT 80. This has also received similar revisions to JCT 80. There are supplements covering fluctuations and sectional completion.

3. *JCT Agreement for Minor Building Works* — known as MW 80. This form was introduced at the same time as JCT 80 and contains many of the provisions of JCT 80 in a more simplified format.

4. *JCT Standard Form of Building Contract with Contractor's Design* — known as CD 81. This is the JCT form to be used on projects of a design-and-build nature. Again many of the clauses are similar to JCT 80, but special clauses are included to meet and deal with this type of arrangement.

5. *JCT Management Works Contract* — known as JCT 87. This form is used on management contracts and includes the following:
   Works Contract/1: Section 1, Management contractor's Invitation to Tender.
   Works Contract/1: Section 2, Works Contract Tender.
   Works Contract/1: Section 3, Articles of Agreement—Attestation.
   Works Contract/2: Works Contract Conditions.
   Works Contract/3: Employer/Works Contractor Agreement.

6. *General Conditions of Government Contracts for Building and Civil Engineering Works* — known as GC/Works/1. This form is published by HMSO and is used extensively by central government departments. The third edition with supplementary conditions was published in 1989. The body responsible for its contents, updating and revision is the Property Services Agency of the Department of the Environment. There are other related forms for both mechanical and electrical services and a minor-works form known as GC/Works/2 (1980).

7. *Conditions of Contract and Form of Tender, Agreement and Bond for use in connection with Works of Civil Engineering Construction* — known as ICE form. The sixth edition was revised in January 1991. Its sponsors include the Institution of Civil Engineers, the Association of Consulting Engineers and the Federation of Civil Engineering Contractors, who jointly keep the document and its use under review.

8. *Conditions of Contract (International) for Works of Civil Engineering Construction*, third edition 1977 — known as the FIDIC form and prepared by the International Federation of Consulting Engineers. It is also approved by several other organizations representing the construction interests of various other countries.

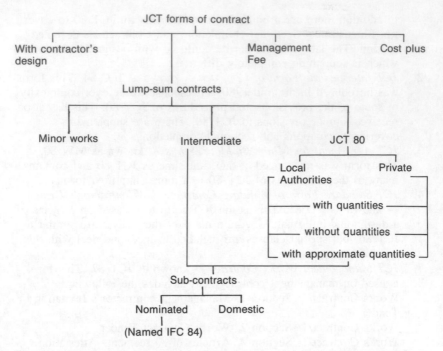

Fig. 5.1   JCT family of forms of contract (adapted from Parris, J. *The Standard Form of Contract.* Collins, 1985)

9. *Association of Consultant Architects Form of Building Agreement* — know as the ACA Form, has been designed as an alternative to JCT 80. Its compilers, clearly disenchanted with the JCT forms, claim that it is short, clear and legally precise and has been prepared with the advice of legal experts and in consultation with clients, contractors and the professions.

10. *Nominated sub-contracts for JCT 80.* There are references in JCT 80 to the nomination procedures to be followed. These contemplate the use of the following documents and forms:
    NSC/1 Forms of Nominated Sub-Contract Tender and Agreement.
    NSC/2 Standard Form of Employer Nominated Sub-Contractor Agreement where Tender NSC/1 has been used.
    NSC/3 Standard Form of Nomination of Sub-Contractor where NSC/1 has been used.
    NSC/4 Nominated Sub-Contract, for Sub-Contractors who have been tendered on NSC/1.

11. *Nominated suppliers forms of tender under JCT 80.* This complies with JCT 80 clause 36, and although its use is not mandatory it is advisable to adopt it. The forms include:

TNS/1 Standard Form of Tender by Nominated Supplier Tender and Schedules 1 and 2.

TNS/2 Form of Tender by Nominated Supplier Schedule 3.

12. *Domestic form of sub-contract*. These forms of subcontract have been prepared by BEC for use with the non-nominated subcontractors, i.e., those appointed directly by the contractor. They include the following:

DOM/1a Sub-Contract Articles of Agreement.

DOM/1c Sub-Contract Conditions for use with the Domestic Sub-contract.

DOM/2 Domestic Sub-Contract Articles of Agreement: for use with Contractors Design 1981.

IN/SC Domestic Sub-Contract Articles of Agreement: for use in connection with IFC/84.

13. *Named sub-contractors for use with IFC 84*. These include the following forms:

NAM/T Form of Tender and Agreement: for a person to be named by the employer as a subcontractor under the IFC/84.

NAM/SC Sub-Contract Conditions: for subcontractors named under the IFC/84.

ESA/1 Employer/Specialist Agreement: for use between the employer and a specialist to be named under IFC/84.

14. *Labour-only Sub-contract Form*. This is used for work which is sub-let by the main contractor under clause 19 of JCT 80. It is published by BEC.

15. *JCT Fixed Fee Form of Prime Cost Contract*; for use on cost-plus type contractual arrangements.

16. *Renovation grant forms*. There are essentially two forms of contract for work of this nature. One is for lump-sum contracts where an architect is employed to prepare drawings and a specification. The other is where an architect is not used, and is on the basis of cost estimated by the contractor.

Other forms are also available, notably those prepared by the large industrial corporations who undertake a substantial amount of building work. Even in those cases where separate forms are not used, it is not uncommon to find a few additional pages being added as supplementary conditions. These conditions are generally to place the standard form more in favour with the building owner. Greater risk than normal is therefore placed with the contractor, and this is often reflected in the contract price submitted at tender stage.

The expected contractual position under JCT 80 is shown diagrammatically in Fig. 5.2. The terminology used is that referred to by JCT 80, although similar terms are used on the other forms of contract. Although this is the 'expected' position, the more likely contractual

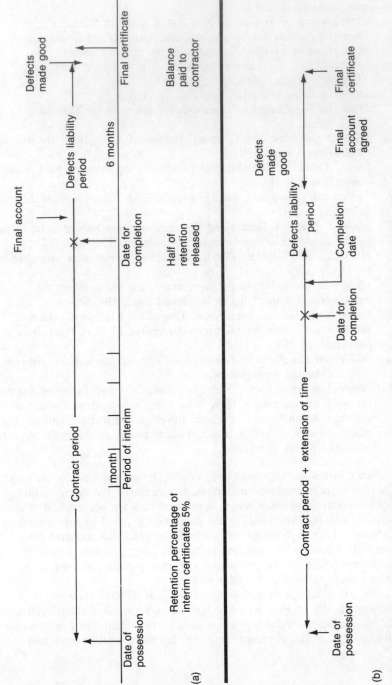

Fig. 5.2 Contractual terminology: (a) expected contractual position; (b) likely contractual position

position is also shown for comparison purposes. The expected position assumes that nothing will go wrong on the project, but all of those connected with construction know only too well that this is often a Utopia type situation. This terminology is described and referred to throughout this book.

Chapter 6

Contract strategy

Appetite for change

A little over thirty years ago the clients of the construction industry had only a limited choice of procurement methods which they might wish to use for the construction of a new building. The RIBA form of contract, although even then not used universally, had yet to experience extensive rivalry from elsewhere, or even from within its own organization for a serious alternative. Bills of Quantities were becoming the preferred document in place of the specification, and the mistrusted cost-plus type contracts which had been a necessity a few years earlier for the rapid repair of war-damaged property were already in decline.

We now live in a world of endless change. In recent years there have been many developments in the technologies that are used, in the types of societies in which we live, and amongst professional attitudes. The causes of these changes which have been experienced are not difficult to find. Society generally is on the look-out for something new, and the construction industry in a way mirrors that change to avoid being thought of as outdated or old-fashioned. The search is also for improvement, knowing that we have not as yet found the perfect system; even if one at all exists. In this context, largely due to improved geographical communications of the twentieth century, the construction industry has looked with interest to both east and west, to the way that others around the world arrange the procurement of capital works projects. Not surprisingly, it is the countries which appear to have been the most successful which have received most of the attention. The methods adopted in the USA or Japan for their construction industries have been in the forefront of our ideas for change.

The apparent failure of the construction industry to satisfy the perceived needs of its customers, particularly in the way it organizes and executes its projects has been another catalyst for change. Various pressure groups too, have evolved to champion the causes of the different organizations who perhaps have particular axes to grind. The 1970s oil-price crisis, which had a massive influence on inflation and hence industries' borrowing requirements, also motivated the construction industry to improve its own efficiency through the way it managed and organized its work. The depression of the 1970s, like other slumps previously, encouraged firms of all kinds to attempt to persuade employers to build, by using what were then innovative approaches to contract procurement.

Figure 6.1, below, is a graph which highlights the interest in the alternative procurement and contract systems which are used in the building industry. It has been derived from the numbers of published papers concerned with these alternative systems. It excludes the large number of books and chapters in books, and seminars and conferences which have taken place over these years on contract procurement.

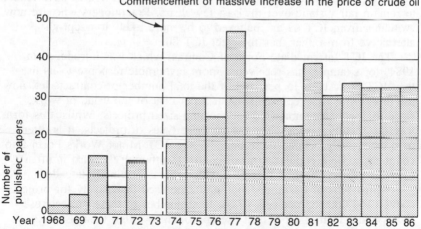

Fig. 6.1   An indicator of interest in alternative systems (derived from the numbers of published papers concerned with alternative systems by years of publication). *Source: Further horizons for chartered builders: Building Procurement — evolving alternative systems*, CIOB, 1988

Contracts in use

It is difficult to measure the size of the construction industry and therefore difficult to generalize about trends. It is diverse by its very nature. In 1987 the output of the construction industry stood at about £20kM (*The Housing and Construction Statistics, HMSO*). This figure is perhaps a little misleading since it excludes repair and maintenance work which might easily double this amount.

In the past twenty years changes in the procurement paths have probably been the most fundamental single change that has affected the construction industry. A number of different organizations attempt to monitor the use of contract procurement systems in the construction industry. The following comments do, however, relate largely to new building projects as distinct, for example, from civil engineering or repair and maintenance work.

What is perhaps surprising among these surveys, is the amount of work still being let on the now outdated 1963 forms of contract. In 1987, for example, over 10 per cent of the value of new orders carried out by consultants and local authorities used a variant of this form. The figure is reducing but it must be remembered that it is almost ten years since it was replaced by JCT 80. About 85 per cent of the actual number of contracts let by consultants and local authorities used one of the family of JCT forms. This figure however reduces considerably when contractors' own design-and-build forms and central government projects are taken into account. The JCT 80 forms represent about 75 per cent when measured by the value of the work undertaken. These figures have tended to remain fairly static over the past few years. Practitioners who are now switching from JCT 63 are believed to be more likely to adopt an alternative form rather than to select JCT 80.

The JCT Intermediate Form of Contract which was introduced in 1984, for example, has received a more favourable response to its use than JCT 80. About 15 per cent of the total number of contracts let, now use this form. This represents about 5 per cent of the value of work, since its use is recommended for medium-sized projects. Whilst this form was specifically designed for use on these types of projects, it is often used extensively beyond these bounds. The JCT Minor Works Form also continues to be a popular form of contract, although this also is often used for projects beyond those for which it was originally intended.

Whilst bills of quantities continue to be used extensively for projects above £150,000 (65 per cent of the total number of these projects use BOQs and a further 5 per cent use approximate bills), their usage nevertheless continues to be in decline. Bills of Quantities are now used on about 50 per cent of all new building projects. However, on the larger types of project other forms of contract documentation are being used in preference. Drawing and specification contracts currently account for almost 20 per cent of the value of all new building projects. This sounds as if the wheel has turned its full circle, but it needs to be remembered that a large proportion of these projects are at the smaller end of the market. On projects of up to £150,000 drawings and specifications account for over 80 per cent of the actual number of contracts. Their popularity also continues to increase. Prime cost contracts currently account for only about 5 per cent of all new building projects across the full range of contract types and values.

There continues to be an increase in the use of design-and-build contracts across a whole range of buildings prices. It is difficult to measure the full extent of their penetration in the market, since the different sides of industry collect their own statistics separately. A general consensus would tend to put the figure at about 15−20 per cent of the value of all new buildings within this category of procurement. It is supposedly at its most popular for projects in the £1−2 m. price range. Management contracting of one sort or another continues to be used for the larger projects, but its growth is declining compared with the earlier years of the 1980s when this method of procurement then was at its peak. In terms of the value of work it represents about 10 per cent, but only about 1 per cent in terms of the number of new building contracts. This has gone full circle. Traditionally architects used to employ a range of subcontractors to do the construction work; now they call it management contracting! Figure 6.2 outlines some of the trends in the methods of contract procurement based upon the value of projects.

Forms of contract

There are a wide variety of forms of contract in use within the construction industry. The extensive use of standard forms within the industry is partly accounted for by the practical impossibility of writing a

Type of procurement	Percentage of contracts by value		
	1984	1985	1987
Lump sum — firm BOQ	58.73	59.26	52.07
Lump sum — approximate BOQ	6.62	5.44	3.43
Lump sum — specifications	13.13	10.20	17.76
Prime cost — fixed fee	4.45	2.65	5.37
Design and build	5.06	8.05	12.16
Management contract	12.01	14.40	9.41
Totals	100.00	100.00	100.00

Fig. 6.2 Trends in methods of procurement (1984−87) *Source:* RICS JO (QS) survey

48

new set of conditions for every contract. The choice of a particular form will depend upon a number of considerations such as

- private client or public authority
- method of procurement selected
- type of work undertaken
- status of designer
- size of project
- type of contract documentation used.

Although the general contents of many of these forms are similar there are wide differences in the detail and the interpretations of the particular clauses and conditions. There is, however, a continuing increase in the numbers of such forms which are available for use within the construction industry. Revisions, clause amendments and case law are now a common characteristic of the construction industry.

General matters

Consultants v. contractors

The contracts survey referred to above under-estimates the total amount of design-and-build type projects because it is almost entirely a survey of consultant organizations. The arguments for engaging a consultant rather than a contractor as the main employer's adviser are inconclusive. The respective advantages and disadvantages may be summarized as follows:

Advantages of a contractor-centred approach are said to be
- better time management
- single point responsibility
- inherent buildability
- certainty of price
- teamwork
- inclusive design fees.

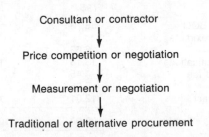

Fig. 6.3 Developing a contract procurement strategy

Disadvantages may be
- problems of contractor proposals matching with employer requirements
- payment clauses
- emphasis may be away from design towards other factors
- employers may still need to retain consultants for payments, inspections, etc.

Competition v. negotiation

There are a variety of ways in which a builder may seek to secure business. These include speculation, invitation, reputation, rotation, arrangement, recommendation and selection. Irrespective, however, of the final contractual arrangements which are made by the employer, the method of choosing the contractor must first be established. The alternatives which are available for this purpose are either competition or negotiation.

Some form of competition on price, time or quality is desirable. All of the evidence which is available, suggests that the employer under the normal circumstances of contract procurement is likely to strike a better bargain if an element of competition exists. There are, however, a number of circumstances which can arise in which a negotiated approach may be more beneficial to the employer. Some of these include

- business relationship
- early start on site
- continuation contract
- state of the market
- contractor specialization
- financial arrangements
- geographical area.

The above list is not exhaustive nor should it be assumed that negotiation would be preferable in all of these examples. Each individual project should be examined on its own merits, and a decision made bearing in mind the particular circumstances concerned and specific advantages to the employer.

Certain essential features are necessary if the negotiations are to proceed satisfactorily. These include equality of the negotiators in either party, parity of information, agreement as to the basis of negotiation and a decision on how the main items of work will be priced.

Measurement v. reimbursement

There are essentially only two ways of calculating the costs of construction work. Either the contractor adopts some form of measurement and is paid for the work on the basis of quantity multiplied by a rate, or the contractor is reimbursed his actual costs. A drawing and specification contract, for example, relies upon the contractor measuring and pricing the work, even though he may only disclose a single sum to the employer. The measurement contract allows for the payment for risk to the contractor, the cost reimbursement approach does not. Many of the measurement contracts may include for a small proportion of the work to be paid for under dayworks (a form of cost reimbursement) but it is more unusual to find cost reimbursement contracts with any measurement aspects. The points to be borne in mind when choosing between measurement or cost reimbursement contracts include the following.

- Contract sum. This is not available with any form of cost reimbursement contract.
- Final price forecast. This is not possible with any of the cost reimbursement methods or with measurement contracts which rely extensively on approximate quantities.
- Incentive for contractor efficiency. Cost reimbursement contracts can encourage wastage which must then be passed on to the employer.
- Price risk. Measurement contracts allow for this, employers may therefore pay for such non-events.
- Cost control. The employer has little control over costs where any form of cost reimbursement contract is used.
- Administration. Cost reimbursement contracts require a large amount of clerical work.

Traditional v. alternatives

Until recent times the majority of the major building projects were constructed using single-stage selective tendering. This method of procurement has many flaws, and as such, alternative procedures have been devised in an attempt to address the issues which it raised. The newer methods, or alternative procurement paths, whilst overcoming the failures of the traditional approach created their own particular problems. In fact if a single method was able to be devised which addressed all of the problems then the remaining methods would quickly fall into disuse. In choosing a method of procurement, therefore, the following issues are of importance. They are more fully described in a later chapter.

- Project size
- Costs, inclusive of the design
- Time, from brief to handover
- Accountability
- Design, function and aesthetics
- Quality assurance
- Organization and responsibility
- Project complexity
- Risk placing

- Market considerations
- Financial provisions.

The framework of society

The correct application of contractual procurement systems is influenced by a number of factors which are present within any society. Such factors, although external to the construction industry, do have implications for the successful completion of each individual project. The appropriate recommendations today may also have different implications in the future, because the framework of society is a constantly evolving one. In selecting the right method, therefore, the following factors should be considered and evaluated:

- *Economic* — interest rates, inflation, land costs, investment policies, market levels, taxation opportunities, opportunity costs.
- *Legal* — contract law, case law, arbitration, discharge of contracts, remedies for breach of contract.
- *Technological* — new techniques, off-site manufacture, production processes, use of computers.
- *Political* — government systems, public expenditure, export regulations and guarantees, planning laws, trade-union practice, policies.
- *Social* — demography, ageing population, availability of potential employees, retraining, the environment.

Many of these factors are unstable even in a well-run economy or for the duration of the contract period, due to the influences from other world markets. An employer's satisfaction with the project relies upon the procurement adviser's skill and to some extent the intuition which can be provided, in being able to reflect on how the above are likely to influence the method recommended for contract procurement.

Employer's essential requirements

Employers when buying a particular service seek to ensure that it fully meets their needs. The consultant or contractor employed needs to identify with the employer's objectives within the context in which the employer has to operate and particularly any constraints which may be present. *A study of quantity surveying practice and client demand* (RICS 1984), identified some of the following criteria as important requirements for the majority of employers:

- impartial and independent advice;
- trust and fairness in all dealings;
- timely information ahead of possible events;
- implications on the inter-reactions of time, cost and quality;
- options from which the employer can select the best possible route;

- recommendations for action;
- good value for any fees charged;
- advice based upon a skilled consideration of the project as a whole;
- sound ability and general competence;
- reliability of advice;
- enterprise and innovation.

Responding to change

The construction industry is constantly examining new initiatives, and responding to changes. The following are some of these changes which impinge upon contract procurement and influence the path to be followed.

1992

In 1992 all of the trade barriers which have previously prevented the EC from being a single trading entity will have been removed. The opportunities lie in the perceived increase in the mobility of capital reflecting the removal of artificial barriers on trade and labour. Europe is the world's largest and perhaps most prosperous market with some 320 million people. This new opportunity for firms based in Britain will be matched by foreign firms seeking a foothold in business in the United Kingdom. Both the contractual arrangements and the procurement methods used throughout the EC are not uniform. They are, however, more uniform within mainland Europe than between Britain and the other countries. It is very unlikely, even in the long term, that the approach to procurement and contracts will be unified, although there will be moves in that direction. The examination of the current plethora of arrangements which exist in the United Kingdom alone are still wide and varied. There will in the early days up to and after 1992 be a certain amount of jockeying for position. More important will be a knowledge of the working of the local or national industry and the contractual arrangements which already prevail.

CCPI

Research at the Building Research Establishment on fifty representative building sites has shown that the biggest single cause of events which stop site managers, architects or tradesmen from working together is unclear or missing project information. Another significant cause is unco-ordinated design, and at times the entire effort of site management can be directed to searching for missing information or reconciling inconsistencies in that which is available. To overcome these weaknesses, the Co-ordinating Committee for Project Information (CCPI) was formed with the task of developing a common arrangement for work sections for building works that could be used throughout the various forms of documentation.

CCPI has consulted widely to ensure that the proposals are practicable and helpful, and its work has been performed by practising professionals who are themselves fully aware of the pressures involved. Is it really more economical to produce incomplete and inconsistent, if not contradictory, project information during the design process, and then to spend time wrestling with and trying to rectify the problems on site, with the attendant waste of time in dealing with claims? Is it not better to produce complete and co-ordinated information once and thus avoid such problems? If properly co-ordinated project documentation is produced much abortive work will be avoided and costs will be so much less.

Regardless of the procurement method selected it is important that the principles of CCPI are adopted and put into practice. Procurement methods which are unable to incorporate such principles may be severely flawed in practice.

Quality assurance

The Building Research Establishment and others have shown that 50 per cent of all building failures have their origins in design faults, and 40 per cent of the failures are due to construction faults. An investment in quality assurance can therefore reap substantial long-term dividends by reducing such failures and saving on repairs and legal costs. Quality assurance is therefore a good thing for the construction industry. Contract procurement methods therefore which fail to address this problem adequately are really of little value to anyone. The use of consultants and contractors who operate quality assurance systems and have been independently assessed and registered provides some protection before the event, rather than after it, when of course the damage has been done.

Value for money

Employers are rightly concerned with obtaining value for money. Cheapness is in itself no virtue. It is well worth while to pay a little more if as a result the gain in value exceeds the extra costs. Value for money, in any context, is a combination of subjective and objective viewpoints. There are some items which can be measured but there are other items which can only be left to opinion or at best expert judgement. The former of these can largely be proven, or at least it could if our knowledge was fully comprehensive. The professionals skill is, however, largely in the judgement area. The procurement method recommended to the employer needs to be that which is able to offer him the best value for money. The need for careful assessment is required to obtain the desired results.

Procurement management

It is of considerable importance to employers who wish to have buildings erected that the appropriate advice is provided on the method of procurement to be used. The advice offered must be relevant and reliable and based upon skill and expertise. There is, however, a dearth of objective and unbiased advice available. It is often difficult to elicit the relevant facts appropriate to a proposed building project. Construction employers will tend to rely on the advice from their chosen consultant or contractor. The advice provided is usually sound, and frequently successful according to the criteria set by the employer. It may, however, tend to be biased and even in some cases tainted with self interest. It is perhaps sometimes given on the basis of 'who gets to the client first'. Methods and procedures have now become so complex, with a wide variety of options available, that an improvement in the management approach to the procurement process is now necessary to meet the employer's needs. The need to match, for instance, the employer's requirements with the industry's response is very important if customer care and satisfaction are to be achieved. The employer's procurement manager must consider the characteristics of the various methods that are available and recommend a solution which best suits the employer's needs and aspirations. The manager will need to discuss the level of risk involved for the procurement path recommended for the project under review.

The process of procurement management may be broadly defined to include the following:

- determining the employer's requirements in terms of time, cost and quality;
- assessing the viability of the project and providing advice in terms of funding and taxation;
- advising on an organizational structure for the project as a whole;
- advising on the appointment of consultants and contractors bearing in mind the criteria set by the employer;
- managing the information and co-ordinating the activities of the consultants and contractor, through the design and construction phases.

The simplistic view is that architects design and contractors build. Those are their strengths. It is important, however, that someone is especially responsible for the contractual matters surrounding the contract.

The NEDO publication *Thinking about Building* suggests the following regarding procurement:

- DO make one of your in-house executives responsible for the project.
- DO bring in an outside advisor if the in-house resources and skills are inappropriate.
- DO take special care to define the needs for the project.
- DO choose a procurement path to fit the defined priorities.

- DO go to some trouble to select the organizations and individuals concerned.
- DO ensure that a professional appraisal is done before the scheme becomes too advanced.

The effectiveness of a procurement path is a combination of the following:

- the correct advice and decision on which procurement path to use;
- the correct implementation of the chosen path;
- the evaluation during and after its execution.

Conclusions

Procurement procedures today are a dynamic activity. They are evolutionary, to suit the changing needs of society and the considerations in which the industry finds itself operating. There are no standard solutions, but each individual project, which invariably represents a one-off project, needs to be considered independently and analysed accordingly. A wide variety of factors have to be taken into account before any practical decisions can be made. The various influences concerned need to be weighed carefully, and always with the best interests of the employer in mind.

Chapter 7

Contract procurement

Introduction

The execution of a construction project requires both design work and the carrying out of construction operations on site. If these are to be done successfully, resulting in a satisfactorily completed project, then some form of recognized procedure must be employed at the outset to deal with their organization, co-ordination and procedures.

Traditionally a client who wished to have a building constructed would invariably commission an architect to prepare drawings of the proposed scheme and if the scheme was sufficiently large employ a quantity surveyor to prepare appropriate documentation on which the builder could prepare a price. These would all be based upon the client's brief, and the information used as a basis for competitive tendering. This was the common system in use at the turn of the century and still continues to be widely used in practice.

Particularly since the mid 1960s a small revolution has occurred in the way designers and builders are employed for the construction of buildings. To some extent these are the results of initiatives taken by the then Ministry of Works in the early 1960s and the Banwell committee which recommended several changes in the way that projects and contracts were organized, one of which was an attempt to try to bring the designers and the constructors closer together. The construction industry continues to examine and evaluate the methods available, and to devise new procedures which address the shortfalls and weaknesses of the current procedures.

There is, however, no panacea for the present difficulties. In fact it may be argued that change is occurring so fast that a present-day solution may be quite inappropriate for tomorrow. Each of the methods described have their own characteristics, advantages and disadvantages. All have been used in practice at some time; some more than others largely due to the familiarity and the consequent advantage of ease of application. New methods will evolve to meet the ever rapidly changing circumstances of the construction industry. These will occur in response to current deficiencies and to changes in the culture of the construction industry.

Methods of price determination

Building and civil engineering contractors are paid for the work which they carry out, on the basis of one of two methods, either measurement or cost reimbursement.

Measurement

The work is measured in place on the basis of its finished quantities. The contractor is paid for this work on the basis of quantity multiplied by a rate. Measurement may be undertaken by the employer's quantity surveyor, or by the contractor's surveyor or estimator. In the first example an accurate and detailed contract document can be prepared. In the latter the document prepared will be sufficient only to satisfy the particular builder concerned. The work may be measured as accurately as the drawings allow prior to the contract being awarded, in which case it is known as a lump-sum contract. Alternatively, the work may be measured or remeasured after it has been carried out. In the latter case it is referred to as a remeasurement contract. All contracts envisage some form of remeasurement to take into account variations. In such cases both the employer's and the contractor's surveyors measure the work together. Measurement contracts, unless they are entirely of a remeasurement type, allow for some sort of final cost to be recalculated. This offers advantages to the client for budgeting and cost-control purposes. Building contracts are more often lump-sum contracts, whereas civil engineering projects are typically of the remeasurement type.

Cost reimbursement

With these types of contractual arrangements the contractor is able to recoup the actual costs of the materials which have been purchased and the time spent on the work by his operatives, plus an amount to cover the contractor's profit. Dayworks accounts are valued on much the same basis.

Measurement contracts

The following are the main types of measurement contracts used in the construction industry.

Drawings and specification

This is the simplest type of measurement contract and is really only suitable for small works or simple projects. In recent years there has been a trend towards using this approach on schemes much larger than was originally intended. Each contractor has to measure the quantities from the drawings and interpret the specification during pricing in order to calculate the tender sum. The method is wasteful of the contractor's estimating resources, and does not easily allow for a fair comparison of the tender sums received by the employer. Interpreting the specification can be a hazardous job even for the more experienced estimator. The contractor has also to accept a greater proportion of the risk, since, in addition to being responsible for the prices, he is also responsible for the measurements based upon his interpretation of the contract information. In order to compensate for possible errors or omissions, evidence might suggest that contractors tend to overprice this type of work.

Performance specification

This method is a much more vague approach to tendering and the evaluation of the contractor's bids. In this situation the contractor is required to prepare a price based upon the employer's brief and user requirements alone. The contractor is left to determine the method of construction and choose the materials that suit these broad conditions. The contractor in practice is likely to select materials and methods of construction which satisfy the prescribed performance standards in the least expensive way. Great precision is required in formulating a performance specification if the desired results are to be achieved.

Schedule of rates

With some projects it is not possible to predetermine the nature and full extent of the proposed building works. In these circumstances, where it is desirable to form some direct link between quantity and price, a schedule of rates may be used. This schedule is similar to a bill of quantities, but without any actual quantities being included. It should be prepared using the rules of a method of measurement. Contractors are invited to insert their rates against these items, and they are then used in comparison against other contractors' schedules in selecting a tender. Upon completion of the work it is remeasured and the rates are used to calculate the final cost. This method has the disadvantages of being unable to predict a contract sum, or an indication of the probable final cost of the project. Contractors also find it difficult realistically to price the schedule in the absence of any quantities.

Schedule of Prices

An alternative to the Schedule of Rates is to provide the contractors with a ready-priced schedule, similar to the *Property Services Agency's (PSA) Schedule of Rates*. The contractors in this case adjust each rate by the addition or deduction of a percentage. In practice a single percentage adjustment is normally made to all of the rates. This standard adjustment is unsatisfactory since the contractor will view some of the prices in the Schedule as high prices, and others as being inadequate in terms of covering costs. It does, however, have the supposed advantage of producing fewer errors in the pricing in the tender documents compared with the contractor's own price analysis of the work.

Bill of Quantities

Even with all the new forms of contract arrangement the Bill of Quantities continues to remain the most common form of measurement contract, and the most common contractual arrangement for major construction projects in the United Kingdom. The contractors' tenders are able to be judged on the prices alone since they are all using the same qualitative and quantitative data. This type of documentation is recommended for all but the smallest projects.

Bill of Approximate Quantities

In some circumstances it is not possible to measure the work accurately. In this case a Bill of Approximate Quantities might be prepared and the entire project remeasured upon completion. The *JCT Standard Form of Building Contract with approximate quantities* could then be used. Whilst an approximate cost of the project can be obtained, the uncertainty in the design data makes any reliable forecast impossible.

Cost reimbursement contracts

These types of contract are not favoured by many of the industry's employers, since there is an absence of a tender sum and a forecasted final account cost. Some of these types of contract also provide little incentive for the contractor to control costs, although different varieties of cost reimbursement build in incentives for the contractor to keep costs as low as possible. They are therefore often used only in special circumstances as follows:

- emergency work projects, where time is not available to allow the traditional process to be used;
- when the character and scope of the works cannot be readily determined;
- where new technology is being used;
- where a special relationship exists between the employer and the building contractor.

Cost reimbursement contracts can take many different forms but the following are three of the more popular types in use. Each of the methods repay the contractor's costs with an addition to cover profits. Prior to embarking on this type of contract it is especially important that all the parties involved are clearly aware of the definition of contractor's costs as used in this context.

Cost plus percentage

The contractor receives the costs of labour, materials, plant, subcontractors and overheads and to this sum is added a percentage to cover profits. This percentage is agreed at the outset of the project. A major disadvantage of this type of cost reimbursement is that the contractor's profits are directly geared to the contractor's expenditure. Therefore, the more the contractor spends on the building works the greater will be the profitability. Because it is an easy method to operate, this tends to be the selected method when using cost reimbursement.

Cost plus fixed fee

With this method the contractor's profit is predetermined by the agreement of a fee for the work before the commencement of the project. There is therefore some incentive for the contractor to attempt to control the costs. However, because it is difficult to predict the cost with sufficient accuracy beforehand, it can cause disagreement between the contractors and the employer's own professional advisers. The result is that the *fixed fee* may thus need to be revised on completion of the project.

Cost plus variable fee

The use of this method requires a target fee to be set for the project prior to the signing of the contract. The contractor's fee is then composed of two parts, a fixed amount and a variable amount. The total fee charged then depends upon the relationship between the target cost and the actual cost. This method provides a supposedly even greater incentive to the contractor to control the construction costs. It has the disadvantage of requiring the target cost to be fixed on the basis of a very 'rough' estimate of the proposed project.

Examples

Cost plus percentage

Estimated cost	£100,000	Final cost	£111,964
Agreed percentage profit 10%	£10,000	10% profit	£11,964
Tender	£110,000	Final account	£123,928

Cost plus fixed fee

Estimated cost	£100,000	Final cost	£111,964
Fixed fee	£12,500	Fixed fee	£12,500
Tender sum	£112,500	Final account	£124,464

Cost plus variable fee

Estimated cost	£100,000	Final cost	£111,964
Fixed fee	£10,000	Fixed fee	£10,000
Variable fee 10% +100,000		Variable fee 10% 11,964	−1196
Tender sum	£110,000	Final account	£120,768

The above are examples only. It cannot be assumed that the final accounts would follow these patterns. These are the simple theories of the calculations. In practice the financial adjustments are often very complex.

Contractor selection

There are essentially two ways of choosing a contractor, either by competition or negotiation. Competition may be restricted to a few selected firms or open to almost any firm who wishes to submit a tender. The options described later are used in conjunction with one of these methods of contractor selection.

Selective competition

This is the traditional and most popular method of awarding construction contracts. In essence a number of firms of known reputation are selected by the design team to submit a price. The firm who submits the lowest tender is then awarded the contract. The NJCC (1989) have developed a *Code of Procedure for single-stage Selective Tendering*, which although not mandatory does provide guidance on the awarding of construction contracts. The Code is frequently revised to take into account the changes in buildings procurement and the general principles take into account the recommendations of the National Economic Development Office (NEDO) reports: *The Public Client and the Construction Industries; The Placing and Management of Contracts for Building and Civil Engineering Work* (The Banwell Report); *Action on the Banwell Report*. The following are some of the more important points from this Code:

1. The Code assumes the use of a standard form of building contract with which the parties in the construction industry are familiar. If other forms of contract are used, some modification of detail may be necessary. There are clear advantages to all parties in the knowledge that a standard procedure will be followed in inviting and accepting tenders.

2. The Code recommends that the number of tenderers should be limited to six. The number of tenderers is restricted because the cost of preparing abortive tenders will be reflected in prices generally throughout the building industry.

3. In preparing a short list of tenderers, the following must be borne in mind:

   - the firm's financial standing and record;
   - recent experience of building over similar contract periods;
   - the general experience and reputation of the firm for similar building types;
   - adequacy of management;
   - adequacy of capacity.

4. Each firm on the short list should be sent a preliminary enquiry to determine its willingness to tender. The enquiry should contain

   - job title
   - names of employer and consultants
   - location of site and general description of the works
   - approximate cost range
   - principal nominated subcontractors
   - form of contract and any amendments
   - procedure for correction of priced bills
   - contract under seal or under hand
   - anticipated date for possession
   - contract period
   - anticipated date for despatch of tender documents
   - length of tender period
   - length of time tender must remain open for acceptance
   - amount of liquidated damages
   - bond
   - special conditions.

5. Once a contractor has confirmed an intention to tender, he should do so. If circumstances arise which make it necessary for him to withdraw, he should notify the architect before the tender documents are issued or, at the latest, within two days thereafter.

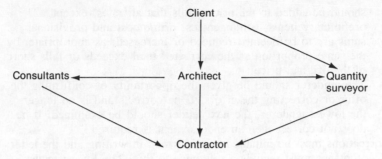

Fig. 7.1 Traditional relationships

6. A contractor who has expressed a willingness to tender should be informed if he is not chosen for the final short list.

7. All tenderers must submit their tenders on the same basis.
   - Tender documents should be despatched on the stated day.
   - Alternative offers based on alternative contract periods may be admitted if requested on the date of despatch of the documents.
   - Standard forms of contract should not be amended.
   - A time of day should be stated for receipt of tenders and tenders received late should be returned unopened.

8. The tender period will depend on the size and complexity of the job, but be not less than four working weeks, i.e., twenty days.

9. If a tenderer requires any clarification he must notify the architect who should inform all tenderers of this decision.

10. If a tenderer submits a qualified tender, he should be given the opportunity to withdraw the qualification without altering his tender figure, otherwise his tender should normally be rejected.

11. Under English law, a tender may be withdrawn at any time before acceptance. Under Scottish law, it cannot be withdrawn unless the words 'unless previously withdrawn' are inserted in the tender after the stated period of time the tender is to remain open for acceptance.

12. After tenders are opened all but the lowest three tenderers should be informed immediately. The lowest tenderer should be asked to submit a priced bill within four days. The other two contractors are informed that they might be approached again.

13. After the contract has been signed, each tenderer should be supplied with a list of tender prices.

14. The quantity surveyor must keep the priced bills strictly confidential.

15. If there are any errors in pricing the Code sets out alternative ways of dealing with the situation.
    - The tenderer should be notified and given the opportunity to confirm or withdraw the offer. If he withdraws, the next lowest tenderer is considered. If he confirms his offer an endorsement

should be added to the priced bills that all rates, except preliminary items, contingencies, prime cost and provisional sums are to be deemed reduced or increased, as appropriate, by the same proportion as the corrected total exceeds or falls short of the original price.

- The tenderer should be given the opportunity of confirming the offer or correcting the errors. If he corrects and is no longer the lowest tenderer, the next tender should be examined. If he does not correct then an endorsement is required.

16. Corrections must be initialled or confirmed in writing and the letter of acceptance must include a reference to this. The lowest tender should be accepted, after correction or confirmation, in accordance with the alternative chosen. Problems sometimes occur because the employer will see that a tender will still be the lowest even after correction. If the first alternative has been agreed upon and notified to all tenderers at the time of invitation to tender, the choice facing the tenderer should clearly be to confirm or withdraw. The employer may require a great deal of persuading to stand by the initial agreement in such circumstances. The answer to the problem is to discuss the use of the alternatives thoroughly with the employer before the tendering process begins. He must be made aware that the agreement to use the Code and one of the alternatives is binding on all parties. It is possible that an employer who stipulated the first alternative and subsequently allowed price correction could be sued by, at least, the next lowest tenderer for the abortive costs of tendering.

17. The employer does not bind himself to accept the lowest or any tender, nor does he take responsibility for the costs involved in tendering. There may be reasons why he will decide to accept a tender which is not the lowest. Although he is entitled to do so, it will not please the other tenderers. The Code is devised to remove such practices.

18. If the tender under consideration exceeds the estimated cost, negotiations should take place with the tenderer to reduce the price. The quantity surveyor then normally produces what is called 'Reduction or Addendum Bills'. They are priced and signed by both parties as part of the Contract Bills.

19. The provisions of the Code should be qualified by the supplementary procedures specified in EC Directives which provide for a 'restrictive tendering procedure' in respect of public-sector construction contracts above a specified value. Guidance on the operation of this procedure is given in *DOE Circular 59/73 (England and Wales)* and *SDD Circular 47/73 (Scotland)*, both of which are obtainable from HMSO.

This method of contractor selection is appropriate for almost any type of construction project, where a suitable supply of contractors are available.

Open competition

With this method of contract procurement the details of the proposed project are often advertised in the local and trade publications, or through the local branch of the Building Employers Confederation. The contractors who then feel that they are capable and willing to undertake such a project are requested to write in for the contract documentation. This method has the advantage of allowing new contractors or contractors who are unknown to the design team the possibility of submitting a tender for consideration. In theory any number of firms are able to submit a price. In practice a limit on the number of firms who will be supplied with the tender documents usually occurs. Unsuitable firms are removed from the list where the number of firms becomes too large. The preparation of tenders is both expensive and time consuming. The use of open tendering may relieve the employer of a moral obligation of accepting the lowest price, because firms are not generally vetted before tenders are submitted. Factors other than price must also be considered when assessing these tender bids, such as the capability of the firm who has submitted the lowest tender. There is no obligation on the part of the employer to accept any tender should the employer consider that none of the contractors' offers is suitable. Prior to the Second World War, many major building contracts, particularly those in the public sector, were awarded using this method. Although it is still commonly used on minor works its use on larger projects has been curtailed.

Negotiated contract

This method of contractor selection involves the agreement of a tender sum with a single contracting organization. Once the documents have been prepared the contractor prices them in the usual way. The priced documents are then passed to the quantity surveyor, who checks the reasonableness of the contractor's rates and prices. The two parties then meet to discuss the queries raised by the quantity surveyor and the negotiation process begins. Eventually a tender price is agreed which is acceptable to both parties. There is an absence of any competition or other restriction, other than the social acceptability of the price. It normally results in a tender sum that is higher than might have been obtained by using one of the previous procurement methods. Negotiation does, however, have particular applications as follows:

- where a business relationship exists between the client and the building contractor;
- where only one firm is capable of undertaking the work satisfactorily;
- on a continuation contract where the building contractor is already established on site;
- where an early start on site is required by the client;
- where it is beneficial to bring the contractor in during the design

stage, to advise on constructional difficulties and how they might best be avoided;
- to make use of the contractor's buildability expertise.

Competitive tendering can create financial problems for both the industry and its clients due to too keen pricing which in the end benefits no one. Negotiated contracts do result in fewer errors in pricing since all of the rates are carefully examined by both parties. Fewer exaggerated claims to attempt to recoup losses on cut-throat pricing are also less likely on negotiated contracts for similar reasons. This type of procurement can also involve the contractor in some participation during the design stage, which can result in on-site time and cost savings. It should also be possible to achieve greater co-operation during the construction process between the design team and the contractor. The public sector, however, does not generally favour negotiated contracts because of:

- higher tender sums incurred;
- public accountability;
- suggestion of possible favouritism.

Contractual options

The following contractual options are an attempt to address the employer's objectives associated with time, cost and quality of construction. They are not mutually exclusive. For example, it is possible to award a serial contract using in the first instance a design-and-build arrangement. Fast tracking may be used in association with a form of management contracting. All of these options will also need to include either a selective or negotiated approach in respect of choosing a contractor.

Early selection

This method is sometimes known as two-stage tendering. Its main aim is to involve the chosen contractor for the project as soon as possible. It therefore seeks to succeed in getting the firm who knows what to build (the designer) in touch with the firm who knows how to build it (the constructor), before the design is finalized. The contractor's expertise in construction method can thus be harnessed with that of the designer's to improve buildability criteria into the project. A further advantage is that the contractor may be able to start work on site sooner than where the more traditional methods of contract procurement are used. In the first instance, an appropriate contractor must be selected for the project. This is often done through some form of competition and can be achieved by selecting suitable firms to price the major items of work connected with the project. A simplified Bill of Quantities can be prepared which might include the following items:

- site on-costs on a time related basis
- major items of measured works
- specialist items, allowing the main contractor the opportunity of pricing the profit and attendance sums.

The contractors should also be required to state their overhead and profit percentages. The prices of these items will then form the basis for the subsequent and more detailed price agreement as the project gets under way.

The NJCC have also prepared a *Code of Procedure for two-stage selective tendering*. This Code is not concerned with any responsibility for design which may involve the main contractor. It assumes the use of a standard form of building contract after the second stage. During the first stage it is important to

- provide a competitive basis for selection
- establish the layout and design
- provide clear pricing documents
- state the respective obligations and rights of the parties
- determine a programme for the second stage.

Many of the conditions already outlined for single-stage selective tendering apply equally to two-stage tendering. Acceptance of the first-stage tender is a particularly delicate operation. The employer does not wish to find himself in the position of having accepted a contract sum at this stage. The terms of the letter of acceptance must be carefully worded to avoid such an eventuality. Depending upon the circumstances, it may be that a contract has been entered into. The question may be: What are the terms of the contract? There are two pitfalls:

- No contract exists. This is likely in many cases.
- A contract does exist binding the employer to pay and the contractor to build. This could be the far worse situation to arise if insufficient care is given to the drafting of the invitation to tender, the tender and the acceptance.

After a contractor has been appointed, all unsuccessful tenderers should be notified and, if feasible, a list of first-stage tender offers should be provided. If cost was not the sole reason for acceptance, this fact should be stated.

Design-and-build

Design-and-build projects aim to overcome the problem of the separation of the designing and constructing processes by providing for these two separate functions within a single organization. This single firm is generally the building contractor, who may employ the designers in-house or be responsible for employing consultants directly under his control. The major difference is, that instead of approaching the designer for a building, the employer briefs the contractor direct as shown in Fig. 7.2. The employer may choose to retain the services of an architect or quantity surveyor to assess the contractor's design or to monitor the work on site. The prudent employer will want some form of independent advice. The design evolved by the contractor is more likely to be suited to the needs of his own organization and construction methodology and this should result in savings in both time and costs of construction. Some argue that the design will be more attuned to the contractor's construction capabilities, rather than the design requirements of the employer. The final building should result in lower production costs on site and an overall shorter design and construction period, both of which should provide price savings to the employer. There should also be some supposed savings on the design fees even after taking into account the necessary costs of any independent advice. A further advantage to the employer is in the implied warranty of suitability because the contractor has provided the design as a part of the all-in service. Where JCT 81 is used the contractor has only a duty to use proper skills and care. A major disadvantage to the employer is the financial discouragement of possible changes to the design by the employer whilst the project is under construction. Where an employer considers these to be important to keep abreast of changing technologies or needs, excessive costs may be required to either discourage them in the first place, or to allow for their incorporation within the partially completed building. Design-and-build projects usually result in the employer obtaining a single tender from a selected contractor. Where some form of competition in price is desirable then both the type and quality of the design will need to be taken into account. This can present difficulties in practice of evaluation and comparison of the different schemes. Many of these comments relate generally to design-and-build projects, and not specifically to those which may use the JCTCD 81 form of contract with contractor's design.

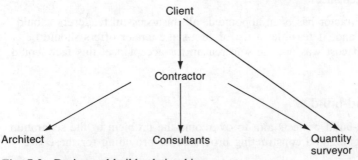

Fig. 7.2 Design-and-build relationships

The advantages claimed therefore for a design-and-build approach include the following.

- The contractor is involved with the project from inception and is thus aware of all of the employer's requirements.
- The contractor is able to use his specialized knowledge and methods of construction in evolving the design.
- The time from inception to completion should be able to be reduced due to the telescoping of the various parts of the design and construction processes.
- There can be no claims for delays due to a lack of design information, since the contractor is in total control of it.
- There is direct contact between the employer and the contractor.

Package deal

In practice the terms 'package deal' and 'design-and-build' are interchangeable. The latter normally refers to a bespoke arrangement for a one-off project. The package deal is, however, strictly a special type of design-and-build project where the employer chooses a suitable building from a catalogue. The employer may also probably be able to view completed buildings of a similar design and type that have been completed elsewhere. This type of contract procurement has been used extensively for the closed systems of industrialized system buildings of timber or concrete. Multi-storey office blocks and flats, low-rise housing, workshop premises, farm buildings, etc., have been constructed on this basis. The building owner typically provides the package-deal contractor with a site and supplies the user requirements or brief. An architect may be independently employed to advise on the building type selected, to inspect the works during construction or to deal with the contract administration. This architect's role is useful to the employer for those items which are outside the scope of the system superstructure. The type of building selected is an off-the-peg type structure that often can be erected very quickly. There is even less scope, however, for variations than with the more usual design-and-build approach, should the employer want to change aspects of the constructional detailing. It cannot be automatically assumed that this type of procurement will be a more economic solution to the employer's needs, either initially or even in the long term. Some system buildings constructed in the 1960s are now very costly to maintain. Standard system buildings are normally constructed more quickly than the traditional solutions owing to the relative completeness of the design, the availability of standard components and the speed of construction on site.

Design-and-manage

This method of procurement is really the consultant's counterpart to contractor's design-and-build. In this case the design-manager who may be an architect, engineer or surveyor has full control, not just of the design phase but also of the construction phase. He effectively replaces the main contractor in this role, which in the present day is one largely of management and organization and the administration and co-ordination of subcontractors. The design-manager is responsible for all of the aspects of construction including the programming and progressing and the rectification of any defects which may arise. The building contract is between the design-and-manage firms and the employer, thus providing for the employer a single point of contractual responsibility. The work is generally let through competition in work packages to individual subcontracting firms. This method of procurement therefore offers many of the advantages of traditional tendering coupled with design and build. The design-and-manage firm will of course need to engage its own construction managers or develop those existing staff who have the potential in this direction. It will also need to consider continuity with this type of work.

It is suitable for all types and sizes of project, but employers undertaking large projects may, due to past experience, prefer to use a more traditional form of procurement using one of the larger contractors. A major disadvantage is with regards to the site facilities which will need to be provided by the design-and-manage consultant which may need to be hired in a similar way to the subcontractors.

This type of procurement method should be able to offer comparative completion times when compared with the other methods that are available. Since there is the traditional independent control of the subcontractor firms this should ensure a standard of quality at least as good as that provided by the other contracting methods. In terms of cost, since the work packages will be sought through competition, this will be no more expensive.

Turnkey method

This form of contracting is still somewhat unusual in the United Kingdom and has thus not been used to any large extent. It has, however, certain notable successes in the Middle East and Far East. The true turnkey contract includes everything. This normally means everything from inception up to occupation of the finished building. The method receives its title from the 'turning-the-key' concept whereby the employer, when the project is completed can immediately start using the project since it will have been fully equipped including furnishings by the turnkey contractor. Some turnkey contracts also require the contractor to find a suitable site for development for this purpose. An all-embracing agreement is therefore formed with the one single administrative company for the entire project procurement process. It is therefore an extension of the traditional design-and-build arrangements, and in some cases it may even include a long-term repair and maintenance agreement. On industrial projects the appointed contractor is also likely to be responsible for the design and installation of the equipment required for the employer's manufacturing process. This type of procurement method can therefore be appropriate for use on highly specialized types of industrial and commercial construction projects.

The entire project procurement and maintenance needs can therefore be handled by a single firm accepting sole responsibility for all events. It has been argued, however, that the employer's ability to control costs, quality, performance, aesthetics and constructional details will be very variable and severely restricted by using this procurement method. A contractor who undertakes such an all-embracing project will have a variety of strengths and weaknesses and may well have fixed ideas about the importance of the different aspects of the scheme.

Management contract

Management contracting evolved at the beginning of the 1970s in the United Kingdom with an aim of building more complex projects in a shorter period of time and for a lower cost. It may be argued, therefore, that the more complex the project the more suitable management contracting may be. This method is also appropriate to a wide range of medium-sized projects.

The term 'management contract' is used to describe a method of organizing the building team and operating the building process. The main contractor provides the management expertise required on a construction project in return for a fee to cover the overheads and profit. The intention is to place the main contractor in a professional capacity where he is able to provide the management skills and practical building ability for a fee. The contractor does not therefore participate in the profitability of the construction work. The construction work itself is not undertaken by the contractor, nor does the contractor employ any of the labour or plant directly, except with the possibility of setting up the site and those items normally associated with the preliminary works. Because the management contractor is employed on a fee basis, the appointment can be made early on in the design process. The contractor is therefore able to provide a substantial input into the design particularly those associated with the practical aspects of constructing the building. Each trade section required for the project is normally tendered for separately by subcontractors, either on the basis of measurement or a lump sum This should result in the least expensive cost for each of the trades and thus for the construction works as a whole. The work on site needs a considerable amount of planning and co-ordination, more so than a traditional procurement arrangement. This is the responsibility of the management contractor and an inherent part of his acquired skills.

In common with all procurement methods, whilst there are undoubted advantages over its alternatives there are also disadvantages. It is somewhat open-ended, since the price can only be firmed up after the final works package quotation has been received. The later in the contract the work is let, the less time there will be for negotiating price reductions overall without seriously impairing a section of the works.

Management fee

Management fee contracting is a system whereby a contractor agrees to carry out building works at cost. In addition he is paid a fee by the employer to cover the overheads and profit. Some contractors are prepared to enter into an agreement to offer an incentive on the basis of a target cost. This type of procurement is a similar approach to management contracting and cost-plus contracts and has therefore similar advantages and disadvantages.

An alternative approach can also be used where a bill of quantities can be prepared and priced net of the contractor's overheads and profit, or just the profit. These items are then recovered by means of a fee. The system can be as flexible and adaptable as the parties wish. Invariably as with cost-plus contracting the fees are generally percentage related unless some reasonably accurate forecast of cost can be made. Different contracting firms who use management fee contracting have different ways of determining the fee addition. In any case the total cost is largely unknown until completion is achieved and the records agreed. Over-spending is therefore much more difficult to control, and any savings in cost which are needed tend to be required and made on the later sections of the project.

Construction management contracting

This offers a further alternative procedure to the management contract. The main difference is that the employer chooses to appoint a construction management contractor who then is responsible for appointing a design team (see Fig. 7.3) with the approval of the employer. The employer chooses to instruct the constructor rather than the designer. The construction management contractor is thus in overall

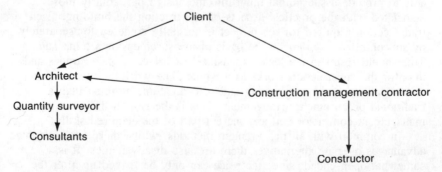

Fig. 7.3 Construction management relationships

project control of both the design and the construction phases. There are
similarities with this method and design and build. A major difference
being that the contractor would invariably appoint outside design
consultants rather than choosing to employ an in-house service. The
employer may thus form some contractual relationship with these
consultants. In reality, it is a reversal of the traditional arrangements.

Project management

Although the definitions of these procurement methods can mean different
things in different parts of the world or even in different sectors of the
construction industry, they are generally those which are understood in
the building industry in the United Kingdom. Project management in this
context is a function which is normally undertaken by the employer's
consultants rather than by a contractor. Contractors do undertake project
management but in a different context from that of contract procurement.
The title of project co-ordinator is similar terminology and perhaps better
describes the role of a project manager. The project manager is appointed
by the employer and he in turn appoints the various design consultants
and selects the contractor (see Fig. 7.4). It is a more appropriate method
for the medium- to large-sized project which requires an extensive
amount of co-ordination. The function of the project manager is therefore
one of organizing and co-ordinating the design and construction
programmes. Any person who is professionally involved in the
construction industry can become a project manager; it is the individual
rather than the profession which is important.

In general terms the need for a project manager is to provide a
balance between function, aesthetics, quality control, economics, and the
time available for constructing. The project manager's aims are to

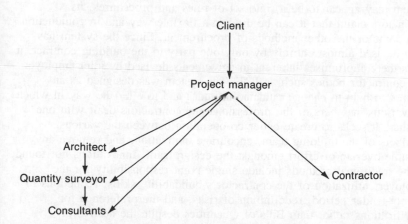

Fig. 7.4 Project management relationships

achieve an efficient, effective and economic deployment of the available resources to meet the employer's requirements. The tasks to be performed include identifying those requirements, interpreting them as necessary, and communicating them clearly to the various members of the design team and through them to the constructor. Programming and co-ordinating all of the activities and monitoring the work up to satisfactory completion are also a part of this role. A significant difference between this system and the majority of the others described, is that the employer's principal contact with his project is through the project manager rather than through the designer.

The British Property Federation System

The BPF represents substantial commercial property interests in the United Kingdom, and is thus able to exert some considerable influence on the building industry and its associated professions. The introduction of this system of building procurement to the industry created considerable interest due largely to the fact that it proposed very radical changes to the established status quo and practices and procedures. Some members of the design team felt threatened as their traditional roles and importance were questioned. The BPF system unashamedly makes the interests of the employer paramount. It attempts to devise a more efficient and co-operative method of organizing the whole building process from inception up to completion by making genuine use of all who are involved with the design and construction process. Its development was due to employer dissatisfaction with the existing arrangements where it was claimed that buildings on the whole cost too much, took too long to construct (when compared with other countries around the world) and did not always produce appropriate or credible results. The BPF manual is the only document which sets out in detail the operation of a system. Whilst the system may appear to be a rigid set of rules and procedures, its originators claim that it can be used in a flexible way and in conjunction with some of the other methods of procurement. Since the system has been devised almost entirely by only one party to the building contract, it lacks the compromises inherent in agreements devised by joint employer and contractor bodies such as JCT. The system was designed as an attempt to help to change outdated attitudes and to alter the way in which the various members of the professions and contractors dealt with one another. It seeks to create better co-operation between the various members of the building team, encourage motivation, and remove any possible overlap of effort amongst the design team. Innovations not found in the traditional methods include single-point responsibility for the employer, utilization of the contractor's buildability skills, reductions in the pre-tender period, redefinition of risks, and the preference for specifications rather than Bills of Quantities despite the desires of contractors for the latter.

Fast tracking

This approach to contracting results in the letting and administration of
multiple construction contracts for the same project at the same time as
outlined in Fig. 7.5. It is appropriate to large construction projects where
the employer's needs are to complete the project in the shortest possible
time. The process results in the overlapping of the various design and
construction operations of a single project. These various stages may

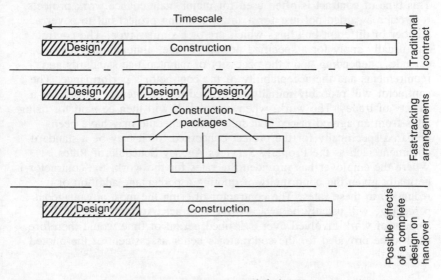

Fig. 7.5 Different contractual arrangements and their effects upon time

therefore result in the creation of separate contracts or a series of phased
starts and completions. When the design for a complete section of the
works, such as foundations, are completed the work is then let to a
contractor who will start this part of the construction work on site while
the remainder of the project is still being designed. The contractor for
this stage or section of the project will then see this work through to
completion. At the same time as this is being done another work section
may be let continuing and building upon what the first contractor has
already completed. This staggered letting of the work has the objective of
shortening the overall design and construction period from inception
through to handover. This type of procurement arrangement requires a lot
of foresight since the later stages of the design must take into account
what has by now already been completed. This type of arrangement will
also require considerably more organization and planning, particularly
from the members of the design team. In practice, where an efficient
application of this procurement procedure is envisaged then a project co-
ordinator will need to be engaged. Although the handover date of the

project to the employer should be much earlier than any of the other methods which might be used, this might be at the expense of the other facets of cost and performance. These aspects may be much inferior to those achieved by the use of the more traditional methods of procurement and arrangement.

Measured term

This type of contract is often used for major maintenance work projects. It is often awarded not just for a single building project but to cover a number of different buildings which are of a similar type. The contract will usually apply for a specified period of time, although this may be extended, depending upon the necessity of maintenance standards and requirements and the acceptability of the contractor's performance. The contractor will probably initially be offered the maintenance work for a variety of trades. The work, when completed, will then be paid for using rates from an agreed priced schedule. This schedule may have been prepared specifically for the project concerned, or it may be a standard document such as the Property Services Agency Schedule of Rates. Where the employer has provided the rates for the work, the contractor is normally given the opportunity of quoting a percentage addition or reduction to these rates. The contractor offering the most advantageous percentage will usually be awarded the contract. An indication of the amount of work involved over a defined period of time would therefore need to be provided for the contractor's better assessment of the quoted prices.

Serial tender

Serial tendering is a development of the system of negotiating further contracts, where a firm has already successfully completed a project for work of a similar type. Initially the contractors tender against each other, possibly on a selective basis, for a single project. There is, however, a contractual mechanism that several additional projects would automatically be awarded using the same contract rates. Some allowances are normally made to allow for inflation, or perhaps more commonly increased costs are added to the final accounts. The contractors would therefore know at the initial tender stage for the first project that they could expect to receive a further number of contracts which would help to provide some continuity in their workloads. Conditions would, however, be written into the documents to allow further contracts to be withheld where the contractor's performance was less than satisfactory. Serial contracting should result in lower prices to contractors since they are able to gear themselves up for such work, for example, by purchasing suitable types of plant and equipment that otherwise might be of a too speculative nature. They should therefore be able to operate to greater levels of efficiency. The employer will also achieve some financial gain since some of these lower production costs will find their way into the contractor's tenders.

A further advantage claimed for the use of serial tendering is that the same design and construction teams can remain involved for each of the projects which form part of the serial arrangement. It is claimed that this regular and close working association aids and develops an expertise which accelerates the production of the work and eases any anticipated problems. In turn the operatives on site improve their efficiency as they proceed from project to project.

Serial projects are particularly appropriate for buildings of a similar nature, such as housing and school buildings in the public sector where a large number of comparable schemes are constructed. This method may also be usefully employed in the private sector in the construction of industrial factory and warehouse units. It has also been successfully used with industrialized system building, where local authorities have worked together in a form of building consortium to gain marketing advantages from the construction industry.

Continuation contract

A continuation contract is an *ad-hoc* arrangement to take advantage of an existing situation. Projects in an expanding economy are often insufficient in size to cope with current demands even before they become operational. During their construction an employer may choose to provide additional similar facilities which may be constructed upon the completion of the original scheme. Such additions, often because of their size and scope, are beyond the definition of extra work or variations. For example, a housing project may be awarded to a contractor to build 300 houses. Due to perhaps an underestimation in demand and where additional space permits, a continuation contract may be awarded to the same contractor to build an extra 100 houses on an adjacent site. Another example can occur where during the construction of a factory building it becomes apparent that it will be insufficient to meet the increased demands for the factory's product. Extensions to the factory may therefore be agreed on the basis of a continuation contract using the same designers and constructors and the same contract prices adjusted only to allow for increased costs caused by inflation.

A continuation contract can be awarded as an add on to the majority of the contractual arrangements. Continuing with the same building team, where this has already proved to be satisfactory to the employer, is a sensible arrangement under these circumstances. Each of the parties will already be familiar with each other's working methods and will be able to offer some cost savings since they are already established on the site. Both the employer and the contractor may wish to review the contractual conditions and the new market factors which may have changed since the original contract was signed. It is also not unreasonable to expect that the contractor will want to share in the monetary savings that will be available from the already established site organization from the initial project.

Speculative work (Develop and construct)

Because of the market demand, many building firms have organized a part of their function into a speculative department. Some contractors are entirely speculative builders. These firms or divisions purchase land, obtain planning approvals, design and construct buildings for sale, rent or lease. It is also described as develop and construct. Housing is the common type of speculative unit but factories, whole industrial estates, new office buildings and refurbishment projects may also fall into this category. The contractors are often in partnership agreements with financial institutions and developers who have established that the demand for a particular type of development exists in a certain geographical area. Such assumptions are based upon a detailed market research of the area which is undertaken prior to the development getting under way. The developer or speculative builder may employ their own in-house design staff or may employ consultants to do the work for them. Whilst design and build is done for a particular employer, speculative building is carried out on the basis that there is a need for certain types of buildings and that these will be purchased at some later date.

Direct labour

Some employers, notably local authorities and large industrial firms, have departments within their organizations which undertake building work. In some cases they may restrict themselves to repair and maintenance works alone or minor works schemes. Others are much larger and are capable of carrying out any size of building project. The employer, in order to execute construction projects in this way, needs to have either an extensive building programme or to be responsible for a large amount of repair and maintenance work. In-house services of this type allow the employer, at least in theory, much greater control than using some of the other methods which have been described. In practice the level of control achieved may be less than satisfactory, due to the accounting procedures which may be employed. Employers who choose to undertake their building works by this method often do so for either political or financial reasons.

Review

At the inception stage of any construction project both the designers and the contractors should ask themselves about the employer's real objectives. Almost without exception the employer's needs will be an amalgam of functional and aesthetic requirements, built to a good standard of construction and finish, completed when required, at an appropriate cost, offering value for money and easily and economically maintained. The contractual procurement arrangements used must aim to satisfy all of these requirements; some in part and others as a whole, trading between them to arrive at the best possible solution.

The traditional approach has been to appoint a team of consultants to produce a design and estimate, and to select a constructor. The latter would calculate the actual project costs, develop a programme to fit within the contract period, organize the workforce and material deliveries and build to the standards laid down in the contract documentation. In practice the quality of the workmanship was often poor, costs were higher than expected, and even where projects did not overrun the contract period they took longer to complete than in other countries around the world. Traditionally little attention or consideration has been given towards future repairs or maintenance aspects.

The obvious deficiencies in the above, largely supposedly due to the separation of the design role from that of the construction effort have been known for some time. Employers, however, have generally wished to retain the services of an independent designer, believing that such would serve their needs better than the contractors with their own vested interests. They also wished to retain the competition element in order to keep costs down and to help to improve the efficiency of the contractor's organization. In more recent years they have seen some benefits from buildability which have been achieved through the early and integrated involvement of the contractor during the design stage. This has also had a spin-off effect in reducing costs and the time that the contractor is on site. Employers were, however, still loath to commit themselves to a single contractor at the design stage when costs might still be imprecise, and where their bargaining position might be seriously affected before the final deal could be struck.

Increasingly, however, contractors attempted to market their design-and-build approach as a possible solution to the employer's dissatisfaction with existing procedures. The benefits of a truly fixed price, a single point of responsibility and where the contractor assumed the full responsibility for both the design and the subsequent construction of the building were attractive propositions. Remedies open to the employer in the case of default or delay were now no longer a matter for discussion between the designer and the builder. If necessary the employer could always employ his own professional advisers to oversee the technical and financial aspects of the project.

The entrepreneurs of the construction industry are always seeking out new ways of satisfying the increasing demands of clients. Some are busy examining the methods that are in use in the USA, and thus seek to import systems which they believe are superior and improve the image of the construction industry. Others feel that the employers' interests would be better served by an over-arching project manager or construction manager. Contractors are themselves also going through a major evolutionary change in the way in which they employ and organize their work-force. An increase in subcontracting has occurred as fewer and fewer operatives are directly employed by main contractors. Management contracting recognizes and encourages these developments as trends which are desirable.

The construction industry will continue to evolve and adapt its systems and procedures to meet the new demands. New procurement methods will be developed which utilize new technologies and new ways of working. Construction projects are different from the majority of manufactured goods, because they are procured in advance of their manufacture. The majority of the projects are also different from the previous ones and often incorporate some new characteristics. Some projects are almost wholly original and all depend upon their peculiar site characteristics. In order to achieve value for money and client satisfaction, the appropriate procurement procedures must be selected or adapted to suit the individual needs of the employer and his project.

Chapter 8

Contract selection

Introduction

The selection of appropriate contract arrangements for any but the
simplest type of project is difficult owing to the diverse range of options
and professional advice which are available. Much of the advice is in
conflict. For example, design-and-build contractors are unlikely to
recommend the use of an independent designer. Such organizations are
also likely to believe that the integration of design and construction is
more likely to result in the provision of better buildings and to improve
client satisfaction. Many of the professions hold the opposite viewpoint,
and believe that their approach will produce the best solution, particularly
in the long term. In the past few years there has been a significant shift
in the way that construction projects are procured. This is partially in
response to the changes which have occurred within the construction
industry. Individual experiences, prejudices, vested interests, the desire to
improve the system and the familiarity with particular methods are factors
which have influenced capital project procurement recommendations.
Those who have had bad experiences with a particular procurement
method will be reluctant and cautious in recommending such an approach
again. When this is suggested they will attempt to resist such a course of
action and where the results are as expected, then this further reinforces
the view that such a method of procurement has only limited use.
  In reality too little is known and too little research has been

undertaken properly to evaluate the various procurement options. In practice, this is difficult because there are both successful and unsuccessful projects that have used identical means and methods of contract procurement. Personal human factors and external circumstances have a major influence upon the possible outcomes. Nevertheless more reliable information, based on empirical evidence is desirable to at least attempt to eliminate hearsay and folklore opinion.

The advice given should always be that which recommends a course of action which best serves the client's interests, and not that which is perhaps more beneficial or easy to operate for the individual who is offering the advice. This is professionalism, even though it may mean losing a commission. The employer may need to be convinced that a particular method and procedures which are recommended should be adopted as the most appropriate approach to be used. This may at times be against the employer's own better judgement or preferences, particularly where there is some familiarity with the other options that are being suggested. Some clients are resistant to change, and may require persuasion to adopt what might appear to be radical proposals. It may be necessary also to accept that because of the mechanisms employed, a better course of action cannot easily be explained until after the event, and that such a recommendation may be rejected at the outset as being speculative. Overseas clients working in a different cultural environment may find that the traditional contractual procedures used are alien to their needs and expectations. They may require even greater assurances that their project should be constructed using a particular procurement method. Individuals working within the same team will also have different expectations and views on the optimum procurement path.

Procurement advisers should offer advice in the absense of any vested interests or personal gains. Any associated interests which might influence the judgements should be declared, in order to avoid possible repercussions at a later stage. Whilst the professional institutions retain codes of conduct and disciplinary powers governing their members' activities, there has been a blurring of commercial and professional attitudes with the former vying for position with the latter. Outmoded approaches and procedures should be removed when they no longer serve any useful purpose. Sound, reliable and impartial advice is necessary from those who have the proficient skills, knowledge and expertise.

Employer's requirements

A confirmed cynic once described the construction industry as 'the design and erection of buildings that satisfy the architect and constructor alone and not the employer'. In addition, buildings often failed to function correctly, were too expensive and took too long to construct. As in most cynicism the case is vastly overstated, yet there is enough truth in the statement not to dismiss it out of hand.

One of the procurement adviser's main problems is in separating the employer's wants and needs. The employer's main trio of requirements are shown in Fig. 8.1. The numerical values result from research and attempt to weigh these broad objectives in order of their relative importance. They reflect the 'average' or typical client, and offer some guidance on the main issues associated with a construction project. The attempted optimization of these factors may not necessarily achieve the desired solution. For example, an employer may desire exceptional standards of quality and the future-use performance of the project. To achieve these he may be prepared to incur extra costs or a longer contract period. Alternatively a client may require the early use of the project as the main priority and be prepared to sacrifice a bespoke design or even high quality standards in order to achieve this. Clients may also choose to set contrasting objectives which are difficult to achieve using conventional procurement procedures. This may require the adviser to devise ingenious methods of procurement in order to satisfy such objectives.

In broad terms the employer's objectives are a combination of the following and the procurement path will need to identify the following priorities:

- An acceptable layout for the project in terms of function and use.
- An aesthetically pleasing design not only to the employer, but also as viewed by others.
- The final cost of the building should closely resemble the estimate.
- The quality should be in line with current expectations.
- The future performance of the building and the associated costs-in-use should fit within specified criteria.
- The project is available for handover and occupation on the date specified for completion of the works.

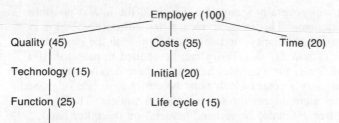

Fig. 8.1 Employer's requirements (after Walker, A. *Project Management in Construction*, p. 125)

Factors in the decision process

The following need to be considered when choosing the most appropriate procurement path for a proposed project:

- size
- cost
- time
- accountability
- design
- quality assurance
- organization
- complexity
- risk
- market
- finance.

Size of project

Projects of a small size are not really suited to the more elaborate forms of contractual arrangements, since such procedures are likely to be too cumbersome and not cost effective. Smaller-sized schemes therefore rely upon the traditional and established forms of procurement, such as a form of competitive tendering or design and build. The medium- to large-scale schemes can use the whole range of options which are available. On the very large schemes a combination of different arrangements may be required to suit the project as a whole.

Cost

Open tendering will generally secure for the client the lowest possible price from a contractor. This is the evidence that competition helps to reduce costs through efficiency, and lowers the price to the customer. There are limits to how far this theory can be applied in practice. If a large number of firms, for example, have to prepare detailed tenders then this increases industry's costs, which must be either absorbed or passed on to the industry's employers through successful tenders. There is no such thing as a free estimate! Negotiated tenders, on the other hand, supposedly add around 5 per cent to the contract price. In the absence of competition, contractors will price the work 'up to what the traffic will bear'. Projects which require unusually short contract periods incur cost penalties, largely to reflect the demands placed upon the constructor for overtime working and rapid response management. The imposition of conditions of contract which favour the client or insist upon higher standards of workmanship than is usual also push up building costs. The employer under these circumstances may end up paying more for the stricter conditions which might not need to be used or for a quality of workmanship which adds little to the overall ambience of the project.

Employers in the past have been overly concerned with a lowest tender sum often at the expense of other factors, such as the principles behind the indeterminate life cycle cost. Cash-flow projections which might have the effect of reducing the timing of expenditures are often ignored except perhaps by the most enlightened employers. A cash-flow analysis, for example, may be able to show that the lowest tender is not always the least expensive solution. The timing of cash flows on a large project may have a significant effect upon the real costs to the employer. With projects that include options on construction method then the cash-flow analysis becomes even more important. Procurement and contractual arrangements which take into account these factors should be considered more frequently.

The cost of the project is a combination of land, construction, fees and finance, and the employer will need to balance these against the various procurement systems which are available. In terms of cost savings a less expensive site elsewhere, rather than reducing the costs of quality, may be more appropriate.

Design-and-build projects show some form of cost savings in terms of professional fees, although the precise amount of these is difficult to calculate since they are absorbed within other charges submitted by the contractor in the bid price. Where the building is of a relatively straightforward design such as a standard warehouse unit or farm building, then it can be more cost effective to use a builder who has already completed similar projects rather than to opt for a separate design service. Cost reimbursement appears to be a fair and reasonable way of dealing with construction costs in a fair world. Society is not, and such an arrangement is often too open-ended for many of the industry's employers. Some clients may choose to use it out of necessity, setting objectives other than cost more highly. The majority of employers, however, will need to know as a minimum the approximate cost of the scheme before they begin to build, and there is nothing new in this (St Luke's Gospel Chapter 14 verse 28).

Where a firm price is required before the contract is signed then one of several procurement arrangements can be used. A firm price arrangement relies to a large extent on a relatively complete design being available. Where more price flexibility is possible then one of the more advanced forms of procurement might be used whilst at the same time achieving a measure of cost control.

Provisions exist under most forms of contractual arrangement for a fixed or fluctuating price agreement. The choice is influenced by the length of the contract period and the current and forecasted rates of inflation. Where the inflation rate is in small percentage terms and falling, then a fixed-price arrangement is preferable. When the rate of inflation is small and stable then it is common to find projects of up to 36 months' duration on this basis. When the rate of inflation is high, and particularly when it is rising then contractors will be reluctant to submit fixed-price tenders for more than about one year's duration. Although a fixed price is attractive to the employer, it cannot be assumed that this will necessarily be less expensive than a fluctuating type arrangement. Some contract conditions limit fluctuation reclaims to increases caused directly by changes in government legislation.

It is difficult to make cost-procurement comparisons, even where similar projects are being constructed under different contractual arrangements. It can be argued that competition reduces price, price certainty in the case of premeasurement or fixed price might not be the most economic, and that using serial tendering, bulk-purchase agreements and similar concepts are ways of reducing building costs. Cash flows and projected life-cycle costs on larger projects should be considered in any overall cost evaluation. The following are the cost factors to consider:

- price competition/negotiation
- fixed-price arrangements
- price certainty
- price forecasting
- contract sum
- bulk-purchase agreements
- payments and cash flows
- life-cycle costs
- cost penalties
- variations
- final cost.

Time

The majority of employers, once they have made the decision to build, want the project to be completed as quickly as possible. The design and construction phases in the United Kingdom are lengthy and protracted. Some of the apparent delays are linked to the protracted planning processes rather than the design or the construction phases. It is difficult to make comparisons on a global basis since there are a wide variety of influences to be considered such as methods of construction, safety, organization of labour, quality assurance, etc. Construction techniques also vary and these in turn produce different qualities and costs. The time available will also influence the type of construction techniques which might be used. A need for rapid completion may force the employer to consider using an 'off-the-peg' type building which can be constructed quickly.

In order to secure the early completion of the project several different methods of procurement have been devised with this objective in mind. Such approaches have implications for the other factors under consideration such as design, quality or cost. There is an optimum time solution depending upon the importance which is attached to these other considerations. For example, in terms of cost, shorter or longer periods of time on site tend to increase building costs. The former is due in part to overtime costs, the latter to extended site on-costs. Some clients are prepared to pay extra costs in order to achieve earlier occupation. Different types of project also have different time concepts. A shopping centre redevelopment may require rapid completion, since earlier revenue may easily account for the extra costs. Different techniques of design and construction may also need to be used to achieve early completion. New educational building completions are linked to school term times, whereas housing starts and completions are at the rate at which they can be either let or sold.

Some research has shown that construction work should not commence on site until the project has been fully designed and ready for construction with only the minimal involvement thereafter by the designer. Variations will still be allowed, but are not encouraged. Such an approach helps to eliminate a large amount of construction uncertainty which is common on many supposedly designed projects today. This approach allows the contractor to plan the organization and management of the project better and to spend less time awaiting drawings and details. Overall the design and construction period is shortened and earlier completion is achieved. The contractor is on site for a shorter period of time which results in the saving of building costs. The difficulty of adopting this approach is that the client wants to see work beginning on site as soon as possible.

Many of the newer methods of contract procurement have been devised specifically to find a quicker route through the design and construction processes. In some ways they have been assisted by changes in the techniques used for the construction and assembly of the building products and materials. Early selection was developed to allow the construction work to start on site whilst some of the scheme was still at the design stage. It also allowed the contractor an early involvement with the project. Some form of cost forecasting and control can be used but these will be much less precise than with some of the more conventional methods of procurement. Critical path analysis can be used to find the quickest way through the construction programme, and the American fast-track system was imported for the sole purpose of securing an early completion of the project. Inaccurate design information coupled with a need for speed in completion of the works has often resulted in abortive parts of the project, poor quality control and higher costs to both the contractor and the employer. The later forms of management contracting offer some solution to the time delay problem. Project management contracts, where an independent organization controls both the design and the construction teams has provided some good examples in terms of project co-ordination.

Faster Building for Commerce (National Economic Development Office, 1988) was a study aimed at helping the industry achieve earlier completions of its projects. The study claimed that the major influences on projects' time performance were customer participation, design quality and information, contractor's control over site operations and the integration of the subcontractors with design and construction. The study showed that fast times were 20–25 per cent shorter than the average, and the slowest times could take twice as long as the average. Overall, one-third of commercial projects finish on time, the rest overrun by a month or more, often because of extensive design alteration. These were claimed as the largest single factor affecting delays. Common ingredients in fast projects are organization to promote unity of purpose, competent management at all stages of the project and working practices which interlock smoothly and leave no gaps between activities and responsibilities. Many of the delays result from a lack of information, an under-estimating of the supervision of subcontractors and late changes in requirements by employers. In some cases quality control was a problem where work needed to be redone and hence caused delays. Slow reactions by the utilities companies can cause extensive delays, especially on sites with high services contents. The following are the time factors to consider:

- completion dates
- delays and extensions of time
- phased completions
- early commencement
- optimum time
- complete information
- fast tracks
- co-ordination

Accountability

Accountability according to the dictionary definition is the responsibility for giving reasons why a particular course of action has been taken. In essence it is not simply having to do the right things, but having to explain why a particular choice was made in preference to others that were available. It is of greater significance when dealing with public employers where it is necessary to justify why a particular course of action was taken. It has also become increasingly important with all types of employers where an emphasis is placed on achieving value for money on capital works projects. The documentation used for construction works is often complex and the technical and financial implications are considerable.

Employers need the assurance that they have obtained the best possible procurement method against their list of objectives. The possible trade-offs between competing proposals will need to be evaluated. It is difficult to satisfy the accountability criteria in respect of price, where tenders are sought in the absence of any form of competition. There is also the difficulty of justifying subjective judgements where these appear to be in conflict with common practice, but the process of selection will never solely be a mechanistic process. The elimination of procedural loopholes should be such as to provide the employer with as much peace of mind as is possible.

Accountability is interlinked with finance and an emphasis on paying the smallest price for the completed project. It may be easy to demonstrate to some employers that to pay more for a perceived higher quality or earlier completion is worthwhile. Other employers may need more convincing and some will feel doubtful about non-monetary gains.

The procedure for the selection, award and administration of contracts must be as precise as possible. Auditing plays a useful role in the tightening up of the procedures used, with *ad-hoc* arrangements that breach these procedures being discouraged. Systems that require huge amounts of documentation and the subsequent checking and cross-checking of invoices, time sheets, etc., are not favoured because of loopholes that can occur. Open-ended arrangements which are unable to provide a realistic estimate of cost are fraught with difficulties in terms of accountability. They provide difficulties in demonstrating value for money at the tender stage, since any forecast of cost will be too imprecise for reliability purposes. The following are the accountability factors to consider:

- contractor selection
- *ad-hoc* arrangements
- contractual procedures
- loopholes
- simplicity
- value for money.

Design

There is a good argument that the best design will be obtained from someone who is a professional designer. The design will then not be limited by the capabilities of the constructor or restrained to those designs which might be the most profitable to such a firm. However, the design-and-build contractor is more likely to be able to achieve a solution which takes into account buildability, and produces a design which is sound in terms of its construction. There are examples where the employer, having been provided with an unsatisfactory building, has to wait impatiently while the consultant and constructor argue about the liability. There are also examples where design and build projects, some using industrialized components, have had to be demolished after only a few years of life, because of their poor design concept, impossible and costly maintenance problems and unacceptable user environment which they have helped to create.

Contractors have on the whole been better at marketing their services and these have reaped benefits in the growing increase in design-and-build schemes. Designers have to some extent been thwarted in their response to this upsurge in activity due to the restrictions imposed on advertising by their profession and to a failure to react to the changes that have taken place. Only in recent years has the design-and-manage approach been introduced.

The traditional methods of contract procurement fail in many aspects of building design, not least because of the absence of any constructor input. They still, however, represent the most common method of procurement and more publicized failures might thus have been expected. Some of the forms of management contracting, which still largely retain the independence of the designer, have gained in their popularity amongst employers. Where the employer has been encouraged to form a contractual relationship with a single organization, then this has on the whole been beneficial.

Designs which evolve and develop only marginally ahead of the construction works on site must be of questionable worth in design solution terms, unless they are working within the constraints of either previously completed schemes or the confines of an existing structure. The following are the design factors to consider:

- aesthetics
- function
- maintenance
- buildability
- contractor involvement
- standard design
- design before build
- design prototypes

Quality assurance

Open tendering can result in a lower standard of workmanship than might have been achieved by using a builder who submitted a higher price. The statement 'you only get what you pay for' is true in terms of construction quality. Where a builder has had to submit an uneconomical price at cost, then quality may suffer unless improved supervision is provided. Consistent and good quality-control procedures are lacking in the construction industry and are often relegated in favour of other criteria in the list of objectives.

The quality of buildings depends upon a whole range of inputs from the soundness of the design, a correct choice of specification, efficient working details, adequate supervision and the ability of the builder. The skills of the operatives are also important, perhaps even more so today than a decade ago, now that the designs are tending to become more complex in their detailing and a higher level of craftsmanship is expected. The choice of a contractor who has a good reputation for the type and quality of work envisaged is important in achieving this objective. The use of labour-only operatives and the general subcontracting phenomena has sometimes resulted in a deterioration in quality performance, due to poor site co-ordination and supervision by site management.

The quality of design-and-build schemes depends largely upon the reputation of the builder selected, particularly where the employer chooses not to involve any professional advisers. The quality of the materials and workmanship will be regulated entirely by the builder alone. Speculative building schemes where the quality assurance is determined solely by the builder are not renowned for their high-quality work. Fast-track procurement methods which can involve a number of contractors on the same project can, without adequate supervision, result in widely varying standards of workmanship. There is also the difficulty of co-ordinating different contractors on the site, such as occurs with work packages on management contracts. The use of selective tendering, properly managed, continues to offer a good solution in terms of quality control.

Quality standards cannot be judged at the building's completion alone, but need to be considered in the long term. A virtually complete design prior to the commencement of work on-site is likely to be beneficial in improving the qualitative aspects of the project rather than the more *ad-hoc* design approach to problems as they occur on site.

The turnkey method where the designer−contractor has contractual responsibility for the long-term repair and maintenance of the project offers advanges, particularly in terms of quality assurance. Under this method of procurement there is the incentive that the designer−contractor will wish to reduce the likelihood of future defects arising by a more careful design and effective site management during construction. This may result in less innovation but this is preferable to inconvenience and costly failures in the future. Progress in construction is necessary, but not at the expense of protype designs which result in poor quality assurance

Although serial and continuation contracts using the same design and detailing should improve the quality aspects, in practice this has not been achieved and poor design, detailing and construction methods have unfortunately been repeated. The following are quality-assurance factors to consider:

● quality control
● independent inspection
● team working
● co-ordination

- subcontracting
- buildability
- future maintenance
- design and detailing
- reputation of craftsmen.

Organization

Allowing the contractor total control of the building project, as in design-and-build or management contracting, removes a layer of organization and eliminates dual responsibility. This should result in fewer things being overlooked or forgotten, work left undone or subcontractors being unable to complete their work on time owing to a lack of information. The additional tier of organization has the disadvantage of the parties blaming each other when disputes arise. However, the traditional methods of contract procurement have to a large extent set the lines of demarcation between designer and constructor quite clearly. In practice the designer probably relies too heavily on the constructor. Elaborate conditions of contract, to cope with the organization of construction work, have had to be drawn up to anticipate most of the eventualities that might arise.

The employment of a single firm, such as a design-and-build contractor, allows for quick response management, the ability to deal with problems as they occur, and more freedom in the execution of the works. The extent of such freedom will vary with the conditions of contract being used. Where a separate designer is used the response time is often much longer and this can result in delays to the contract. Where complex or difficult contract arrangements are employed these can have the effect of removing the initiative from the contractor.

The more parties involved with a building project the more complex will be the organization and the contractual arrangements. The employment of a group design practice should therefore result in fewer organizational difficulties than where individual firms are used. Management contracting is based upon awarding individual work packages to a range of specialist and general subcontractors. This can create problems of organization and co-ordination. There is much less control over such firms than when directly employed operatives of the main contractor are used. General contracting is, however, now unusual since about 90 per cent of construction work is subcontracted regardless of the method of procurement being used. These individual firms need to be programmed for precise periods of time, and a delay in allowing them to proceed with their work or a failure by them to complete on time can have a knock-on effect for the whole project. This presents even greater difficulties with tightly scheduled construction programmes. The following are the organizational factors to consider:

- complexity of arrangements
- single responsibility
- levels of responsibility
- number of individual firms involved
- lines of management.

Complexity

Projects which are complex in design or construction require more precise and comprehensive contractual arrangements. Complexity may be the result of an innovative design, the utilization of new constructional methods, the phasing of the site operations or the necessity for highly specialized work. It can also be the result of employing several contractors on the same site at one time in order to achieve rapid progress or the complicated refurbishment of an existing building whilst still in use by its occupants. It is often necessary in circumstances of these types to devise new contractual arrangements and to apply different types of procedures to the varying parts of the construction work. Where work can be reasonably well defined and forecasted, then traditional estimating processes can be used and the work paid for on the usual basis. Where the work is indeterminate, of an experimental type or requiring a solution from the contractor, then a lump-sum or cost-reimbursement approach with contractor design may need to be employed. In the latter case the contractor is given the opportunity to offer an acceptable solution to the problem as a part of the contract.

Where the project is very complex then the employer is likely to choose a separate designer with the skills which are required to produce the right solution. It is, however, important to involve the constructor as soon as possible with the project, particularly where this might influence the sequencing of site operations. A form of two-stage tendering might therefore be appropriate against this eventuality. The following are the organizational points to consider:

- nature of complexity
- capabilities of parties
- main objectives of employer.

Risk

Risk is inherent in the design and construction of a building. The employer's intentions will be to transfer as much of this as possible to either the consultants or the contractor. Risk may be defined as possible loss resulting from the difference between what was anticipated and that which actually occurred. Risk is not entirely monetary. An unsatisfactory design although completed successfully can result in a weakening of the designer's reputation with a consequent loss of future commissions. Risk can be reduced but it is difficult to eliminate it entirely. For example, the risk associated with a very specialized form of construction can be reduced by selecting a contractor with the appropriate experience.

The transfer of risk from the employer to others involved with the project may appear to satisfy the accountability criteria. It may be argued as an appropriate course to follow for the employer, but it may not be a fair and reasonable approach. It may also not be the best route for the employer to follow, since the risk needs to be evaluated. All contractors' tenders contain a premium to cover contractual risk. Where the risk does not materialize then this becomes a part of the contractor's profit. The employer may thus be better advised to assess and accept some of the risk involved and thereby reduce the contractor's tender sum and his own costs accordingly. This is a more common way of dealing with risk on construction projects.

The lump-sum contract with a single price, which is not subject to any variation is at one extreme, and at the other is cost reimbursement, where risk and financial predictability are uncertain. In the former the employer is paying for eventualities which might not occur. In the latter the client is accepting the risk but only pays for events that happen. A balance has to be drawn. Risk should always be placed with the party to the contract who is in the best position to control it. Where this is not possible then it should at least be shared, although it may be difficult to convince the employer that this course of action is the most financially appropriate. Some projects involve a large amount of risk in their execution. In some cases the risk may be so high that it is impossible to get a contractor even to consider tendering under conventional arrangements. Some form of risk sharing may then become essential in order for the project to proceed. The following are risk factors to consider:

- risk evaluation
- risk sharing
- risk transfer
- risk control.

Market

The selection of a method of procurement will be influenced by the state of a country's economy and the industry's workloads. An appropriate recommendation for today may have different implications for some time in the future. When there is an ample amount of work available, contractors are able to choose those schemes which are the most financially lucrative. Under these circumstances employers will be unable to insist upon onerous contractual arrangements and conditions. Where the risk involved is high it will be even more difficult to persuade contractors to tender for the work. Employers may need to be advised to delay their building projects at such times, and to wait until the economy is more favourable. Many employers will, however, be unable or unwilling to follow this advice.

When construction prices are low, then a form of cost reimbursement or management fee approach can be expensive. During times like this, contractors are sometimes prepared to do work at cost, and take a gamble with the risk factors that nothing of financial significance will go wrong. Conversely in times of full order books the opposite is true, and paying contractors their actual costs plus an agreed amount for profit can be a better proposition. When work is plentiful, contractors often have difficulty in recruiting a competent workforce of skilled operatives and this, coupled with similar restrictions in the availability of good supervision, can result in a deterioration in quality standards. When the amount of construction work available is restricted, then the standards of workmanship coupled with more intensive inspection, is likely to enhance the overall quality of the project. The following are the market factors to consider:

- availability of work
- availability of contractors
- economy affects procurement advice.

Finance

The usual way of paying the contractor for the building work is through monthly or stage payments. These payments help the contractor to offset the financial borrowing that is required to pay for wages and salaries and goods and materials. Two alternatives to this can be used. The first is a delayed payment system similar to that used on speculative developments. The employer effectively pays for the work by way of a single payment upon completion of the project. The employer has to accept the design as it is built, but acquires immediate occupation of the project. The financial borrowing requirements of the contractor are higher, but the employer makes savings by paying for the work at the end of the project. The other alternative is for the employer to fund the work in advance and thereby reduce the contractor's interest charges that are otherwise included in his tender. In these situations there are cautions of which the client needs to be aware. The industry is notorious for the number of insolvencies, and the employer would thus want to ensure the financial soundness of the appointed contractor. Contractors also tend to be less interested in a project once they have received payment for work. The employer can devise remedies to deal with these factors. With the former, a performance bond can be adopted and with the latter, liquidated damages can be applied. The following are financial factors to consider:

- payment systems
- financial soundness of parties
- financial remedies
- contract funding.

Conclusions

The choice of a particular method of contract procurement for a construction project involves identifying the employer's objectives, balancing these with the procurement methods which are available and taking into account the considerations outlined above. Figure 8.2 provides a comparison of some of the payment methods. It compares factors such

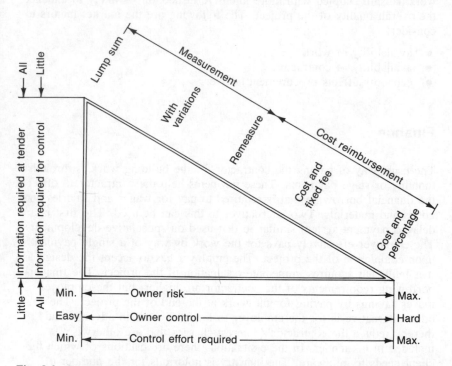

Fig. 8.2 Range of contract types (adapted from Burgess, R. A. (ed.) *Construction Projects, their Financial Policy and Control*, Longman, 1980, p. 149)

as the information requirements with the control and risk considerations. If an employer's main priority, for example, is for a lump sum price from a contractor, then the full information at the tender stage must be provided for an accurate price to be prepared. Risk and control effort throughout the duration of the contract, will then be minimal to the employer. On large and complex projects the ability to provide this detailed information is difficult. The quality and reliability of the design information will detemine how precise the buildings costs can be forecasted and controlled. The poorer and more imprecise it is, the greater will be the risks to the employer. The risk, of course, may never materialize and hence there will be no loss to the employer.

The three broad areas of concern to the employer, and the expectations that are required from any building project have already been identified in Fig. 8.1. The balance of these will vary but their analysis will help to influence and select the most appropriate procurement method.

Figure 8.3 offers a checklist of questions to help to determine an appropriate contract strategy. It is based upon an EDC report entitled *Thinking about Building*, but has been adapted accordingly. It provides examples of some of the more usual contractual arrangements which are available. It docs, however, need to be emphasized that the solutions recommended are based largely upon judgement rather than objective analysis. In answering the questions users can be provided with appropriate solutions. Under differing circumstances or where other factors need to be taken into account then the solutions must be adjusted accordingly. The questions themselves are not weighted and users will need to do this in order of importance. Some employers may wish to emphasize only a single aspect such as quality, and choose a method and contractor which arc capable of securing this. The majority of employers are, however, interested in an amalgam view, trading off the various factors against each other. It is inappropriate to use the chart in an incremental fashion by adding the various answers together.

The correct choice of a procurement method is a difficult task owing to the wide variety of options which are available. Some of the changes in methods of procurement are the result of a move away from the craft base to the introduction of off-site manufacture, the use of industrialized components and the wider application of mechanical plant and equipment. The improved knowledge of production techniques coupled with the way in which the work-force is organized have enabled the contractor to be able to analyse the resources involved and move towards their greater optimization. Contractors have also a much greater influence upon the design of the project and the recognition of buildability has had an influence both upon the design and the way the work is carried out on site and hence the quality of the finished work. The time available for construction and the subsequent costs involved have also been affected by these changes.

	Traditional selective tendering	Early selection	Design and build	Construction management	Management fee	Design and manage
TIMING — Is early completion important to the success of the project						
Yes:		*	*	*	*	*
Average:	*	*		*	*	*
No:	*					
VARIATIONS — Are variations to the contract important?						
Yes:	*	*		*	*	*
No:			*			
COMPLEXITY — Is the building technically complex or highly serviced?						
Yes:	*	*		*	*	*
Average:		*	*	*	*	
QUALITY — What level of quality is required?						
High:	*	*		*	*	*
Average:	*	*	*	*	*	*
Basic:			*			
PRICE CERTAINTY — Is a firm price necessary before the contracts are signed?						
Yes:	*		*	*		
No:		*			*	*
RESPONSIBILITY — Do you wish to deal only with one firm?						
Yes:			*			*
No:	*	*		*	*	
PROFESSIONAL — Do you require direct professional consultant involvement?						
Yes:	*	*		*	*	
No:			*			*
RISK AVOIDANCE — Do you want someone to take the risk from you?						
Yes:	*		*	*	*	*
Shared:						
No:						

Fig. 8.3 Identifying the client's priorities (adapted from 'Thinking aloud about Building,' EDC Report)

Chapter 9

Contract documents

The contract documents under any building project should include, as a minimum, the following information:

1. *The work to be performed.* This generally requires some form of drawn information. It assists the client by way of showing him schematic layouts and elevations. Even the non-technical employer is usually able to grasp a basic idea of the architect's intentions. Drawings will also be necessary for planning permission and building regulations approval. Finally, they will be needed by the prospective builder in order that he can carry out the architect's intentions during estimating and construction. On all but the simplest types of project, therefore, some drawings will be necessary.
2. *The quality of work required.* It is not easy on drawings alone to describe fully the quality and performance of the materials and workmanship expected. It is usual, therefore, for this to be detailed either in a specification or in a bill of quantities.
3. *The contractual conditions.* In order to avoid any future misunderstandings it is preferable to have a written agreement between the employer and the builder. For simple projects the conditions appropriate to minor works may be sufficient. On more complex projects one of the more comprehensive forms of contract should be used.
4. *The cost of the finished work.* This should be predetermined, wherever possible, by an estimate from the builder. On some projects it may only be feasible to assess the cost once the work has been

carried out. In these circumstances the method of calculating this cost should be clearly agreed.

5. *The construction programme.* The length of time available for the construction work on site will be important to both the client and the contractor. The client will need to have some idea of how long the project will take to complete in order to plan his own arrangements for the handover of the project. The contractor's costs will, to some extent, be affected by the time available for construction.

The contract documents on a building contract therefore normally comprise the following:

1. Form of contract.
2. Contract drawings.
3. Bill of quantities or specification.

On a civil engineering project it is more usual to include both a bill of quantities and a specification. The JCT forms used on building contracts allow only one of these documents.

Form of contract

This is the principal contract document and will generally comprise one of the preprinted forms described in Chapter 5. It takes precedence over the other contract documents (JCT clause 2.2). The conditions of contract seek to establish the legal framework under which the work is to be undertaken. Although the clauses aim to be precise and explicit, and to cover any eventuality, disagreement in their interpretation does occur. In the first instance, an attempt would be made to resolve the matter by the parties concerned. Where this was not possible, it may be necessary to refer the disagreement to arbitration. The parties to a contract agree to take any dispute initially to arbitration rather than to court. This can save time, costs and adverse publicity that may be damaging to both parties. If the matter still cannot be resolved, it is now taken to court to establish a legal opinion. Such opinions, if held, eventually become case law and can be cited should similar disputes arise in the future.

It is always preferable to use one of the standard forms available, rather than to devise one's own personal form. There are, in practice, several private forms that have been established by the large industrial corporations for their own use. The imposition of conditions of contract which are biased in favour of the employer are not to be recommended. Contractors will tend to overprice the work, even in times of shortage of work, to cover the additional risks involved. Unless there are very good reasons to the contrary, the architect should do all within his power to persuade the building owner to use one of the standard forms available. The modification of some of the standard clauses, or the addition of special clauses, should only be made in exceptional cases.

The majority of the standard forms of contract comprise, in one way or another, the following three sections:

Articles of agreement

This is that part of the contract which the parties sign. It should be noted that the contract is between the employer (building owner) and the contractor (building contractor). The blank spaces in the articles are filled in with:

(a) the names of the employer, contractor, architect and quantity surveyor;
(b) the date of the signing of the contract;
(c) the location and nature of the work;
(d) the list of the contract drawings;
(e) the amount of the contract sum.

If the parties make any amendments to these articles of agreement or to any other part of the contract, then the alterations should be initialled by both parties.

In some circumstances it may be necessary or desirable to execute the contract under seal. This is often the case with local authorities and other public bodies. The spaces for the signatures are then left blank and the seals are affixed in the appropriate spaces indicated. After sealing, the contract must be taken to the Department of Customs and Excise, where upon payment of stamp duty, a stamp will be impressed on the document. Without this the contract will be unenforceable.

Conditions of contract

The conditions of contract in any of the forms in general have a large degree of comparability, but are different in their details. They include, for example, the contractor's obligations in carrying out and completing the work shown on the drawings and described in the bills to the satisfaction of the architect (or supervising officer). They cover matters dealing with the quality of the work, cost, time, nominated suppliers' and subcontractors' insurances, fluctuations and VAT. Their purpose is to attempt to clarify the rights and responsibilities of the various parties in the event of a dispute arising. The *JCT Standard Form of Building Contract* contains 41 clauses, the last three of which deal with fluctuations and are published separately from the other clauses. The clauses from the *JCT Standard Form of Building Contract* are discussed in detail in Chapters 11–19.

Appendix

The appendix to the conditions of contract needs to be completed at the time of the signing of the contract. The completed appendix includes that part of the contract which is peculiar to the particular project in question.

It includes information on the start and completion dates, the periods of interim payment and the length of the defects liability period for which the contractor is responsible. The appendix includes recommendations for some of the information.

Contract drawings

The contract drawings should ideally be complete and finalized at tender stage. Unfortunately this is seldom the case, and both clients and architects rely too heavily upon the clause in the conditions allowing for variations. Occasionally it is due to insufficient time being made available for the pre-contract design work or, frequently, because of indecision on the part of the client and his design team. One of the intentions of SMM7 was only to allow bills of quantities to be prepared on complete drawings. Tenderers should, however, be given sufficient information to enable them to understand what is required in order that they may submit an accurate and realistic price. The contract drawings will include the general arrangement drawings showing the site location, the position of the building on the site, means of access to the site, floor plans, elevations and sections. Where these drawings are not supplied to the contractors with the other tendering information, they should be informed where and when they can be inspected. The inspection of these and other drawings is highly recommended since it may provide the opportunity for an informal discussion on the project with the designer.

The preparation of the architect's drawings should comply with the appropriate British Standard, BS 1192. Each drawing should include:

(a) the name and address of the consultant (architect, engineer or surveyor);
(b) the drawing number, for reference and recording purposes;
(c) the scale, and if more than one scale is used they should be of such dissimilar proportions that they are readily distinguishable by sight;
(d) the title, which will indicate the scope of the work covered on the drawing.

When the contractor signs the contract he will be provided with two further copies of the contract drawings. The contract drawings may include copies of the drawings sent to the contractor with the invitation to tender, together with those drawings that have been used in the preparation of either the bill of quantities or specification. In JCT 80 the contract drawings are defined in the first recital of the articles of agreement as those which have been signed by both parties to the contract. It will probably be necessary during the construction phase for the architect to supply the contractor with additional drawings and details. These may either explain and amplify the contract drawings, or because of variations identify and explain the changes from the original design.

The contractor must ensure that he has an adequate filing system for all of his drawings. Superseded copies should be clearly marked. They should not, however, be discarded or destroyed until the final account has been agreed, since they may contain relevant information used for contractual claims. The drawings should be clear and accurate, but because paper expands and contracts, only figured dimensions should be used. Scaling dimensions is therefore very much a last resort. Depending upon the size and type of the project, the architect may supply the building contractor with some or all of the following drawings:

Drawing title	Suggested scale
Survey plan	1 : 1,250
Site plan and draining	1 : 500
Floor plans	1 : 200
Roof plan	1 : 200
Foundation plan	1 : 200
Elevations	1 : 200
Sections	1 : 100
Construction details	1 : 10, 1 : 5
Engineering services	1 : 200

Return of drawings

Once the contractor has received his final payment under the terms of the contract he may be requested to return to the architect all drawings, details, schedules and other documents which bear the name of the architect (clause 5.6). The copyright of the design is vested in the architect. If either the building owner or building contractor wishes to repeat the work, then a further fee must be paid to the architect. None of the documents prepared especially for the project can be used for any other purpose than the contract (clause 5.7). Also, the contractor's rates must not be divulged to others or used for any purpose other than the contract.

Schedules

The preparation and use of schedules is particularly appropriate for items of work such as:

(a) windows;
(b) doors;
(c) manholes;
(d) internal finishings.

Schedules provide an improved means of communicating information between the architect and the builder. They are also invaluable to the quantity surveyor during the preparation of his bill of quantities. They have several advantages over attempting to provide the same information by way of either correspondence or further drawings. The checking for possible errors is simplified, and the schedules can also be used for the placing of orders for materials or components.

During the preparation of schedules two questions must be borne in mind.

1. Who will use the schedule?
2. What information is required to be conveyed?

The architect must supply the building contractor with two copies of these schedules that have been prepared for use in carrying out the works (clause 5.3.1.). This should be done soon after the signing of the contract, or as soon as possible thereafter should they not be available at this time.

Contract bills

A bill of quantities should be prepared for all types of building projects, other than those of a minor nature. The bill comprises a list of items of work to be carried out, providing a brief description and the quantities of the finished work in the building. A bill of quantities allows each contractor tendering for a project to price on the same information using a minimum of effort. The bill may include firm or approximate quantities depending upon the completeness of the drawings and other information from which it was prepared.

Uses

Although the main use of a bill of quantities is to properly assist the contractor during the process of tendering, it can be used for many other purposes, such as:

(a) preparation of interim valuations in order that the architect may issue his certificate;
(b) valuation of variations that have either been authorized or sanctioned by the architect;
(c) ordering of materials if care is properly exercised in the checking of quantities and future variations;
(d) preparation of the final account; the bill is used as a basis for agreement;
(e) production of a cost analysis for the building project;
(f) determination of the quality of materials and workmanship by reference to preamble clauses;

(g) useful in obtaining domestic subcontract quotations for sections of the measured work.

Preparation

The preparation of bills of quantities should always preferably be undertaken by the quantity surveyor. The items of work should have been measured in accordance with a recognized method of measurement. Building projects are generally measured in accordance with the *Standard Method of Measurement of Building Works* (SMM7). There are several other methods of measurement available to the construction industry. On mass housing projects it may be preferable to use a simplified version such as the *Code of Measurement of Building Works in Small Dwellings*. Methods also exist for work of a civil engineering nature, and many countries abroad have developed their own rules for measurement. The descriptions and quantities are derived from the contract drawings and SMM7, on the basis generally of the quantities of finished work in the completed bulding.

Contents

The contents of a bill of quantities are briefly as follows:

1. Preliminaries

This covers the employer's requirements and the contractor's obligations in carrying out the work. SMM7 provides a framework for this section of the bill. It includes, for example,

(a) names of parties;
(b) description of the works;
(c) form and type of contract;
(d) general facilities to be provided by the contractor.

In practice, although the preliminaries may comprise over 20 pages of the bill, only a small number of items are priced. The remainder are included for information and contractual purposes. The value of these items may account for 15 per cent of the contract sum.

2. Preambles

The preamble clauses contain descriptions relating to:

(a) the quality and performance of materials;
(b) the standard of workmanship;
(c) the testing of materials and workmanship;
(d) samples of materials and workmanship.

Some government departments have now replaced this section of the bill with a set of standard and comprehensive preamble clauses. The contents of the usual preambles bill are generally extracted from sets of standard clauses. Contractors rarely price this section of the bill.

3. Measured works

This section of the bill includes the items of work to be undertaken by the main contractor or to be sublet for his own domestic subcontractors. There are several different forms of presentation available for this work, for example:

Trade format The items in the bill are grouped under their respective trades. The advantages of this format are that similar items are grouped together, there is a minimum of repetition, and it is useful to the contractor when subletting.

Elemental format This groups the items according to their position in the building, on the basis of a recognized elemental subdivision of the project, e.g. external walls, roofs, wall finishes, sanitary appliances. This type of bill should, in theory, help in tendering by locating the work more precisely. In practice contractors tend to dislike it since it involves a considerable amount of repetition. It is, however, useful to the quantity surveyor during cost planning.

A recognized order for the inclusion of the various items is important, in order to provide quick and easy reference.

4. Prime cost and provisional sums

Some parts of the building project are not measured in detail but are included in the bill as a lump sum item. These sums of money are intended to cover work not normally carried out by the general contractor (prime cost sum) or for work which cannot be entirely foreseen, defined or detailed at the time that the tendering documents are issued (provisional sum). They are separately described as for defined or undefined work. Prime cost sums cover work undertaken by nominated subcontractors, nominated suppliers and statutory undertakings.

5. Appendices

The final section of the bill includes the tender summary, a list of the main contractors and subcontractors, a basic price list of materials and nominated subcontractor's work for which the main contractor desires to tender.

The form of tender is the contractor's written offer to 'undertake and execute the works in accordance with the contract documents for a contract sum of money', and will also state the contract period and whether the contract is on the basis of a fixed price. The tenders are submitted to the architect who will then make his recommendations regarding the acceptance of a tender to the client. If the client decides to go ahead with the project, the successful tenderer is invited to submit his bill of quantities for checking. The form of tender may also state that the employer

(a) may not accept any tender;
(b) may not accept the lowest tender;
(c) has no responsibility for the costs incurred in their preparation.

Contract specification

In certain circumstances it may be more appropriate to provide
documentation by way of a specification rather than a bill of quantities.
The types of project where this may be appropriate include:

(a) minor building projects;
(b) small-scale alteration projects.

The specification is similar to a bill of quantities. The difference is
that it does not include a measured works section, but this is replaced by
detailed descriptions of the work to be carried out. A specification is used
during:

(a) tendering, to help the estimator to price the work that is required to
be carried out; and
(b) construction by the designer in order to determine the requirements
of the contract, legally, technically and financially, and by the
building contractor to determine the work to be carried out on site.

Schedule of rates

A schedule of rates is a compromise between a specification and a bill of
quantities. It is essentially a bill of quantities that has omitted to include
any quantities for the work to be carried out. Its main purpose is
therefore in valuing the items of work once they have been completed
and measured. A schedule of rates may be used on:

(a) jobbing work;
(b) maintenance or repair contracts;
(c) projects that cannot be adequately defined at the time of tender;
(d) urgent works;
(e) redecoration projects.

Master programme

The contractor must provide the architect with a master programme
showing when he will carry out the works (clause 5.3.1.2). Unless
otherwise directed by the architect, the type of programme and the details
to be included are to be at the discretion of the contractor. If the architect

agrees to a change in the completion date because of an extension of time (clause 25.3.1) or wage damage (clause 33.1.3) then the contractor should provide the architect with amendments and revisions to the programme within 14 days.

Contractual provisions

Copies of contract documents

Clause 5.2 requests the architect to supply the contractor with the following documents:

(a) one copy of the form of contract certified by the employer;
(b) two further copies of the contract drawings;
(c) two copies of the unpriced bill of quantities.

Clause 5.1 states that the contract drawings and the contract bills will remain in the custody of the employer. These are to be available for inspection at all reasonable times.

Where there are no bills of quantities, then the building contractor will be provided with copies of a specification or schedule rates as may be appropriate.

Availability of documents on site

Clause 5.5 requires the building contractor to keep one copy of the following documents on site at all times for reasonable inspection:

(a) contract drawings;
(b) bills of quantities (unpriced);
(c) descriptive schedules;
(d) master programme;
(e) additional drawings and details.

Discrepancies in documents

Clause 2.3 asks the contractor to write to the architect should he find any discrepancies between the documents. Only the form of contract takes precedence over the other documents. The contractor cannot therefore assume that the drawings are more important than the bills. He can, however, assume that large-scale drawings will take precedence over the smaller scale drawings.

Clause 6.1.2 expects the contractor to adopt a similar course of action should he find a divergence between statutory requirements and the contract documents.

Part 3

Process and parties

Chapter 10

Process and parties associated with construction contracts

The following is a brief summary of processes used during the design stage and the construction stage of a building project.

Construction process

There are several different ways of describing the process which might be used for the construction of a building. Perhaps the most commonly referred to is the RIBA Plan of Work. This has been adapted and modified in all sorts of ways but essentially comprises the following range of tasks and activities. There are basically two separate groupings; pre-contract and post-contract. Some writers, however, identify four separate stages by separating the tentative (feasibility) from the definite (design) and the construction from the maintenance aspects. Certainly the latter aspect of property care has been greatly under-valued and under-utilized, and in terms of its time span and the need to protect an investment it has become of much greater significance in recent years. Figure 10.1 illustrates a process which might be used.

112

Architect	Quantity surveyor	Engineer	Contractor
	Client's brief		
Identifying the client's needs and wants in terms of space, function and aesthetics	Guide cost information Financial factors such as taxation and funding		Only involved if negotiation, design-and-build or two-stage tendering
	Investigation		
Feasibility and viability	Approximate estimate	Site survey and investigation	
Planning possibilities	Initial cost plan	Preliminary structural calculations	
Alternative sorts/types of construction			
Outline design approval			
	Sketch design		
Outline planning permission	Final cost plan		
Major planning problems solved	Life-cycle cost plan		
	Design		
Development of sketch plans	Cost implications and cost checking	Constructional methods decided	
Constructional details determined		Preliminary schemes for services	
Constructional methods decided		Design schemes for structure	

Pre-contract process

This is the period during which the need for the project, and the idea in terms of size, function and appearance, are formulated into plans that are capable of being used for the construction of a complete building.
Although variations are expected even after the work has commenced on site, this should not provide an excuse for a delay in the design requirements. Indications are currently showing that this lack of decision, prior to commencement on site, is an important factor affecting the trio of time, cost and quality of the finished project.

Architect	Quantity surveyor	Engineer	Contractor
	Working drawings		
All construction drawings and details completed	Quotations from specialist firms Final cost checks Bills of quantities	All construction drawings and details completed	
	Tender stage		
All members of the design team check their calculations			Contractors prepare tenders
	Receipt of tenders and tender checking		Materials and subcontractor quotations
			Determination of market factors
			Contractor's method statements
	Post-contract construction		
Inspection of quality Subcontractor nomination Issue of instructions Issue of certificates	Valuations, forecasts and payments	Inspection of quality	Construction programme agreed Planning and progress control Subcontractor control

Maintenance

Contractually up to the end of the defects liability period in-use repair and maintenance, changes in use, conservation, demolition, alteration and reconstruction, asset valuation, etc.

Fig. 10.1 The construction process

Client's brief

On a traditional project the client will first approach the architect regarding his requirements. In other circumstances he may decide to go straight to the builder for a design-and-build scheme, or to a firm who can offer an 'off-peg' project that may suit his requirements. The purpose of this first meeting is to distinguish between the client's needs and wants in respect of the design and spatial requirements. The majority of clients today will have a precise idea on how much they intend to spend. This they will have determined on the basis of their capital resources and funding ability. The architect would be wise to obtain some cost information from the quantity surveyor, rather than to attempt to go it alone. The quantity surveyor should therefore be able to provide guide costs based upon the floor area or some other functional requirement. He should also be able to suggest in very general terms the comparative costs of alternative design suggestions.

Investigation

Assuming that the initial requirements can be agreed, the project then moves towards a second stage. During this period many of the aspects are examined to ascertain the viability of the project. A site survey and investigation should be carried out to determine the nature of the ground and site conditions, and to locate the building's position on site. Bad ground conditions may have implications on the overall aspects of the design. They will also inevitably increase construction costs. Alternative methods of construction both in terms of design and costs will be considered. The quantity surveyor should by now have prepared his approximate estimate. Once the outline design is approved he will begin to formulate his cost plan. Preliminary ideas from the structual engineer may also be necessary, where this can significantly alter the design or the building costs.

Sketch design

During this stage the architect will be able to obtain outline planning permission. He will previously have discussed with the planners the possibility of such a scheme being approved. This he will have been able to assess upon the knowledge of the structure and district plans. The major planning problems will thus be solved, and the quantity surveyor's cost plan finalized.

Design

This is the period during which the sketch plans are developed and the constructional details and methods are selected. Preliminary schemes should now be available for the engineering services and structure. The quantity surveyor will need to know the cost implications of these various solutions and whether or not the cost plan is on target.

Working drawings

All of the drawn information should be completed during this stage. The practice of leaving parts of the design until later is to be deprecated. If the scheme has been fully designed, it should now be possible to obtain quotations from nominated suppliers and tenders from nominated subcontractors. The quantity surveyor, prior to preparing the bill of quantities, should complete extensive cost checks to satisfy himself that the design does not exceed the projected costs, when pace during the design stage will now have speeded up as the project moves towards the general tender period.

Tender stage

During this stage of the project tenders are invited from those firms who have already expressed their willingness to submit a price. While tenderers are busy pricing the documents, the architect and the other consultants will be checking through their own calculations. The pressure for progress has now moved, however, entirely to the contractor. During pricing he will obtain domestic subcontractor quotations, and current information from his various suppliers on the costs of materials. He will also need to be aware of the current state of the market in order that he can submit a price that is the most favourable. Tenders will be returned by a stated date, and the process of their checking and reporting is largely that of the quantity surveyor. Finally, a tender will be recommended for acceptance, and once the contract has been signed the project moves into the post-contract phase.

Post-contract process

Construction

The project should have been completely designed prior to release to the contractor for tendering purposes. Although the contract allows for and expects the occurrence of variations, this should not provide an excuse for only a partly finished design. One of the architect's main duties during this stage is to ensure that the contractor has all the information that he requires for construction purposes. In addition he will be responsible for the smooth running of the works. As the work is carried out, the architect's role is largely that of a supervisor ensuring that the contractor complies with all the requirements. He may employ a clerk of works, whose duties consist almost entirely of inspecting the work and materials during construction. The clerk of works may also act as a liaison officer on site, and his relationship with the contractor can either improve or reduce the overall success of the project.

The quantity surveyor during the construction of the works will prepare the valuations for the interim certificate. Certification is, however, entirely the responsibility of the architect. It is preferable if the varied or provisional works can be remeasured and agreed soon after it has been completed. In this case the work items will still be clear in everyone's minds, and the possibility of errors arising is therefore reduced.

116

The various subcontractors will come onto the site to carry out their own work. Even the major subcontractors will only be on site for a relatively short period of time, compared with the main contractor. The architect is unlikely to have completed the process of nomination for every firm, and some of these will therefore need to be done during the construction stage.

The local authority will have little to do with the building project in the majority of circumstances, but may choose to inspect the works at different stages. This will be done to make sure that each stage complies with the appropriate building regulation. The local authority will, however, take action where local regulations are infringed or where a nuisance is caused to nearby properties.

Maintenance

The project becomes officially complete when the architect issues his certificate of practical completion. The contractor is responsible for making good any of his defects from this date for about six months. The actual length of time will be specified in the appendix to the conditions of contract. The architect should ensure that all defects are made good prior to the issue of the final certificate. The quantity surveyor during this period will prepare and agree his final account with the contractor's surveyor. At the commencement of the defects liability period, one-half of the retention is released to the contractor, with the other half being paid with the final certificate. Although the contractor is contractually responsible for his work up to the end of this period, his liability under common law will extend for a much longer period.

Parties involved with the construction process

Local authorities

The construction industry is subject to a variety of controls, some of which are mandatory. Both the design and the contracting organizations must naturally comply with the general laws of the country, but in addition there are special regulations appertaining only to the construction industry. Such laws and regulations initially arise by an Act of Parliament, but their administration is generally undertaken by local government.

Local government is broadly divided into county councils and district councils, each with their own function. A major reorganization of local authorities was introduced by the Local Government Act 1972, which came into operation in 1974. The allocation of the various functions appropriate to construction are as follows:

Building regulations — district council.

Highways — county council, although much of the maintenance work is undertaken on their behalf, and with their agreement, by the district council.

Housing — district council.

Refuse — collection by the district council; disposal by the county council. This means that it is the county council's responsibility to find tipping sites.

Town planning — structure plans by the county council and local plans by the district council. This means that the county authority determines the outline plan for an area with the district council completing the details.

Water and sewage — dealt with by the regional water authorities.

Local government is restricted in the way it can exercise its powers as follows:

1. *Area* — It is generally confined to a defined geographical area. It works with adjoining authorities on matters of common interest through joint committees and joint boards.
2. *Central government* — The control of a local authority is exercised through the Secretary of State for the Environment. In some governments a local government Minister has been appointed to carry out this control. Central government control may be exercised by way of supervision where a statutory inspection can take place, and because a local government relies to a large extent on the finances from central government. All the local authority's accounts must be properly audited. In some cases the Minister concerned has powers to carry out a local authority's functions in cases where it defaults.
3. *Judicial control* — Because local authorities are created by statute, they derive their powers and functions in this way. They must therefore act within the laws afforded to them. Building owners and contractors are likely to encounter the local authority concerned initially for the approval of planning permission, where an appropriate fee is payable, and during construction where they must conform to the building regulations and other statutory documents.

During the 1980s there was political direction from Parliament via central government which has resulted in the privatization of certain aspects of local government services. This has in many cases required local authorities to tender against private companies for the services which they have traditionally provided.

The Crown

The Crown is used in this context to denote the governmental powers which are exercised through the civil service. This means central government offices rather than local government. Central government has many powers conferred upon it by Parliament. It does, for example, exert a certain measure of control over local government. This may be achieved by:

1. *Supervision.* The Secretary of State has power through statutes to supervise the activities of local authorities. For example, some town planning decisions may need to be referred to the Secretary of State. Some local services such as fire, police and education are subject to statutory inspection.
2. *Finance.* Much of a local authority's finances are obtained from central government. The Minister therefore can exercise considerable pressure on proposed expenditure, and also through the auditing of the local authority's accounts.
3. *Supersession.* In some cases the Minister concerned has power to supersede in certain functions in case of default by a local authority.

Because government is a major spender in the construction industry they are considered to be a very important client. They can also severely restrict and regulate how the work will be carried out. Although the Property Services Agency (PSA) undertake a large amount of central government's building work, other departments also have extensive construction programmes. Much of the central government's work is undertaken on the GC/Works/1 form of contract.

Public corporations

These operate the nationalized industries and are therefore essentially companies which are owned by and run for the benefit of the State. They have almost all been created by statute since 1945 and include: British Airways; National Coal Board; British Steel Corporation; Gas Board. Many of these have been privatised by the recent Conservative government. The majority of these companies exercise a complete monopoly, although there are exceptions. Each statute provides for a Minister to be answerable to Parliament for the industry concerned. He has the power both to appoint and to dismiss members of the board, and to give general directives in the national interest.

The employer

The purpose of construction is to provide a project for the building owner or client. The clients of the industry are both wide and varied and include those of the public sector and those of private organizations. Public sector clients include local and central government departments, and those industries or services that have been nationalized. Each separate organization is given a considerable amount of autonomy by the government of the day, and it is interesting to note the wide diversification in the methods used for the procurement and execution of major capital works projects. Little uniformity exists either in the design procedures employed or the contract conditions that are used. The private sector includes all those organizations that are not directly funded by some form of government money supply. It must be stressed, however, that even in the private sector individuals and companies may be able to secure funds for a variety of types of building work. For example, grants may be available for housing improvement and renovation or for the attraction of industry to a particular location.

Clients in the public sector may be influenced by both social and political trends and needs, and the desire to build may be limited by these factors. They will, nevertheless, be restricted in their aspirations by the amount of capital they are allowed to borrow for these purposes. The private sector, which encompasses the individual house owner and the large multi-national corporation, will probably direct its capital spending to the ventures that are considered to be monetary profitable. In both sectors, however, there has in recent years been a particular emphasis upon securing value for money. This has tended to be viewed on a building's life-cycle rather than upon initial construction costs alone.

The employer is one of the parties to the contract, the other being the contractor. Each client will have different priorities but essentially there will be a combination of:

(a) *Performance* in terms of quality, function and durability;
(b) *Time* available for completion by the date agreed in the contract documents; and
(c) *Cost* as determined in the budget estimate and the contract sum.

If employers are to be satisfied with the product (i.e. their construction project), then these three conditions must be critically examined.

The important references to the employer in JCT 80 are as follows:

(a) appointment of the architect;
(b) powers regarding insurances;
(c) duty to give possession of the site to the contractor;
(d) powers in respect of damages for non-completion;
(e) powers to determine the employment of the contractor;
(f) powers to engage directly employed contractors;
(g) duties regarding certificates;
(h) procedure in respect of arbitration.

The architect

The architect has traditionally been the leader of the design team. In the building process, where design and construction are separate entities, it is the architect who receives the commission from the client. Under the Architects' Registration Act 1938 it is an offence for anyone to carry on the business of an architect unless he is registered with the Architects' Registration Council (ARCUK). Because projects today require a large amount of specialized knowledge to complete the design, the architect may require the assistance of consultants from other professional disciplines.

The architect's function is to provide the client with an acceptable and satisfactory building upon completion. This will involve the proper arrangement of space within the building, shape, form, type of construction and materials used, environmental controls and aesthetic considerations — all within the concept of total life-cycle design.

The architect's duties and powers are described under the *JCT Standard Form of Building Contract* 1980. A contractor who believes that the architect is attempting to exercise powers beyond those assigned to him under the contract, can insist that the architect specifies in writing the conditions that allow him such powers (clause 4.2). The architect will generally operate under the rules of agency on the part of the employer. This means that if he gives instructions to the contractor, the employer will pay the agreed amount when necessary.

In some forms of contract the architect is termed the supervising officer. This is the name used, for example, in the GC/Works/1 form of contract, and is one of the alternative titles suggested in JCT group of forms. It is used in the GC/Works/1 form since the designer may be an engineer rather than an architect, and the terminology has been extended to the JCT form for a similar assumption.

The scope of the work undertaken by the architect may be broadly divided into pre-contract and post-contract duties. Although it is more common for an architect to provide a fully comprehensive design and supervision service, he can sometimes be requested to provide a design service only. It is much less common to expect him to supervise construction work only, although it could arise in situations where prefabricated buildings are used. However, even in these circumstances, the architect is more likely to be asked for advice on a particular system building, during the design stage.

In the normal pre-contract stage the architect's basic duty is to prepare a design for the works. This may involve three facets: architectural design, constructional detailing and administration of the scheme. This latter aspect will entail integrating the work of the various job architects and other consultants, and ensuring that the information is available for a start on site when required. The architect during his work must exhibit reasonable skill and care in the design of the works. This duty may be established in accordance with normal trade practice. The architect will also generally be held responsible for any work that he delegates to another. In the JCT form of contract, for example, although the quantity surveyor is responsible for most of the financial arrangements, the architect is ultimately responsible regarding the certification of monies to be paid. If part of the design is undertaken by a nominated subcontractor, then some protection may be afforded by means of a warranty from that firm.

During the post-contract stage the work undertaken by the architect is largely supervision and administration. Some drawings and details may still need to be prepared, particularly where such information is reasonably requested by the contractor. The purpose of supervision is to ensure that the works are carried out in accordance with the contract. The amount of supervision necessary will vary from project to project. A complex refurbishment project will require more frequent visits than the construction of a large warehouse shed. On very large contracts the architect may even be resident on the site. The duties of administration are used to describe the various functions, such as issuing instructions to the contractor, that must be carried out during the progress of the works. The post-contract stage involves those duties described in the *JCT Standard Form of Building Contract*, some of the more important of which are as follows:

1. Instructions

- Discrepancies and divergencies between documents
- Justification of instructions
- Instructions to be in writing
- Confirmation of verbal instructions
- Divergence between statutory regulations and project documents
- Opening up of work for inspection
- Removal from site of work, materials or goods which are not in accordance with the contract
- Exclusion from the works of any person
- Instructions given to person-in-charge
- Variations requirements
- Expenditure of prime cost and provisional sums
- Sanction in writing of variations created by the contractor
- Defects in the contractor's work
- Postponement of any work
- Execution of protective work after an outbreak of hostilities
- War damage
- Antiquities
- Nominated subcontractors
- Nominated suppliers

2. Certificates

- Practical completion of works
- Completion of making good defects
- Estimate of the approximate total value of partial possession
- Completion of making good defects after partial possession
- Failure to complete the works by the completion date
- Determination
- Interim certificates
- Final certificate

3. Other matters

- Provision of documents, schedules and drawings
- Stating levels and setting-out the works
- Access to site and workshops
- Limitation of assignment and subletting
- Granting an extension of time
- Reimbursement of loss and expense to the contractor
- Arbitration

The quantity surveyor

The quantity surveyor has developed from the function of a measurer to a building accountant and a cost advisor. The emphasis of the quantity surveyor's work has moved from one solely associated with accounting functions, to one involved in all matters of forecasting finance and costing.

The function of the quantity surveyor in connection with construction projects is therefore threefold: first, as a cost advisor, attempting to forecast and evaluate the design in economic terms both on an initial and life-cycle cost basis; second, preparing of much of the tendering documentation used by contractors; and third, in an accounting role during the construction period where he will report on interim payments and financial progress and the preparation and control of the final expenditure for the project.

Quantity surveyors are employed on behalf of both the building owner and the building contractor, the latter tending to specialize in post-contract functions or commercial management. The duties of the quantity surveyor are listed below.

1. Pre-contract stage

- Initial cost advice
- Approximate estimating
- Cost planning
- Bills of quantities and tender documentation
- Specification writing (where the bills are not required)
- Tender evaluation

2. Post-contract stage

- Valuations for interim certificates
- Final accounts
- Remeasurement of the whole or part of the works
- Measuring and valuing variations
- Daywork accounts
- Adjustment to prime cost sums
- Increased cost assessment
- Evaluation of contractual claims
- Cost analysis

In addition, the contractor's surveyor will be involved in the agreement of subcontractors' work, other duties of a commercial nature and possible bonus payments and ancillary functions.

Although the quantity surveyor has been accepted in the building industry as an essential member of the construction team, the situation is somewhat different in engineering. The acceptance of the quantity surveyor, for example, in civil engineering has not been easy, although there is considerable evidence that this is now changing. Many engineers now accept that the employment of the QS is essential if financial control is to be properly exercised. Of course, civil engineering contractors have been employing quantity surveyors since the turn of this century. A similar situation occurs in environmental services engineering and the petro-chemical industry. The quantity surveyor's work often extends beyond that described above. Loss adjusting, arbitration and auditing are other areas where quantity surveyors are employed.

His role within the JCT form of contract, although vague, is more precise than in other forms of contract. In the ICE form these duties are placed with the engineer, but in practice it is the quantity surveyor who will carry them out. In JCT 80 the quantity surveyor is mentioned in the following list of operations:

(a) confidential nature of contractor's prices;
(b) valuing variations;
(c) calculation of loss and expense;
(d) preparation of interim valuations;
(e) preparation of the final account;
(f) accounts of nominated subcontractors and suppliers;
(g) fluctuations.

Quantity surveying is only one branch of the surveying profession, which includes land surveyors, building surveyors and general practice surveyors among their number. Quantity surveyors account for over 40 per cent of the membership of the Royal Institution of Chartered Surveyors.

The clerk of works

The clerk of works is employed under the direction of the architect as an inspector of the works under construction. The clerk of works may give instructions to the contractor, but these are of no effect unless they are subsequently authorized by the architect.

The contractor must give the clerk of works every reasonable facility to allow him to carry out his duties. He is the counterpart of the person-in-charge employed on behalf of the contractor. His duties, therefore, are to ensure that the contract in terms of the specification and further instructions from the architect are fully complied with. He will attempt to make sure that the materials used and the workmanship carried out are in accordance with the contract requirements. This will involve: inspecting the materials prior to their incorporation within the works; obtaining samples where necessary for the approval of the architect; testing materials such as concrete, bricks and timber to the specified codes of practice; and generally ensuring that the construction work complies with accepted good practice.

The engineer

There is a wide range of different types of engineers employed in the construction industry. These may range from civil and structural engineers to building services engineers. Civil engineers are responsible for the design and supervision of civil and public works engineering, and are employed in a similar way to that of architects employed on a building contract. In addition, the engineer's counterpart working for the contractor is often a civil engineer. Their work can be very diverse, and may include projects associated with transportation, energy requirements, sewage schemes or land reclamation projects. Structural engineers are usually employed by the architect on behalf of the client. They act as consultants to design the frame and the other structural members in buildings. The building services engineers are responsible for designing the environmental conditions that are required in today's modern buildings. There has in recent years been an upsurge in their membership as greater attention is paid towards this aspect of building design.

Engineers are not mentioned by name in JCT 80, although the supervising officer that is mentioned in some of the forms may equally be an engineer or a surveyor or an architect, depending upon who is largely responsible for the design and supervision of the works.

The engineering profession is very diverse, with several institutions coming under the umbrella of the Chartered Engineering Institute, such as the Institution of Civil Engineers, Institution of Structural Engineers, and the Chartered Institute of Building Services. In addition the Association of Consulting Engineers, acting as a voice for the various practices, has a wide membership.

Person-in-charge

The person-in-charge is responsible for the effective control of the contractor's work and workpeople on site. He will be responsible for organization and supervision on the contractor's behalf, and for receiving instructions from the architect. Depending upon the size and nature of the works and the type of firm, he may be a general foreman, or a site agent, or a project manager. He may have received his initial training as a trade craftsman or he may be a chartered builder or engineer. His responsibilities will vary with the size of the project and company policy. On the larger projects he may receive considerable assistance from other site staff. The person-in-charge, whatever his title, is the site manager on behalf of the main contractor and he is very often a member of the Chartered Institute of Building.

Main contractor

The majority of the construction work in the United Kingdom is undertaken by a general contractor. These firms, which will be public limited companies (plc), will vary in size, having from just a few to many hundreds of employees. Many of the larger companies are household names and have developed only since the beginning of the twentieth century. Although there is no clear dividing line between building and civil engineering works, many firms tend to specialize in only one of these sectors. Even in the larger companies, separate divisions or companies exist, often trading and structured in entirely different ways depending upon the sector in which they are employed. The majority of construction firms will be members of either the Building Employers Confederation (BEC) or the Federation of Civil Engineering Contractors (FCEC). Even the operatives' unions and the rules under which they are engaged are different.

The smallest building firms may specialize in one trade, and as such may act as either domestic subcontractors or jobbing builders carrying out mainly repairs and small alterations. The medium-sized firms may be a combination of trades operating as general contractors within one town or region. These firms may specialize in certain types of building projects or be speculative house builders. The largest firms may be almost autonomous units, although it is uncommon even in these companies to find them undertaking a complete range of work. On the very large projects it is generally usual to find specialist firms for piling, steelwork and high-class joinery.

It has been suggested that one-quarter to one-third of the work of the construction industry is minor in nature, being largely of repairs and maintenance. This work is often carried out by the smallest companies. A recent survey also indicated that one-third of the building firms in Britain do not employ any operatives, but the work is carried out by the partners of the firm. The larger companies may be represented by only 200–300 firms throughout the country. In more recent years there has been a trend away from the multi-million pound project, resulting in a slight reduction in the number of these firms. Overseas projects of this size have helped to keep such firms viable within the UK. The reduction in the size of projects has also meant the breaking down of some of the larger firms into smaller sized units working on a more localized basis.

The contractors under JCT 80 and the other forms of contract agree to carry out the works in accordance with the contract documents and the instructions from the architect. They agree to do this usually within a stipulated period of time and for an agreed amount of money. The main contractor must also comply with all statutory laws and regulations during the execution of the work, and ensure that all who are employed on the site abide by these conditions. The contractor will still be responsible contractually for any defects that may occur, for the period of time stipulated in the conditions of contract (normally six months). The responsibility, however, of the contractor for the project does not end here. In common law the rights of the employer will last for 6 years and 12 years respectively, depending upon whether the contract was under hand or seal.

The contractor is mentioned extensively in the conditions of contract, largely because, along with the employer, he is one of the parties to the contract. Some of the more important provisions are listed below.

1. Quality
- Contractor's obligations
- Compliance with architect's instructions
- Duties in setting-out
- Compliance with the standards described
- Responsibility for faulty workmanship
- Duty to keep on site a person-in-charge
- Requirement for access for the architect to the site and workshops
- Limitations on assignments and subletting
- Right to object to nominated subcontractors
- Duty to employer's directly employed contractors

2. Time
- Procedure for partial possession
- Necessity to proceed diligently with the works
- Liabilities in the event of non-completion
- Duty to inform the architect of any delays
- Rights in cases of determination of the contract

3. Cost
- Duty to ask for any loss or expense
- Responsibility for payment to nominated subcontractors
- Procedure for certificates and payments

4. Others
- Liability for injuries to persons and property
- Duties regarding insurances

Suppliers

Building materials delivered to a site may be described under one of three headings: materials, components, and goods.

Materials are the raw materials to be used for building purposes and include, for example, cement, bricks, timber, plaster, etc. The items included within this description will, in total, probably represent the largest expense on the traditional building site. As more and more of the construction processes are carried out off site, so the value of this section will diminish.

The second category of items, the components, represent those items delivered to site in almost 'kit' form. They may include joinery items such as door sets or joinery fittings to be assembled on site. The industrialized building process is based to a large extent on the assumption that many items can come to site in component form to be assembled very quickly for a very small amount of money.

The third section, described as goods, includes those items that are generally of a standard nature which can be purchased directly from a catalogue — for example, sanitary ware, ironmongery, electrical fittings, etc.

The contractor's source of supply for these items may vary, but must in all circumstances comply with those specified in the contract documents, regarding quality and performance. The contractor will probably make extensive use of builders' merchants, because they stock a wide variety of items that can be purchased at short notice. Some of the items will need to be obtained directly from the manufacturer, and in other circumstances specialist local suppliers of timber or ready-mixed concrete will be used. Contractors are able to secure trade discounts for the items that they purchase, and such discounts will be increased either to attract trade or because of large orders. Some clients, who undertake extensive building work, are able to arrange with suppliers a bulk purchase agreement. This helps to reduce their own costs of construction because they are able to secure very reasonable rates for the items. The contractor must then obtain the appropriate items described from such suppliers.

The *JCT Standard Form of Building Contract* refers to two special types of suppliers: i.e. named suppliers and nominated suppliers. A named supplier is a firm specified in the contract documents from whom the contractor should obtain certain materials, components or goods. It is usual to suggest a list of alternative suppliers or sometimes to add the words 'other equal and approved'. The contractor would then need to show that the items he proposed to purchase for the work complied with those specified. In other circumstances a single supplier or manufacturer may be named, where the intention of the architect is not to diverge to any other alternative. This is often the case in respect of sanitary ware, where a particular design is selected, or for suspended ceilings and kitchen fittings.

In some situations the architect may choose to nominate a particular supplier to provide some of the various materials, components or goods. In these circumstances the architect chooses to include these items as a prime cost sum in the bills. The appropriate conditions of clause 36 then apply, and these are described in the context of that clause.

Subcontractors

It is very unusual today for a single contractor to undertake all the
contract work with his own workforce. Even in the case of minor
building projects the main contractor is likely to require the assistance of
specialist trade firms. Work undertaken by firms other than the main
contractor are often described as subcontractors, although in some
situations it is not uncommon to find specialist firms working on the site
beyond the normal jurisdiction and confines of the main contractor.

The employer may, for example, choose to employ such firms
directly, and in this context these firms are not to be considered as
subcontractors of the main contractor. Provision is made in the conditions
of contract for such firms in order that they may have access to the
contractor's site (clause 29). For example, a firm constructing a sculpture
may come into the confines of this clause. Second, the employer may
choose to nominate particular firms to undertake the specialist work that
will be required. In these cases the employer may adopt this approach in
order to gain a greater measure of control over those who carry out the
work. These subcontractors enjoy a special relationship with the
employer, as discussed in clause 35. Although after nomination they are
often supposedly treated like one of the main contractor's own
subcontractors, they do have some special rights, for example, in respect
of their payment.

The architect may also choose to name subcontractors in the bills of
quantities or specification, who will be acceptable for the execution of
some of the measured work. This procedure avoids the lengthy process of
nomination, but still provides a substantial measure of control on the part
of the architect. Provisions are found within the conditions of contract,
clause 19, and a requirement is to name at least three firms who will be
acceptable to the architect. This provides for some measure of
competition and allows the contractor a choice of firms. The contractor
may also add to this list with the approval of the architect, and this
should not unreasonably be refused.

All the remaining work is still unlikely to be carried out by the main
contractor, and provision is also made for the use of the contractor's own
subcontractors. These subcontractors are referred to in the conditions as
the main contractor's domestic subcontractors (clause 19). Named
subcontractors are employed to undertake that work (a) for which the
contractor makes no provision within his company, or (b) when his own
employed labour are busy elsewhere. The contractor must seek the
approval of the architect in this respect, but it is unusual for this approval
not to be given.

A further group of subcontractors are those described as statutory
undertakers, e.g. gas, water, electricity. These are separately described
for the following reasons: the employer and contractor often have no
choice in employing them because of their statutory rights; they
sometimes require payment in advance; and they refuse to give any cash
discount for prompt payment.

The Intermediate Form of Contract identifies another type of subcontractor, known as the named subcontractor, who is akin to the nominated subcontractor. More about these is mentioned in Chapter 24 covering the IFC.

Direct labour

The public-sector employer is a large client of the construction industry. They carry out work ranging from multi-million pound engineering projects to the repair and maintenance of local authority dwellings. Although there has been some discussions regarding a publicly owned national building corporation operating on a regional basis, this has not yet been developed and is not in practice. There are, however, the direct labour construction departments employed within the majority of borough and county councils. The expansion or contraction of all of these organizations is a politically sensitive issue and opinions regarding their efficiency and necessity will depend much on one's viewpoint. In some local authorities the direct labour departments may be responsible for no more than building and highway maintenance. In others they may be large enough to undertake major projects. They will generally only work within the confines of their geographical area, although they have been known to tender for other local authorities' building work. They do not work in the private sector, nor do they work for other publicly controlled organizations such as, for example, the health service. Where capital projects are envisaged they are usually required to tender for this work against private contractors. Maintenance work may be undertaken by the direct labour department as a matter of course, although even within this sphere of work some element of competition is now envisaged.

The building surveyor

Traditionally the building surveyor's role was in assisting other colleagues and clients with the maintenance and repair of buildings and preparing survey reports for the prospective purchasers and users of real estate. Building surveying is today a rapidly expanding profession. Some of this is due to the growing popularity of building conversion and renovation and the poor and deteriorating nature of our buildings stock. It is also due to some extent to the nature of our society with its make-do-and-mend approach and the desire for the conservation of older properties. As a profession it is somewhat unusual in being largely restricted to the United Kingdom and some of its ex-colonies at the present time. Building surveyors are, however, rarely concerned with projects of a large size, and are not specifically referred to in the forms of contract.

The peripheral professions

There is a wide range of other professions who are associated with the construction industry. One's viewpoint will determine whether these represent an unnecessary fragmentation of the industry or a desirable specialization. The clear demarcation of activities has now become blurred, particularly as we look forward towards the end of the century and consider the characteristics of the European community and the USA. Certainly the amount of knowledge which is now available and the skills which are required are too great for a single person to control and some specialization even within a conglomerate of the professions is essential. Figure 10.2 lists the major professional bodies which currently exist in the United Kingdom and the following list describes some of the other activities involved.

Building control officer — normally employed on behalf of the local authority to ensure that the building plans and proposals comply with the building regulations and by-laws made under the public health and building laws.

Estimator — responsible for calculating in advance of building, the cost of the project to a particular contractor based upon the total costs of all the labour, materials and plant that will be needed.

General practice surveyor — responsible for the acquisition of the building site for the owner or developer and negotiating with adjoining owners before, during and after construction and the disposal (sales or lettings) of the scheme upon completion.

Interior designer — developing the internal shell of buildings to provide good aesthetic and working conditions to create an acceptable ambience for the owner and user.

Landscape architect — helps to create the all-important context and space in which the building is set. Increasingly in modern buildings this often includes internal spaces.

Planner — involved with the legislative aspects of the building's location in interpreting the structure and district plans of local authorities.

		Membership
Royal Institution of Chartered Surveyors	RICS	84,500
Institution of Civil Engineers	ICE	74,000
Royal Institute of British Architects	RIBA	31,000
Chartered Institute of Building	CIOB	29,000
Institution of Structural Engineers	IStrutE	20,000
Royal Town Planning Institute	RTPI	12,500
Chartered Institution of Building Services Engineers	CIBS	11,000
Incorporated Society of Valuers and Auctioneers	ISVA	7,500
Chartered Institute of Arbitrators	CIArb	6,000
British Institute of Architectural Technicians	BIAT	5,500
Society of Surveying Technicians	SST	5,000

Fig. 10.2   Professional institutions in the construction industry

Part 4

Standard Form
of Building
Contract

Chapter 11

Introduction, Articles of agreement and the appendix

Introduction

The Standard Form of Building Contract is known throughout the industry as JCT 80. It replaced the previous form of 1963. Since 1980 there have been eight amendments and these have been listed in Chapter 5. Some of these deal with a single change to a particular clause whereas others deal with a multiplicity of amendments. The content of the JCT 80 form is as follows:

Articles of Agreement.
Conditions — Part 1. General clauses.
Part 2. Nominated subcontractors and nominated suppliers.
Part 3. Fluctuations.
Part 4. Settlement of dispute — arbitration.

The principle of the form is that it is an entire contract which is modified by a number of its own provisions. Separate editions are available for private clients as distinct from local-authority clients. The differences

134

between the two are, however, minimal. Financially it is a lump-sum
contract using three variants of with quantities, without quantities, or with
approximate quantities. The two parties involved are the employer (client)
and the contractor. The employer is responsible for making payments to
the contractor, who in turn has obligations to complete the works in
accordance with the contract provisions. Neither the architect nor the
quantity surveyor are parties to the contract. The former acts on behalf of
the employer but sometimes in an impartial way. The quantity surveyor
accounts for the financial transactions.

Articles of agreement

The articles of agreement precede the conditions of contract, and include
the information that is specific to a particular contract. They define the
various persons referred to in the contract, and also describe the
procedure to be followed in the case of arbitration. The following
information therefore needs to be written into the articles of agreement.

1. *The date.* This is the date when the agreement is made. It is not the
   date of tender, which may have some significance in respect of
   fluctuation contracts; nor is it the date when the project will start on
   site. This date is defined in the appendix as the date of possession
   and included in clause 1. The date in the articles of agreement will
   therefore have little significance as far as the contract is concerned.
2. *The parties.* The contract is between the employer and the contractor,
   and their names and addresses must be inserted in the articles of
   agreement. These names are used consistently throughout the
   conditions of contract.
3. *The works.* The employer requires the contractor to complete the
   works in accordance with the drawings and bills of quantities. The
   works are essentially the building project, but by implication in the
   conditions of contract may also mean the site. A description of the
   project and its location (address) should be given. The contractor is
   given possession of the site on the date of possession as stated in
   clause 23 and detailed in the appendix.
4. *The drawings and bills of quantities.* These, together with the form
   of contract, constitute the contract documents. They are defined in
   clause 1 and discussed in clause 2 of the conditions of contract. The
   contract drawings are formally registered by their numbers and
   should be signed by both parties. The contract bills, which are a
   priced copy of the bills of quantities, are also to be signed by the
   parties.
5. *The architect.* The drawings and bills of quantities are prepared
   under the direction of the pre-contract architect. It emphasizes that
   the design is the responsibility of the architect and not the contractor.

On some contracts the designer may not be the person who supervises the work on site. The architect referred to in the conditions comes within this latter definition. In the event of the architect's death, or when he no longer fulfils his function, the employer must nominate a replacement architect. If the contractor has a reasonable objection, then the employer must appoint an architect with whom the contractor approves. Such an appointee must not revoke decisions already acted upon by the contractors. He can of course, ask the contractor to rebuild part of the completed works, but if these have previously been accepted then the contractor is entitled to an appropriate payment. In some cases the supervisor of the works may not be an architect within the definition of the Architects' Registration Act 1938. In this case the term supervising officer is used to refer, perhaps, to an engineer or surveyor.

In the local authorities version the term architect has been substituted by architect/contract administrator. This reflects the view held by some, that some contractual matters are probably better dealt with by someone other than the architect.

6. *The quantity surveyor* (article 4). This refers to the client's quantity surveyor. In the event of his death, or when he is replaced by the architect, this must be done with the approval of the contractor.
7. *The contract sum* (article 2). The employer's main obligation is towards the payment of the contractor for the work executed. The total amount is described as the contract sum (clause 14) and this will be paid by instalment (clause 30). Although this sum is agreed upon by the two parties, it will be subject to adjustment within the terms of the contract (clause 30) as the project progresses.
8. *The employer.* The status of the employer for the purpose of the statutory tax deduction scheme must be stated in the appendix. This refers to clause 31 and generally to labour only subcontractors.
9. *Contractor's obligations* (article 1). The contractor's obligations under the terms of the agreement are to carry out and complete the works in accordance with the contract documents. These obligations are further reinforced in clause 2 of the conditions.

Settlement of disputes — arbitration (article 5)

Where disputes or differences of opinion occur between the employer (or architect) and the contractor, the parties agree to attempt to settle the matter first of all through arbitration. Arbitration is described in the Arbitration Act of 1979. Article 5 constitutes an arbitration agreement under the said Act. Disputes that may be referred to arbitration can arise both during and after construction or should the works be abandoned.

Arbitration is now covered in clause 41 and the JCT Arbitration Agreement. Disputes may occur for a variety of reasons. The following instances will not generally be referred to arbitration:

(a) differences in the interpretation of the statutory tax deduction scheme — the appropriate Act may direct some alternative method of resolving such a dispute;
(b) disagreements regarding the possibility of exemption of the VAT agreement.

The reason why the above matters are not referred to arbitration is largely due to the statutory powers and responsibilities of the various government departments. The interpretation of the various acts is therefore largely their own prerogative.

Attestation

The attestation page is for the parties to sign the contract and for the signatures to be witnessed. The signatories must have the necessary authority to sign for this purpose to provide validity to the contract. The contract may be executed under seal or under hand, and the Limitation Act of 1963 states that actions become barred after 12 years and 6 years, respectively. The current ruling suggests that the cause of action begins to accrue when the damage is discovered, or when it should reasonably have been discovered. The actual time of discovery may therefore not be relevant. There is no contract between the parties until the articles of agreement have been executed, unless the facts show otherwise. The carrying out of work prior to contract may indicate an intention on both parties, and therefore, if the project does not proceed, a claim for *quantum meruit* may result.

The appendix

The appendix (see Fig. 11.1) provides a considerable amount of information about the contract that is of particular importance to the project. The purpose is to set out in one place a schedule of these details. The completion of the appendix is necessary to give the conditions their full meaning. Each subject listed in the appendix is discussed in detail under the clause concerned. There are, however, some differences in principle between the treatment of items in the appendix. Some items will always need to be completed to make sense, whereas others can be left blank. In other circumstances the appendix makes a recommendation, and unless anything is entered to the contrary this suggestion will apply.

Appendix

	Clause etc.	
Statutory tax deduction scheme – Finance (No. 2) Act 1975	Fourth recital and 31	Employer at Base Date *is a 'contractor'/is not a 'contractor' for the purposes of the Act and the Regulations *(Delete as applicable)
Base Date	1·3	
Date for completion	1·3	
Defects Liability Period (if none other stated is 6 months from the day named in the Certificate of Practical Completion of the Works)	17·2	
Assignment by Employer of benefits after Practical Completion	19·1·2	Clause 19·1·2 *applies/does not apply *(Delete as applicable)
Insurance cover for any one occurrence or series of occurrences arising out of one event	21·1·1	£
Insurance – liability of Employer	21·2·1	Insurance *may be required/is not required Amount of indemnity for any one occurrence or series of occurrences arising out of one event £_____[y·1] *(Delete as applicable)
Insurance of the Works – alternative clauses	22·1	*Clause 22A/Clause 22B/Clause 22C applies (See Footnote [m] to Clause 22) *(Delete as applicable)
Percentage to cover professional fees	*22A 22B·1 22C·2 *(Delete as applicable)	
Annual renewal date of insurance as supplied by Contractor	22A·3·1	
Insurance for Employer's loss of liquidated damages clause 25·4·3	22D	Insurance *may be required/is not required *(Delete as applicable)
	22D·2	Period of time
Date of Possession	23·1·1	

Footnote

[y·1] If the indemnity is to be for an aggregate amount and not for any one occurrence or series of occurrences the entry should make this clear.

Amendment 4: 1987

	Clause etc.	
Deferment of the Date of Possession	23·1·2 25·4·13 26·1	Clause 23·1·2 *applies/does not apply Period of deferment if it is to be less than 6 weeks is _____ *(Delete as applicable)
Liquidated and ascertained damages	24·2	at the rate of £ _____ per _____
Period of delay: [z·1]	28·1·3	_____
Period of delay: [z·2]	28A·1·1 28A·1·3	_____
Period of delay: [z·3]	28A·1·2	_____
Period of Interim Certificates (if none stated is one month)	30·1·3	_____
Retention Percentage (if less than 5 per cent) [aa]	30·4·1·1	_____
Work reserved for Nominated Sub-Contractors for which the Contractor desires to tender	35·2	_____
Fluctuations: (if alternative required is not shown clause 38 shall apply)	37	clause 38 [cc] clause 39 clause 40
Percentage addition	38·7 or 39·8	_____
Formula Rules	40·1·1·1	
	rule 3	Base Month _____ 19 ____

It is essential that periods be inserted since otherwise no period of delay would be prescribed.

Local Authorities Edition only

	rule 3	Non-Adjustable Element _____ (not to exceed 10%)
	rules 10 and 30 (i)	Part I/Part II [dd] of Section 2 of the Formula Rules is to apply
Settlement of disputes – Arbitration – appointor (if no appointor is selected the appointor shall be the President or a Vice-President, Royal Institute of British Architects)	41·1	President or a Vice-President: *Royal Institute of British Architects *Royal Institution of Chartered Surveyors *Chartered Institute of Arbitrators *(Delete as applicable)
Settlement of disputes – Arbitration	41·2	Clauses 41·2·1 and 41·2·2 apply (See clause 41·2·3)

Footnotes

[z] It is suggested that the periods should be:
z·1 one month;
z·2 one month;
z·3 three months.

[aa] The percentage will be 5 per cent unless a lower rate is specified here.

[bb] Not used.

[cc] Delete alternatives not used.

[dd] Strike out according to which method of formula adjustment (Part I – Work Category Method or Part II – Work Group Method) has been stated in the documents issued to tenderers.

Amendment 4: 1987

Fig. 11.1 Appendix

Chapter 12

Quality of work during construction

The following clauses from the conditions of contract have a particular influence in the way that the work is carried out, and hence the resultant quality of the finished project.

Clause 6   Statutory obligations, notices, fees and charges.
Clause 7   Levels and setting out of the works.
Clause 8   Materials, goods and workmanship to conform to description, testing and inspection.
Clause 9   Royalties and patent rights.
Clause 10   Person-in-charge.
Clause 11   Access for architect to the works.
Clause 12   Clerk of works.

The combination of ensuring that the contractor complies with the statutory regulations, and the specification of the works described, should result in a building that achieves the desired standard. In addition, there is the provision for inspection by the clerk of works regularly, and by the architect intermittently. There is also the added precaution for the inspection of goods and materials in the workshops off site, should this be so desired. The contractor, on the other hand, must seek to ensure that he employs competent tradesmen to do the work. He must constantly keep on the site someone who can accept instructions from the architect and who will also be responsible for the daily site management of the project. In addition, there are clauses covering levels and setting out — making sure that the project is off to a correct start. There is also provision for uncovering work for inspection if the architect feels that this is necessary.

Statutory obligations, notices, fees and charges (clause 6)

The contractor must comply with and give all notices required by any Act of Parliament, statutory instrument, regulation or byelaw of any local authority or statutory undertaker which has any jurisdiction with regard to the works. The contractor, however, will not be liable for compliance with this requirement where the works themselves do not comply with these requirements. The contractor should not deliberately execute work that he knows will contravene these regulations, and as such will require future modification. On the other hand, the contractor is not a watchdog to ensure that the architect carries out his duties properly and efficiently.

If the contractor finds any divergence between the statutory requirements and any of the contract documents or architect's instructions he should immediately write to the architect pointing out the discrepancy. The architect must then, within seven days of the receipt of this notice, issue instructions in relation to the divergence. If the instruction requires the work to be varied then this should be treated in the same way as other variations, in accordance with clause 13.

In some circumstances it may be necessary for the contractor to urgently comply with a statutory regulation; for example, where an existing structure on the site is in danger of collapsing or where health is in danger. This may require the contractor to supply materials or execute work prior to receiving instructions from the architect. The contractor should do that which is reasonably necessary to secure the immediate compliance with the statutory requirement. The contractor must then inform the architect of this action. The materials and work executed in these circumstances will then be treated as a variation under clause 13.

The contractor must pay and indemnify the employer against liability in respect of any fees, charges, rates, taxes, etc. These may be required under an Act of Parliament, regulation or byelaw. The amount of such fees and charges will be added to the contract sum unless:

(a) they arise in respect of goods or work done by a local authority or statutory undertaker;
(b) they are included in the contract sum by the contractor;
(c) they are included as a provisional sum in the contract bills.

Level and setting out of the works (clause 7)

The architect is responsible for providing the contractor with all the information necessary in order that the contractor can set out the works at ground level. This information should comprise properly dimensioned drawings and levels. The actual setting out of the works from this information is entirely the responsibility of the contractor. If mistakes are made during this process the contractor must correct them at his own expense. Delays in the presentation of the information from the architect could result in an extension of time. One possible problem could arise from the inaccurate setting out of the works by trespassing on the land of an adjoining owner. In this situation the contractor would be liable to indemnify the employer under clause 20. With the consent of the employer, the architect may instruct that such errors will not be amended and an appropriate deduction for such errors will be made from the contract sum.

Materials, goods and workmanship to conform to description, testing and inspection (clause 8)

This clause seeks to ensure that the quality of materials and workmanship will be as specified in the contract bills. It therefore reinforces the information contained in the bills of quantities. Where the quality specified becomes no longer possible to obtain then, before proceeding with some alternative, the contractor should seek instructions from the architect. The contractor must, whenever required to do so, prove that the materials being used are in accordance with the specified requirements. This may be done by providing the architect with applicable quotations and invoices.

In other circumstances this may involve the contractor in testing the materials, goods or workmanship in accordance with the tests described in the contract bills. If the architect requires tests to be performed that have not been specified, then these must be carried out by the contractor, but will form an additional charge to the contract sum. Routine tests at regular intervals are generally described adequately in the contract bills. The contractor must therefore expect that some of these tests will be required. It may be useful in other circumstances to include a provisional sum for abnormal testing in case this is required.

The architect also has the powers to request the inspection or test of any part of the works up to the issue of the final certificate. This may require the contractor to open up the works for inspection or testing. The purpose of this is to ensure that the work is in accordance with that specified in the contract. The costs of opening up the works for this purpose will be borne by the contractor if the inspection or tests show that it is not in accordance with the contract. Where it is in agreement to that specified, then the costs of opening up and making good will be added to the contract sum. This may also result in other repercussions such as an extension of time (clause 25.4.5.2) or a claim for loss and expense (clause 26.2.2).

The architect may also issue instructions in regard to the removal from site of materials that do not conform with the contract. In other circumstances, once the materials arrive on site they cannot be removed without the architect's permission (clause 16). The materials that are removed must be replaced with materials that do conform, and at no extra expense to the contract. There is no limit in time when such defective materials should be discovered. The architect will, however, seek to inspect the works reasonably as they progress. If, however, a failure in the foundations did not occur until the building was suitably loaded, and such a failure was due to the use of defective materials, the contractor would be liable fully to rectify the problem to the satisfaction of the architect. (Note: article 1 of the articles of agreement.) The architect should, however, express any dissatisfaction within a reasonable time from the execution of the unsatisfactory work.

If any of the work, materials or goods are not in accordance with the contract the architect may

1. Issue instructions for their removal.
2. Allow such work to remain and confirm this in writing to the contractor. This is not to be construed as a variation, but will probably result in an appropriate deduction from the contract sum.
3. Issue instructions requiring a variation but allow no addition to the contract sum or an extension of time.
4. Issue instructions for opening up inspection using the following Code of Practice.

A *Code of Practice* has been written to assist in the operation of clause 8.4.4. The architect and contractor should agree to the amount and method of opening up or testing in accordance with the following criteria

1. The event of the non-compliance is unique and is unlikely to happen again.
2. The need to discover whether any non-compliance in a primary structural element is a failure of workmanship and/or materials such that rigorous testing of similar elements must take place. Where the non-compliance is less significant and can be simply repaired.
3. The significance of the non-compliance having regard to the nature of the work in which it has occurred.
4. The consequence of any similar non-compliance on the safety of buildings, its effect on users, adjoining property, the public, and compliance with any statutory requirements.

5. The level and standard of supervision and control of the works by the contractor.
6. The relevant records of the contractor and where relevant of any subcontractor resulting from the supervision and control referred to above.
7. Any Codes of Practice or similar advice issued by a responsible body which are applicable to the non-complying work, materials or goods.
8. Any failure by the contractor to carry out, or to secure the carrying out of any tests specified in the contract documents or in an instruction to the architect.
9. The reason for the non-compliance when this has been established.
10. Any technical advice that the contractor has obtained in respect of the non-complying work, materials or goods.
11. Current recognized testing procedures.
12. The practicability of progressive testing in establishing whether any similar non-compliance is reasonably likely.
13. If alternative testing methods are available, the time required for and the consequential costs of such alternative testing methods.
14. Any proposals of the contractor.
15. Any other relevant matters.

The architect may also issue instructions excluding anyone from the site. He must not do this unreasonably or to the specific annoyance of the contractor. The contractor should therefore have been previously warned of this impending situation, in order that he may take appropriate corrective action. It is, however, an uncommon occurrence, but it may arise in circumstances where persistently bad workmanship arises or where a member of the contractor's staff has consistently failed to carry out the architect's instructions.

Royalties and patent rights (clause 9)

All royalties and other similar sums included for work described in the contract's bills are deemed to be included in the contract sum by the contractor. The contractor must also indemnify the employer against any actions that might be brought against him in connection with royalties. The contractor may, for example, have used a patented system of scaffolding, the royalties of which are entirely his responsibility.

If, however, the contractor is requested to use a patented system under an architect's instruction, the royalties that may be payable in these circumstances will be added to the contract sum. Presumably in this case such royalties would be agreed when valuing the variation.

Person-in-charge (clause 10)

The contractor must keep a site manager constantly on site. This is the person who is responsible for the daily running of the site, and to whom the architect can give his instructions, or to whom the clerk of works can give his directions. In the construction industry he may have several names from project manager to general foreman. A contracts manager, however, who is often responsible for several sites, will not fit within this description since he is not 'kept up on the works'. The instructions given by the architect will be deemed to have been issued to the contractor. In order to satisfy this last requirement the person-in-charge may delegate an assistant who can receive instructions in his absence. The term 'constantly on site' means at all reasonable times, to ensure that the work is correctly executed and to receive any instructions from the architect.

Access for architect to the works (clause 11)

The architect and his representatives have the right of access, at all reasonable times, to the construction site and the contractor's workshops. This clause is extended to cover the workshops of domestic and nominated subcontractors. The term 'architect and his representatives' can also, presumably, be extended to quantity surveyors and engineers of different kinds. In some circumstances, for example, it may be important for the structural engineer to be allowed access to the fabrication process of the steelworker. The purpose of this clause, therefore, is largely to inspect the quality control of the firm concerned. It should be noted, however, that suppliers are not listed here, since their contract is a contract of sale of completed goods, and inspection may be inappropriate, particularly in the case of mass-produced goods.

Due to the increasing amount of specialist work included in buildings, provision is now necessary and is provided to protect the proprietory interests of the contractor or subcontractor, whilst not detracting from the right of access given to the architect. This might be achieved through confidentiality agreements or limiting the inspections of specialist manufacturing processes where some form of indemnity could be provided.

Clerk of works (clause 12)

The employer has the option of appointing a clerk of works whose duty is to act 'solely as an inspector'. He is employed for this purpose under the directions of the architect. The contractor should provide the clerk of works with all reasonable facilities in order that he can perform his designated duties. The clerk of works is not employed in the capacity of the architect's representative, since he is solely employed for inspection purposes. If he chooses to give the contractor instructions, even in writing, they will have only little contractual effect unless they are confirmed by the architect. This must be done within two working days of the instruction, and must be in writing, which will then constitute an architect's works instruction. If the architect chooses to confirm a clerk of work's suggestion orally, then the appropriate procedures to put this in writing must then be taken up by either the contractor or the architect. The clerk of works is generally resident on site and in constant touch with the works, in circumstances that often require a quick decision. In practice, therefore, the contractor must receive many statements from the clerk of works in good faith.

Chapter 13

Costs of construction

An important factor in any construction contract is the calculation and payment of the sum of money by the employer to the building contractor. The importance of the contract sum and its relationship to the final account, together with the matters relating to the timing of payments, are discussed in this chapter.

Clause 3   Contract sum — additions or deductions — adjustment — interim certificate.
Clause 13   Variations and provisional sums.
Clause 14   Contract sum.
Clause 16   Materials and goods unfixed or off site.
Clause 24   Damages for non-completion.
Clause 26   Loss and expense caused by matters materially affecting regular progress of the works.
Clause 30   Certificates and payments.

The project starts with the contract sum and the integrity of this amount is clarified within the contract conditions. It is extremely unusual for this amount to remain unchanged and be paid as the final account upon completion. Changes beyond the contractor's control will be made, and these must eventually be costed to the appropriate amount. Changes occur particularly in respect of foundation costs, the nomination of specialist firms and variations to the design instigated by the client or architect, and occasionally by the building contractor. Rules are laid down on how these changes are to be evaluated in terms of cost. In some circumstances the contractor may feel that he has been improperly reimbursed, and there is provision in the contract to rectify this should his case be proven. In other circumstances the employer may have suffered damages due to a late completion by the contractor. There is also provision to deal with these circumstances should this situation occur. On the majority of contracts of any size, the contractor will be unable to complete the works without some form of interim payment. Clause 30 describes the procedures involved for calculating the amounts owing to the contractor both during the period of construction and also upon final completion of the contract. Matters covering valuation periods, retention and the time allowed for payment to be made are also included in this clause.

Contract sum — additions or deductions — adjustment — interim certificate (clause 3)

If the conditions refer to the addition to or deduction from the contract sum, then once this adjustment has been calculated it shall be paid and included in the value of the next interim certificate. Several clauses refer back to this clause in respect of extra expense caused by changes to the contract. Some of these items are as follows:

Clause 6	Fees and charges.
Clause 7	Levels and setting out the works.
Clause 8	Opening up for inspection and testing of the works where found to be correct.
Clause 9	Royalties and patent rights.
Clause 17	Repair of defects, the costs of which are accepted by the architect.
Clause 21	Certain insurance matters.

Variations and provisional sums (clause 13)

Most of the forms of contract used in the United Kingdom allow for variations arising at some stages during the contract. The absence of such a clause would necessitate a new contract being arranged if variations did arise. The disadvantage of such a clause is that it allows the architect to delay making some decisions almost until the last possible moment. The building owner will be bound by any variation given by the architect as long as the architect does not exceed his powers under the terms of his contract.

The question sometimes arises as to what constitutes a variation. Clause 13 aptly describes those circumstances where a variation can arise, but it must be presumed and implied that a limit on these change orders will apply in practice. If the nature of the works described in the contract documents can be shown to be 'substantially' different to that carried out then the main contractor will be entitled to reprice the work accordingly. 'Substantially different', however, may require the courts to formulate a decision in individual cases. A variation resulting in a change in the size of a window will be admissible. The increase in the size of a proposed extension from 200 m^2 to 2000 m^2 of floor may not. The contractor may be willing to carry out the work, but on a different contractual basis.

Clause 13.1 attempts to define a variation in normal circumstances. A variation from the contract occurs where the actual work to be carried out changes, or where the circumstances in which the work is to be carried out changes. The first category includes:

(1) the alteration or modification of the design, quality or quantity of works:
(2) the addition, omission or substitution of any work;
(3) the alteration of the kind or standard of materials or goods.

The removal from site of work, materials or goods that were formerly in accordance with the contract is also included under this section.

A change in the circumstances in which the work is carried out also comes within this definition and is defined to include access and use of the site, limitations of working space, limitations of working hours, and a change in the sequence of work.

Clause 13.1.3 does, however, place some restrictions in the way that the architect can go about issuing variation instructions. Work that has been described in the contract bills as the main contractor's (or one of his domestic subcontractors should he have intended to sublet it) cannot be omitted and then awarded to a nominated subcontractor. It can be omitted enitrely and done after the contract has been completed. It can also be awarded to a firm employed directly by the building owner, assuming that the main contractor will allow access to the works, for this purpose, during the contract period. Of course, if the main contractor agrees to this nomination, then this will override the condition.

All instructions from the architect requiring a variation from the contract must be in writing. This is in pursuance of clause 4.3. The quantity surveyor has no power to measure and value varied work unless he has this written instruction (clause 13.4). Any variation made by either the architect or the contractor can be confirmed in writing at any time prior to the issue of the final certificate (clause 4.3.2.2).

The rules for the valuation of variations are detailed in clause 13.5. The two alternative ways of valuing the construction work are described in clause 13.5.1 (by measurement) and clause 13.5.4 (by cost reimbursement). The rules for measurement state that the same principles used for the preparation of the contract bills should be adopted (clause

13.5.3.1). Four situations are described and these are shown diagrammatically in Fig. 13.1.

1. Where the additional or substituted work is the same in character, conditions and quantity to items in the contract bills, then bill rates or prices are to be used to value the variation.
2. Where the additional or substituted work is the same in character, but is executed under different conditions or results in significant changes in quantity, then the bill rates or prices are to be used as a basis for valuing the variation. These are known as pro-rata rates.
3. If the additional or substituted work is different from those items in bills, then a fair method of valuation is to be used.
4. Omissions are valued at bill rates unless the remaining quantities are substantially changed, in which case a revaluation of these items will become necessary using method 3 above.

If any percentage or lump-sum adjustments have been made in the contract bills — for example, for the correction of errors (see clause 14) — then these will need to be adjusted accordingly. Also, if it can be shown that the value of preliminary items have changed as a result of variations, then this will require adjustment.

If the varied work cannot be properly measured or valued, then the contractor or subcontractor is to be paid for the work on a daywork basis. The schedule, 'Definition of prime cost of daywork carried out under a building contract' and issued by the RICS/BEC, together with the

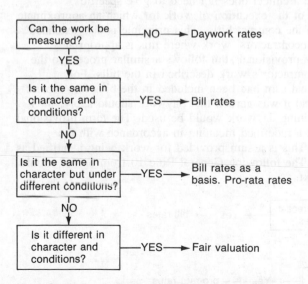

Note: Omitted work at bill rates unless the remaining work changes substantially in quantities, in which case a revaluation of these items becomes necessary.

Fig. 13.1 Valuation of variations

percentage additions determined by the contractor in the bills, should be used. Alternatively, if the work is within the province of any specialist trade, defined as either electrical or heating and ventilating, then their appropriate definition for daywork together with the percentages inserted by the contractor in the bills should be used. Vouchers showing the daily time spent on the work, the workmen's names and the plant and materials employed should be verified. This is recommended to be done weekly by the architect's representative and this is read as the clerk of works. It should be noted here that the verified voucher is an agreed record only; it does not mean that the method of valuation adopted will be daywork.

Amendment 7 issued in July 1988 has extended these rules to cover approximate quantities in bills of quantities. This change is a result of the introduction of *SMM7* as the method of measurement which should be used with *JCT 80*. If the quantity surveyor has included some approximate quantities in the contract bills and these have a close resemblance to the actual quantities as executed, then the rates inserted by the contractor at the time of tender will be used to value them. If the approximate quantities are not a reasonable forecast then the rates used in the bills will only be used as a basis for revaluation. At the extremes, i.e., where the approximate quantity does not change or where it differs by, say, 100 per cent then the above rules can easily be applied. In the 'grey' areas in between these extremes then the test of reasonableness will need to be applied by the parties concerned. This principle only applies where the work as executed is not altered or modified other than by quantity alone. The architect does not need to give specific instructions in respect of the execution of work for which an approximate quantity is included in the contract bills. This principle is also extended to cover nominated subcontractors' work where this is appropriate.

The valuation of a provisional sum follows a similar process to the valuing of the main contractor's work described in the bills. For example, if a provisional sum had been included in the bills for 'repairs to timber staircase', and it was agreed that daywork should apply, then the above rules for valuing daywork would be used. The term provisional sum has also taken on a redefined meaning in accordance with the provisions of SMM7. This is a sum provided for work being identified as defined or undefined. The following General Rule 10 from *SMM7* should be noted in this context.

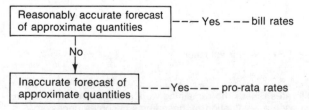

Fig. 13.2   Effect of changes in quantities in approximate quantities (JCT Amendment 7, of July 1988)

10. Procedure where the drawn and specification information required by these rules is not available

10.1

Where work can be described and given in items in accordance with these rules but the quantity shall be given and identified as an approximate quantity.

10.2

Where work cannot be described and given in items in accordance with these rules it shall be given as a Provisional Sum and identified as for either defined or undefined work as appropriate.

10.3

A Provisional Sum for defined work is a sum provided for work which is not completely designed but for which the following information shall be provided:

(a) The nature and construction of the work.

(b) A statement of how and where the work is fixed to the building and what other work is to be fixed thereto.

(c) A quantity or quantities which indicate the scope and extent of the work.

(d) Any specific limitations and the like identified in Section A35.

10.4

Where Provisional Sums are given for defined work the Contractor will be deemed to have made due allowance in programming, planning and pricing Preliminaries. Any such allowance will only be subject to adjustment in those circumstances where a variation in respect of other work measured in detail in accordance with the rules would give rise to adjustment.

10.5

A Provisional Sum for undefined work is a sum provided for work where the information required in accordance with rule 10.3 cannot be given.

10.6

Where Provisional Sums are given for undefined work the Contractor will be deemed not to have made any allowance in programming, planning and pricing Preliminaries.

The contractor in pricing the work at tender stage will be deemed to have made due allowance in pricing for the preliminary items. If the execution of any of this work is subject to variation then an adjustment may need to be made to the value of the preliminary items. The repayment of any direct loss or expense resulting from a variation issued by the architect would be reimbursed and discussed under clause 26.

Variations often necessitate either remeasurement on site or from drawings. Clause 13.6 gives the contractor the right to be present at the time that such measurements are taking place.

Contract sum (clause 14)

The contract sum is assumed to have been calculated on the basis of the quality and quantity of work as described in the bills of quantities. A part of the quantity surveying process on any project is to establish the correctness of the contract sum both arithmetically and technically. This means that the bills should have been checked to see that the item costs have been extended correctly, that page totals add up and that the various collection sheets and summaries have been correctly completed. The adequacy of the contractor's rates should also have been examined in order to avoid difficulties that could arise in the agreement of the final account. Failure, however, on the part of the quantity surveyor to perform these duties efficiently will not provide the contractor with any redress against the building owner. It is the contractor's responsibility to determine the sufficiency of his tender, and he has no alternative but to honour his pricing should any errors occur at a future date during the contract.

Any errors discovered by the quantity surveyor or the contractor prior to the signing of the contract can be corrected by using one of the alternative methods described in the code of procedure for selective tendering (see Chapter 7). It is prudent, therefore, on the part of the quantity surveyor to satisfy himself on the nature of the prices prior to the signing of the contract.

The only errors that can be corrected are those made by the quantity surveyor during the preparation of the contract bills (clause 2.2). These may have occurred because of errors in the quantities or descriptions or because items have been omitted. If the bills depart from the method of measurement stated, and this has not been brought to the contractor's notice, then this will also be deemed to be an error.

Materials and goods unfixed or off site (clause 16)

Materials and goods which have been delivered to the site or placed on or adjacent to works, and are intended for the works, must not be removed from the site unless written consent has been received from the architect. Once the value of these goods and materials has been included in an interim certificate and paid for by the employer they become the property of the employer. However, the main contractor will still be responsible for any loss or damage they may suffer and for the insurance of the same, as long as clauses 22A and 22B are in operation. Although the employer becomes the true owner of the materials and goods concerned, the contractor's insolvency may raise the question of whether the contractor was the reputed owner. The employer would need to ensure that the contractor's title to the goods was not defective.

Where the value of any materials or goods intended for the works, but stored off site, has been included in an interim certificate and paid for by the employer, then these materials will also become the property of the employer. The contractor must not remove these items from the premises except to the project for which they are intended. The contractor, however, continues to be responsible for any loss or damage that may occur, and for their insurance in accordance with clauses 22A and 22B. In these circumstances the architect has exercised his option under clause 30 to pay for materials off site. This clause has particular relevance and importance to factory manufactured components, used with industrialized buildings. In these situations the contractor may be loathe to bring to site items of manufactured joinery until their incorporation in the works is imminent. The option of paying for these materials will assist the contractor's cash flow, and should cause no problems if the provisions of clause 30 are complied with.

Damages for non-completion (clause 24)

If the contractor fails to complete the works by the completion date, then the architect must issue a certificate accordingly. This certificate allows the employer to deduct from monies due to the contractor, the liquidated and ascertained damages at the rate stated in the appendix. The amount of damages claimed is based upon the period between the completion date and the date of practical completion. If there is an insufficient amount owing to the contractor by which to offset the damages, the employer is able to recover the balance as a debt.

The amount stated in the appendix for liquidated and ascertained damages must be a realistic sum related to possible actual damages suffered by the employer. If the amount stated is shown to be a penalty, then the courts will set a fair, but smaller amount, as damages payable by the contractor.

If the architect subsequently fixes a later completion date, then any amounts deducted by the employer are to be repaid to the contractor accordingly.

Loss and expense caused by matters materially affecting regular progress of the works (clause 26)

The main purpose of this clause is to reimburse the contractor in those circumstances where he has suffered loss and expense, and will not be reimbursed elsewhere under the terms of the contract. The loss and expense claim must be directly attributable to matters that have substantially affected the regular progress of the construction of the project.

In order for the contractor to claim for reimbursement he must first make a written application to the architect. In this correspondence he must state that he has incurred, or is very likely to incur, direct loss and expense during the execution of the works, and that he will not be reimbursed under any other provision of the contract. His basis of claim is that the regular progress of the works has been disturbed and this has resulted in the loss and expense. Loss in this context means that he has been inadequately reimbursed for work carried out. Expense implies that additional resources were necessary to complete the works.

The conditions of contract list various matters that could affect the regular progress of works. The contractor must cite one or more of the following items in support of his claim for loss and expense.

1. Delay in the receipt of instructions (including the expenditure of provisional sums), drawings, details or levels from the architect. The contractor must have requested this information in writing from the architect, and have allowed sufficient time to elapse prior to its use on site.
2. Opening up of work for inspection or testing of materials and for their consequential making good. This is providing the items were in accordance with the work specified.
3. Discrepancies between the contract drawings and contract bills.
4. Work being carried out by firms employed directly by the employer.
5. Postponement of any of the work to be executed under the provisions of the contract.
6. Failure on the part of the employer to give ingress to or egress from the works by the appropriate time.
7. Variations authorized by the architect under clause 13.2 or the expenditure in regard to provisional sums for defined work.
8. The execution of work for which an approximate quantity is included in the contract bills which is not a reasonably accurate forecast of the quantity of work required.

Upon receipt of the correspondence from the contractor the architect must then assess whether the claim is justified. First, he will need to satisfy himself that the regular progress of the works had been disturbed by one or more of the eight matters listed above. For this he may need to refer to the contractor's master programme. The mere fact that the project is running behind schedule may also be due in part to the contractor's inability to perform the works adequately. Some allowance on the period of delay may therefore need to be taken for this assumption. Second, either the architect or the quantity surveyor will need to ascertain the amount of the loss and expense incurred by the contractor. In practice the architect may agree that the contractor has a valid argument, but leave the settlement of the financial sum to the quantity surveyor.

The contractor's written application should be made as soon as it is apparent that the regular progress of the works has been affected. He should also submit to the architect the relevant information in support of the claim that will help the architect form his own opinion. He should also provide some indication of the amount of loss and expense he has suffered. If any extension of time has already been agreed by the architect under the appropriate items of clause 25, then the contractor shall be informed accordingly. This may affect the calculation and assessment of the contractor's claim.

A nominated subcontractor can also submit a claim for the loss and expense caused by the disturbance of the regular progress of his subcontract works (JCT form of subcontract, clause 13.1). Such a claim must first be submitted to the contractor. If it is appropriate, then the contractor will in turn submit it to the architect. This claim will then follow a similar process, as described above.

Any amounts that the architect agrees should be paid to the contractor for a claim under this clause are to be added to the contract sum. If they can be agreed during the progress of the works, they can then be included in the next valuation.

The inclusion of this clause within the form of contract provides only one remedy for the contractor. Other courses of action are therefore open to the contractor in the event of the regular progress of the works being affected. Other actions the contractor may wish to take, if they are to succeed with the payment of damages, must not be too remote in the eyes of the law. The loss of profit is, however, a reasonable claim to be made under this heading.

Certificates and payments (clause 30)

Interim valuations are generally prepared by the client's quantity surveyor (clause 30.1.2) in agreement with the contractor's surveyor. Although these may be required at more frequent intervals by the architect, the conditions of contract will stipulate a maximum period for interim certificates. The appendix to the form of contract, which needs completing individually for each project, recommends this period to be one month, although the parties do have the option of stating any period that they desire. The ICE conditions of contract also stipulate that the valuation must achieve a minimum amount (to be stated in the contract) before any monthly payment will be made. There is no comparable condition in JCT 80, although if this was desirable then it could be inserted as a supplementary condition. The purpose of such a recommendation is to attempt to ensure that the contractor is making regular progress of the works. On very large contracts it may be necessary to provide approximate valuations on a weekly basis in order to satisfy the contractor's cash flow. More accurate payments would continue to be made at the monthly interval. This may be required at peak construction periods, for example during the summer months on mass earthmoving contracts.

Valuations will be prepared on a monthly basis (or on whatever basis has been stated in the appendix) until the certificate of practical completion is issued. If the work has been accurately valued at this point, then only retention monies will be outstanding and these can therefore be released with the final certificate. There will therefore be no requirements to issue a certificate between these two certificates. The certificate of practical completion has therefore often been referred to as the penultimate certificate, although there is nothing in the contract to prohibit the issue of further certificates beyond this one. In a real contract situation it is often not possible to value accurately the works at completion, and this therefore results in further certificates being issued.

The final certificate is referred to as the certificate of completion of making good defects, and is issued either at the end of the defects liability period or once the defects have all been made good, whichever date is the later. The certificate of practical completion of the works includes the release of one moiety (one half) of the retention monies, the remainder being released with the certificate of making good defects.

One further point that needs some consideration is the effect of the NEDO formulae on valuations. Using the traditional method of price fluctuation — i.e. increased cost sheets — these were quite independent from the value of the measured works. The interim valuation of the contract works was also looked upon as a means to an end, and as long as it was reasonably correct overall that was all that mattered. The contractor needed to be paid a reasonable sum for the work he carried out, and the employer needed to be satisfied that he was not being overcharged. The introduction of the NEDO formulae has, however, meant that interim valuations must be much more accurate since the appropriate percentages used to calculate the increases (or decreases) use the valuation amounts in their computation. Although at interim valuation time the indices may only be provisional, the work valued must be actual, to closely resemble the work completed. Using the traditional method for calculating price increases, it was generally accepted that it was in the best interest of the contractor to overvalue the works wherever possible, as this helped to improve his cash flow. The adoption of the formulae method will usually result in a higher payment should the contractor wait as long as possible before including the work in his valuation.

In practice, the contractor often prepares the valuation since he is more often on site, and is therefore more familiar with the progress of the works. The quantity surveyor will then visit the site at the appointed date to examine, approve and agree the amount of the valuation. Should there be any dispute between these parties on the amount to be paid, the quantity surveyor's assessment will be used. The valuation is then forwarded to the architect with the provision that the work included is in accordance to the architect's satisfaction. The quantity surveyor should not knowingly include in a valuation work that does not conform to the contract, but the question of quality control is not really his prerogative. If, however, he has any doubts over an item he should bring this to the notice of the architect. The architect will generally accept the valuation and use it for the preparation of his certificate. This is sent to the employer with a copy to the contractor, and should be paid within the 14 days stipulated in the contract. If it is not, then the contractor can determine his contract under clause 28.

Amounts due

The amount stated as due in an interim certificate is the gross valuation agreed between the parties and certified by the architect. In order to calculate the amount payable to the contractor, deductions in the form of retention and payments made under previous certificates are made. The gross valuation includes the following, which are subject to retention as stated in the appendix:

1. The total value of work properly executed by the contractor including variations carried out and agreed in terms of their financial consequences but excluding any restoration, replacement or repair or loss or damage and removal and disposal of debris which in clause 22B.3.5 and 22C.4.4 are treated as if they were a variation.
2. Any adjustments to these values arising as a result of the application of the price adjustment formulae under clause 40.
3. The total value of materials and goods delivered to the site. This, in practice, often only includes those items of a major financial importance. The materials on site will only include those items that are reasonably, properly and not prematurely delivered to site. The inclusion, in the valuation, of sanitary ware that is already on site at the start of the contract may be refused because they have been prematurely brought to the site. The client, when paying for materials on site, will need to be satisfied in every respect regarding their safety from damage or theft. Materials on site for long periods are more susceptible to these occurrences. The provision for payment may also require adequate protection from the weather as a prerequisite condition. This clause also applies in respect of materials from nominated suppliers.
4. The value of any materials off site as agreed with the architect as long as they conform to the requirements of the contract as described in clause 30.3.
5. The amounts of any nominated subcontractor's work that have been properly executed. Included with the subcontractor's invoice may be materials on or off site as appropriate and agreed by the architect. It is normal practice to include these amounts only where the subcontractor supplies an invoice. In addition, in some circumstances the architect or quantity surveyor may require proof that previous payments have been made to nominated subcontractors.
6. The profit of the contractor in respect of nominated subcontractors' invoices. The rates (percentages) stated in the bill of quantities are used. Should nomination be the result of a provisional sum, then these rates will be used as a basis. The contractor's profit on

nominated suppliers' accounts is presumably covered with the supply of the materials under items 3 and 4 above, and would be added as appropriate. Attendance items are properly the main contractor's work and come, therefore, within the definition of 1 above.

In addition the following items are to be included which are not subject to retention:

1. Items which adjust the contract sum resulting from changes in fees and charges (clause 6.2), changes in setting out the works (clause 7), opening up for inspection and testing of the works where found to be correct (clause 8.3), royalties or patent rights resulting from an architect's instruction (clause 9.2), repair of defects accepted by the architect (clause 17.2), certain insurance matters (clause 21.2.3).
2. Loss and expense agreed under clauses 26.1 or 34.3 or in respect of any restoration, replacement or repair or loss or damage and removal of and disposal of debris which in clauses 22B3.5 and 22C4.4 are treated as if they were a variation.
3. Where final payment has been secured to a nominated subcontractor under clause 35.17.
4. Any increased payments in respect of contributions, levies and tax fluctuations under clauses 38 and 39.
5. Any amounts of a similar nature to those described above relating to nominated subcontractors' works.

The following items are not subject to retention but are to be deducted from interim certificates:

1. Amounts in respect of levels and setting out of the works (clause 7); work, materials or goods which although not in accordance with the contract have been allowed to remain (clause 8.4.2); any defects, shrinkages or other faults which have been allowed to remain in the works (clauses 17.2 and 17.3) or any amounts allowable by the contractor to the employer in respect of fluctuations (clauses 38 and 39).
2. Any amount allowed by the contractor to the employer in respect of a reduction in contributions, levies and tax fluctuations.
3. Any similar allowance in respect of a reduction in nominated subcontractors' payments.

Off-site materials or goods

The amount stated as due in an interim certificate may, at the discretion or option of the architect, include the value of such items prior to delivery to the site. There are a number of stipulations that the contractor must comply with before payment may be made for such goods and materials.

1. The materials are intended for incorporation within the works. This would normally be interpreted to mean that the materials or goods

concerned were 'special' to this contract. Common bricks or quantities of standard sized timber which could be used on any project would not normally therefore be allowable item to be included.

2. Nothing remains to be done to the materials prior to their incorporation within the works. This also eliminates the standard type materials and goods that could have been provided by the contractor for any type of contract. The items envisaged therefore assume some form of prefabrication for the project concerned, either at the contractor's workshops or the workshops of a subcontractor.

3. The materials have been set apart from other materials at the place of storage. They must be clearly and visibly marked by letters to identify the employer and the name of the project for which they are intended.

4. If the materials are ordered from a supplier by the contractor or subcontractor, then the supply must be in writing and the goods must pass unconditionally to the contractor or subcontractor.

5. If the materials are manufactured or assembled by a subcontractor, then these similar conditions must also apply.

6. The materials must be in accordance with the contract.

7. The contractor must also provide the architect with reasonable proof of his ownership of the goods and materials.

8. The contractor must show that these goods and materials are properly insured in accordance with the terms of the contract both while they remain in storage and also during their transportation to the site.

Retention

The contractor is not paid the full amount of the valuation, but this is subject to a deduction in the form of retention. The purpose of this retention is to provide some incentive for the contractor to complete the works, and it also provides some security should the contractor default in construction. The employer has only a fiduciary interest in the retention. In this respect he holds the retention on trust only, and need not therefore invest it to accrue interest.

The amount retained by the employer under this clause is recommended as 5 per cent, although a lower rate can be agreed between the parties. It would appear that higher rates of interest are not envisaged under this contract. The percentage amount of retention is shown in the appendix. Where the size of the project exceeds a contract sum of £500,000 then the recommendation of this contract is that the amount retained should be limited to 3 per cent. This would imply a 3 per cent retention throughout, rather than a 5 per cent retention with a limit of 3 per cent of the contract sum. Retention is applied to all those items of work and materials described in clause 30.2.1.

The retention is released to the contractor as follows. One-half of that retained by the employer at the certificate of practical completion of the works, and the remainder with the issue of the certificate of making good defects.

At the date of each interim certificate the quantity surveyor must prepare a statement of retention. This should show the amount of the contractor's retention and the retention for each nominated subcontractor. This statement should be issued by the architect to the employer, contractor and each nominated subcontractor concerned.

The employer may exercise the right to pay a nominated subcontractor direct, because of the contractor's default. He must also inform the contractor of this action and its subsequent effect upon the retention.

Final account

Either during the contract period or within 6 months after practical completion of the works, the contractor shall provide all the documents necessary for the preparation of the final account. These documents should include the appropriate details from nominated subcontractors and nominated suppliers. When this has been complied with, the quantity surveyor must prepare a statement of the final valuation under clause 13. The architect must send a copy of this to the contractor and to each nominated subcontractor. The quantity surveyor should within three months of receiving the information from the contractor ascertain any loss and expense under clause 26.1, 26.4.1 and 34.3 and also prepare a statement of all contract sum adjustments as follows. The following items are to be deducted from the contract sum:

1. Prime cost sums, which include the contractor's profit and attendance items where appropriate. This also includes the value of any work by a nominated subcontractor, whose employment has been determined in accordance with clause 35.24 which was not in accordance with the relevant subcontract but which has been paid or otherwise discharged by the employer.
2. Any amount deductible under levels and setting out of works (clause 7), materials or goods which although not in accordance with the contract have been allowed to remain (clause 8.4.2) or any defects, shrinkages or other faults which have been allowed to remain (clause 17.2 or 17.3).
3. Provisional sums and provisional work in the contract bills.
4. Amounts omitted by reason of variations caused by architect's instructions.
5. Amounts allowable to the employer because of reduction in contributions, levies and taxes.
6. Any other amount which is required by this contract to be deducted from the contract sum, such as liquidated damages.

The following items are to be added:

1. Nominated subcontract sums as finally adjusted or ascertained under the relevant provisions of subcontract NSC/4.
2. The tender sum properly adjusted against prime cost sum items which have been undertaken by the contractor.
3. Nominated suppliers' accounts adjusted within the terms of the contract.
4. The profit and attendance items on nominated subcontractors' and nominated suppliers' items where appropriate.
5. Additional payments authorized by the employer in respect of
   (a) fees and charges;
   (b) levels and setting out the works;
   (c) opening up of the works for inspection and testing where the work complies with the contract;
   (d) royalties and patent rights;
   (e) making good of defects where payment is authorized by the architect;
   (f) insurances where a provisional sum was included in the contract bills for this item.
6. Variations authorized or approved by the architect.
7. The expenditure associated with provisional sums and approximate quantities in the contract bills.
8. Loss and expense ascertained under clauses 26.1 or 34.3.
9. Increases in contributions, levies and taxes under clauses 38, 39 or 40.
10. Any other amount which is required to be added to the contract, such as the agreement of the contractor's claims.

If it is practicable, but at least 28 days before the issue of the final certificate, the architect should issue an interim certificate which should include the amounts of the subcontract sum for all the nominated subcontractors adjusted and ascertained under all the relevant provisions of the contract.

The architect must issue the final certificate and inform each nominated subcontractor of its issue within two months of the last of the following events:

1. End of defects liability period.
2. Date of issue of certificate of making good defects
3. Agreement of the final account.

The final certificate must state:

1. The amounts already paid to the contractor under interim certificates.
2. The contract sum adjusted within the terms of the contract.
3. The difference expressed as a debt to either the employer or the contractor.

The final certificate is conclusive evidence that the quality of materials and the standard of workmanship are to the reasonable satisfaction of the architect. It is also conclusive evidence that the contract sum has been properly adjusted within the terms of the contract. If, however, there has been any accidental inclusion or exclusion of work, or arithmetical errors in computation, these can be corrected. The same is true also in respect of fraud. The final certificate is also conclusive evidence that appropriate extensions of time have been given and that any reimbursement for loss and expense is in final settlement of all and any claims.

If any arbitration proceedings have occurred or have been commenced, then these will affect the issue of the final certificate accordingly. The final certificate will be subject to the terms of any award or judgment of such proceedings. If arbitration is commenced within 14 days after the final certificate has been issued, it shall still remain conclusive evidence in respect of quality of materials and workmanship.

Chapter 14

Time factor
of construction

Several clauses in the conditions of contract are of relevance and importance in respect of the time factor. These have been grouped together for commentary purposes.

Clause 17   Practical completion and defects liability.
Clause 18   Partial possession by employer.
Clause 23   Date for possession, completion and postponement.
Clause 25   Extension of time.
Clause 27   Determination by employer.
Clause 28   Determination by contractor.
Clause 28A   Determination by employer or contractor.

These clauses describe the start and finish of the project and the implications associated with these dates. The difference between these is, of course, the contract period. The distinction between completion date and date for completion should be carefully noted. This is described in clause 1 under the general rules of interpretation and definitions. Should the contractor fail to complete the works by the completion date then the architect must issue a certificate of non-completion of the works as described in clause 24, and damages are then payable by the contractor. Upon the practical completion of the project the contractor is relieved of most of his contractual obligations. He is, however, still responsible for defects that may arise due to his workmanship. This responsibility continues until the end of the defects liability period, which the JCT form recommends should extend for six months after practical completion. In some circumstances the contractor may be able to secure an extension of the contract period for one of the reasons listed in clause 25. The advantages of this course of action to the contractor is either the reduction or elimination of liquidated damages. The date for completion is stated in the appendix and any approved extension of time which is added to this provides the later completion date. The completion date cannot occur prior to the date of completion stated in the appendix, unless the contractor agrees to such a revision. In some extreme circumstances the works may be postponed, perhaps indefinitely, and clause 23 allows for this eventuality. The works may also offer partial possession in the case of a phased project awarded as a single contract. In this case phased completion is treated almost as a separate project as far as time is concerned. Finally, circumstances can, and sometimes do, arise where either the employer or the contractor feels that the contract should be terminated. This usually results because of a breach by the other party. The procedures and position of each party are described accordingly in clauses 27 and 28.

Practical completion and defects liability (clause 17)

Practical completion

When in the opinion of the architect the works become practically complete, he must issue the certificate of practical completion of the works. In practice this certificate may be issued even though minor items of work still need to be carried out within the terms of the contract. This does not presume that these items are either irrelevant or need not be completed. The date of practical completion often coincides with the handover date, and this latter consideration may have resulted in this certificate being issued even though the works are only 'almost' complete. Prior to the issue of this certificate the architect needs to satisfy himself that:

(a) the work has been carried out in accordance with the contract documents and the architect's instructions;
(b) the building is in an appropriate state to be taken over and used by the employer.

The date of practical completion is important since the following take effect automatically:

1. The start of the defects liability period (clause 17).
2. The beginning of the period of final measurement (clause 30).
3. The release of the first moiety of the retention fund (clause 30).
4. The ending of the insurance of the works (clause 21).
5. The end of any liability to liquidated damages by the employer (clause 24).

6. The opening of matters referred to arbitration (article 5).
7. The removal of the liability to frost damage (clause 17).

Many of these items also occur to those parts of a project affected by partial completion (clause 18). Upon achieving practical completion, the contractor is no longer obliged to accept instructions from the architect in respect of additional work since the works are now complete. The contractor may choose to do this work on the basis of a fresh agreement. For example, in connection with the payment for this work, bill rates and interim certificate periods, etc., will no longer apply.

Defects liability

The contractor is responsible for the making good of defects, shrinkages or faults which appear within the defects liability period. These must be due to materials and workmanship which are not in accordance with the contract, or to frost damage occurring before the practical completion of the works. If defects occur because of the inadequacy of the design, the the contractor is not obliged to make these good. The architect cannot also issue a variation order after the issue of the certificate of practical completion in order to remedy his design fault. Items which 'appear' during the defects liability include those presumably that were unnoticed during the contract period. These items must be included on a schedule of defects not later than 14 days after the expiration of the said defects liability period. The length of the defects liability period must be inserted in the appendix to the conditions, although six months is the recommended length. The making good of the contractor's defects should be done within a reasonable time and entirely at his own expense.

When, in the opinion of the architect, the defects requested by him have been made good, and the defects liability period has expired, he will issue his certificate of making good defects. The issue of this certificate releases the remainder of the retention monies due to the contractor, and removes the defects obstacle that would prevent the issue of the final certificate. The contractor, however, is not totally released from the responsibility of his defective work since he will still be affected by the statute of limitations.

The contractor will never be responsible for making good, at his own expense, damage by frost which occurs after the issue of the certificate of practical completion of the works. Should damage of this nature be found there may be some difficulty in practice of deciding when it occurred.

Partial possession by employer (clause 18)

The employer, with the agreement of the contractor, may decide to take possession of a section of the works. This is particularly appropriate where the contract concerned may be in two distinct parts — for example, alterations and extension, two extensions to an existing building or a housing scheme where numbers of units are released at various intervals. Within seven days of the employer taking possession of the relevant part, the architect must issue a certificate of partial possession indicating the approximate value of this part of the contract. This certificate has the same effect on the part completed, as the certificate of practical completion has on the whole. Items 1–7 under 'Practical completion' above apply equally to this part of the works that are now complete, and have received the aforementioned certificate. (See sectional completion supplement to JCT form of contracts.)

Date of possession, completion and postponement (clause 23)

The date for possession of the site by the contractor is stated in the appendix to the conditions of contract. Failure on the part of the building owner to provide the site by this date will result in a breach of contract. There is, however, provision in JCT 80 to allow the employer, without being in breach of contract to defer giving the contractor possession of the site for a period not exceeding six weeks. The deferment of the date of possession is referred to in the appendix and the period of deferment should be stated if less than six weeks. The contractor must start the project and regularly and diligently proceed with the project to the date of completion or the completion date if this has been extended. Failure on the part of the contractor to make regular progess with the works will also result in a breach of contract, this time on the part of the contractor. The employer is able to determine the contractor's employment on the works for this reason (clause 27.1.2).

The completion date is the date at the start of the defects liability period. It is also the date, should the contractor fail to complete by this time, of the starting point of the provisions relating to liquidated damages. It should be noted that the date for completion is the date written into the contract. The completion date is this date amended to take into account any extra time allowed under an extension of time or for the repair of war damage.

The architect can postpone the work for a short period of time or indefinitely. Where postponement exceeds the period of delay stated in the appendix, the contractor can determine his employment. In circumstances where the postponement is a relatively short period of time the usual redress for the contractor is to claim an extension of time under clause 25 and loss and expense under clause 26.

The employer, with the consent of the contractor in writing, may use or occupy the site or the works for the purpose of storage of his goods or otherwise before the date of practical completion. Before the contractor gives this consent the provisions of the insurers should be obtained. If an additional insurance premium is required and the employer continues to use the site then the premium will be added to the contract sum.

Extension of time (clause 25)

Once the main contractor realizes that the progress of the works is likely to be delayed he should write to the architect giving the reasons for the cause of the delay. Where the delay includes reference to a particular nominated subcontractor, this firm should also be given details of the delay. The effect of the successful application of this clause by the contractor is to reduce or eliminate any damages that he may suffer due to non-completion of the works. The initiative to be taken in seeking either an extension of time or a further extension of time must come from the contractor.

The contractor, in giving notice to the architect, should where possible provide particulars of the expected effects of the delay, and also estimate the extent in respect of completion of the works. If the answers to these questions are not known to the contractor, he should nevertheless still inform the architect of a probable delay, and provide this information at a later date.

Upon receipt of the notice of delay, the architect shall decide whether any of the events listed are relevant. If, in his opinion, he does not consider them to be a reasonable basis for an extension of time, he should refuse such an extension to the contractor.

If the reasons listed by the contractor are accepted as a relevant event by the architect, then the architect should write to the contractor giving details of:

(a) the events that, in the opinion of the architect, are relevant in these circumstances for an extension of time;
(b) a new completion date that he has estimated to be fair and reasonable. (If variations of omissions have been issued since the fixing of a previous completion date, then these can be taken into account in the fixing of a new date.)

The new completion date fixed by the architect must be at least 12 weeks from the receipt of the notice, or at the earliest the previously agreed completion date. The architect can therefore bring forward the completion date where the contract work has been significantly reduced. He must, however, give to the contractor reasonable notice of this intention (12 weeks) and in any case it must be shown to be a fair and reasonable action. The architect must also notify the contractor in writing where he considers that it is not fair and reasonable to fix a later date as a completion date.

The architect must, within 12 weeks from the date of practical completion of the works, write to the contractor to fix a completion date. This date may be fixed as follows:

1. The completion date as previously fixed.
2. A later completion date, in order to take into account any extension of time that in the opinion of the architect is justifiable.
3. An earlier completion date, if in the opinion of the architect the construction work has been significantly reduced. This date, however, cannot be fixed earlier than the date for completion stated in the appendix to the form of contract.

The architect can revise the completion date as necessary. He does not have to wait until the contractor informs him that the works will be delayed. If, however, the contractor does not request an extension of time, the architect is not bound to take any action or to attempt to enforce a later completion date than is otherwise stated in the contract.

The contractor must always, to the best of his endeavours, try to prevent any delay in the progress of the works. He must also, to the satisfaction of the architect, proceed with the regular progress of the works.

The following are the relevant events referred to in clause 25:

1. *Force majeure*. The meaning of this phrase is imprecise, but it is generally accepted to mean 'exceptional circumstances beyond the control of either of the parties of the contract'.
2. *Exceptionally adverse weather conditions*. These are weather conditions that could not normally be expected at the time of the year in the location of the building works. For example heavy rainfall during the winter months would not fit within the definition of exceptional unless it was abnormal. In the winter of 1978/79 the total rainfall was 579 mm compared to the average for this period over the preceding years of 452 mm (Manchester Weather Centre). This may have been considered exceptional, but such a decision may rest with the courts of law if the parties cannot agree upon an interpretation.
3. *Loss or damage occasioned by any one or more of the clause 22 perils*. The perils referred to in this clause are generally those items which are an insurable risk, such as fire, lightning, explosion, storm, tempest, etc. The full list of the specified perils are described under 'Definitions' in clause 1.3.
4. *Civil commotion, etc.* This is also included as one of the specified perils. It includes both local and national strikes, and lock-outs by management of any of the trades employed upon the works. It is also extended to similar actions in the preparation, manufacture or transportation of the goods and materials.
5. *Compliance with architect's instructions* — in respect of:

   (a) discrepancies in or divergences between documents (clause 2.3);
   (b) an instruction requiring a variation (clause 13.2);

(c) the expenditure of provisional sums (clause 13.3) except provisional sums for defined work;
(d) the postponement of any work (clause 23.2);
(e) the finding of antiquities on the site (clause 34);
(f) nominated subcontractors' work (clause 35);
(g) nominated suppliers (clause 36).

If the main contractor is required to open up work for inspection or testing, and if the work complies with the contract, then this becomes an admissible event. If the work is not in accordance with the contract any delays ensuing will not be gounds for an extension of time.

6. *Delay in the receipt of instructions, drawings, details or levels from the architect.* If this is to be accepted as a relevant event the contractor must have requested the information beforehand from the architect. The contractor must also use some foresight in respect of when the details are required. He must give the architect reasonable notice so that he can prepare and provide the information by the requisite day. In practice the contractor, by reference to his programme, should be able to ask for such information well in advance. The clause does not, however, assume that the architect will only work at the 'direction' of the contractor, but that he will be diligently preparing the information that he presumes the contractor will require anyway. In the event of this assumption being invalid, the contractor could find himself preparing the architect's checklist, and then being penalized for doing this inadequately.

7. *Delay on the part of the nominated subcontractors or nominated suppliers.* If the main contractor has taken all practicable steps to avoid or reduce these delays this fulfils this condition for an extension of time.

8. *Delay on the part of works or persons engaged by the employer.* This assumes that if the employer decides to undertake some of the work direct, outside the scope of this contract, then such work should be carried out so as not to cause a delay to the main contract. The main contractor here will have minimal control. It is up to the employer, therefore, to take the necessary steps to ensure as little inconvenience as may be expected.

9. *Government intervention.* If, once the contract has been signed, the government restricts the availability or use of labour which is essential to the carrying out of the works, then the contractor may apply for an extension of time. In the case of war, for example, the government may call up all 'able-bodied' men to the armed services thus removing tradesmen from the labour market. In other circumstances it may commandeer the essential building materials. On other occasions it may restrict the use of fuel or energy resulting in limited working, as occurred in 1973 with the three-day

working week. Two points are, however, worthy of note. First, the government intervention must restrict the essential supplies of men, materials, fuel or energy. If the work can be easily performed in some other way, without detriment to the project, then no claim for an extension of time will be permitted. Second, the government intervention must occur after the signing of the contract. If the contractor knew or should have known before he entered into the contract that the government would introduce certain restrictive measures, he cannot then claim this as a basis for his defence.

10. *Contractor's inability to secure labour and material.* The foregoing comments on government intervention apply equally to this relevant event. A sudden unexpected upturn of the construction industry in a certain area may starve some sites of the essential supplies of labour and materials.

11. *Work by local authorities or statutory undertakings.* Although these may be part of the contract, the contractor may have severe difficulties in attempting to control them. In some circumstances the contractor may be delayed waiting for statutory inspections by local authorities. The contractor must, however, have taken all reasonable steps to avoid difficulties occurring in these circumstances.

12. *Failure on the part of the employer to give access.* If the employer is unable to give to the contractor, by the stipulated dates stated in the contract, proper ingress to or egress from the works as defined in the contract documents, then the contractor will be entitled to an extension of the contract period.

13. Inaccurate forecast of an approximate quantity. Where such work is executed by the contractor then it must be a reasonably accurate forecast.

It should be noted under clause 25 that the matters discussed relate only to an extension of the contract period. The relevant events listed will form a good reason on the part of the contractor to this contractual provision. It must not be assumed to be an automatic result following any one of these events. In any case the agreement for an extension of time could result, in some cases, in only a matter of a few days.

Another important factor connected with this clause, is the aspect of any financial adjustment to the contract sum either in connection with damages for non-completion (clause 24) or the loss and expense to the contractor resulting from the delay (clause 26). These matters are discussed more fully with those appropriate clauses.

One further point that needs to be considered is that an extension of the contract period, for any reason, may be unacceptable to the employer. The architect may therefore reasonably expect the contractor to take appropriate action to save time. The contractor may also reasonably expect to be paid for the costs involved in such action. There is, however, no obligation under the contract for the contractor to take such action.

Determination by employer (clause 27)

In certain circumstances the employer is rightfully allowed to terminate the employment of the contractor. If the contractor defaults in one of the following ways the architect may issue a notice to the contractor accordingly. This notice must be delivered by registered post or recorded delivery specifying the default. The reason why the notice must be delivered in this manner is to avoid any claim by the contractor that he did not receive it.

1. The contractor unreasonably suspends the carrying out of the works. This is for the architect to decide.
2. The contractor fails to carry out the works in a regular and diligent manner. This may also put the contractor in breach of clause 23.
3. The contractor fails to comply with an instruction from the architect to remedy defective work, and this results in further damage to the works. (It should be noted that the failure to comply with other instructions merely results in the architect issuing the instructions to

Position as it should have been

		£
Contract sum		500,000
Value of variations		25,000
Theoretical Final Account		525,000

Position at determination

Value of work executed at time of liquidation		340,000
Interim payments	300,000	
Less retention	−15,000	
	285,000	
Nominated subcontractors paid after determination	30,000	
	315,000	315,000
Amount outstanding at determination		25,000

Position at final account

Paid as above, at determination	315,000
New completion contract	250,000
Employer's loss and expense	25,000
	590,000
Less as it should have been	525,000
Cost of determination/bankruptcy	£65,000

Fig. 14.1 Example showing calculation at contractor's insolvency

another firm, and recouping the necessary amount from the contractor.)

4. The contractor has either assigned or sublet a portion of the works without permission (clause 19).

Where the contractor defaults he should be asked to remedy the contract, perhaps unofficially at first. If the contractor continues to ignore the warning from the architect then the notice of determination should be sent to the contractor. The contractor, upon receipt of the notice, has 14 days in which to rectify the problem. The employer may then within 10 days after this date, assuming that the contractor is still in default, issue a notice that effectively terminates the employment of the contractor. The employer must ensure that the issue of the notice is a reasonable course of action to take, and should not be given solely to annoy the contractor.

If a contractor becomes bankrupt, or arranges with his creditors for voluntary winding up (see Insolvency Act 1986 and Fig. 14.1), then the employment of the contractor is automatically terminated. There is, however, provision in the contract for this employment to be reinstated where both the employer and the contractor, or liquidator, agree. In practice, there are immense disadvantages to the employer where bankruptcy of the contractor occurs. It is therefore in his best interests to retain the services of the contractor, where this has been previously satisfactory. The liquidator is in a position of wishing to continue with those contracts that are likely to be profitable and quick to execute. He is therefore more likely to continue with contracts that are nearing completion, and dispense with those that are in the early stages of construction.

The employer is also entitled to terminate the contractor's employment in cases of corruption. This can be extended to all contracts between the employer and the contractor where an irregularity of this nature has occurred in one contract. The contractor may, for example, be already undertaking several different contracts on behalf of the employer. He may then seek by way of a bribe to secure further work. Where this is proved, then all the contractor's work may be terminated. Corruption may result from the method of obtaining work or from the execution of the contract. Corruption can also occur where one of the contractor's employees offers favours which are neither known nor sanctioned by the contractor. The offences would usually come within the remit of the Prevention of Corruption Acts 1889 to 1916. Although corruption is generally well understood, it is often difficult to draw a line between the actions that may be classified as such. For example, many would regard the offer of a bottle of spirits at Christmas time as quite acceptable, and not as a bribe or offered in return for a favour. A crate of spirits would probably prove to be a different situation!

The respective rights of the employer and contractor, upon the termination of the contractor's employment, are as follows:

1. The employer may engage another firm to complete the project. This

firm is to be allowed to use the temporary buildings, plant and equipment until completion free of charge.

2. Unless the termination occurs because of bankruptcy, the contractor must, without payment, assign to the employer any benefits for the supply of goods and materials or for the execution of subcontracts. In practice, the contractor could encourage bad relations to develop in order to deprive the employer of these benefits.

3. Where bankruptcy has not occurred the employer may pay any supplier for materials or goods, or a subcontractor for work executed, who have not previously received payment. The employer may also use his discretion for paying nominated subcontractors, who should have been paid previously under certificates. He will then try to recover these sums from the contractor. In practice, those who should have been paid, but have not been paid because of a default on the part of the contract, may be unwilling to carry on their work unless they receive a payment. The employer may therefore be forced into this situation, in order to see progress in the works, and then try to recover the amounts from the contractor.

4. The contractor must remove his temporary works and other items belonging to him within a reasonable time after receiving an instruction from the architect. If he fails to do this, the employer shall remove and sell the items, and after deducting his costs, pass on the proceeds for the benefit of the contractor.

5. If the employer suffers any loss or expense because of this termination then this will become a debt of the contractor.

6. The employer is not bound to make any further payments to the contractor until the project has been properly completed and the accounts agreed for the project as a whole.

Determination by contractor (clause 28)

A number of situations can arise which may give the contractor the legal grounds for the termination of his contract. The contractor, should he decide to take this course of action, must issue a notice to either the employer or the architect of his intent to do so. The notice should be sent by registered post or recorded delivery and must not be issued unreasonably or for the annoyance of the employer or the architect. This does not imply that the contractor must take into account the peculiar state of the employer in respect, for example, of the employer's temporary shortage of funds in terms of cash flow. The most usual case, however, resulting in determination by the contractor, will arise because an employer has failed to honour a certificate. Grounds that may give rise to determination are listed below, although the contractor may take an alternative course of action that he considers to be more prudent. Determination generally results because of a series of events or a repetition of one of the events listed. It is also largely accepted that the contractor will probably suffer in terms of his reputation, or even financially, and this procedure is certainly a very last resort as far as he is concerned.

1. The employer fails to pay a certificate within the period of 14 days as stated in the contract (clause 30), and continues to default for a further 7 days after the receipt of a formal notice. This notice should be sent by registered post or recorded delivery, to ensure that the employer receives it. The notice will state that it is the intention of the contractor to terminate his employment forthwith. The first time this occurs the contractor is more likely to approach the architect regarding the absence of payment. The persistent occurrence of this event will then result in the notice. The certification of monies to the contractor is not a matter for discussion by the client. If the client has any misgivings about the project, then this should be brought to the attention of the architect prior to certification.

2. The employer interferes with or obstructs the issue of any certificate. The employer cannot deduct sums of money from amounts already certified by the architect. This may occur where a dispute arises between the contractor and the employer's directly employed workforce.

3. The project has been suspended by the architect, or the employer, or other persons, such as the local authority. The period of delay is entered on the appendix, but should this be omitted then one month may be taken as normal. Suspension of the works may occur because of:

   (a) compliance with an architect's instruction issued under clause 2.3 (Discrepancies between documents), clause 12.3 (Variations) or clause 23.2 (Postponement);
   (b) delay in the receipt of information requested from the architect;
   (c) delays on the part of the work being carried out by the employer's own contractors;
   (d) opening up of work for inspection where shown to be in accordance with the contract;
   (e) failure of the employer to give in due time ingress to or egress from the site of the works through or over any land or buildings.

4. The employer becomes bankrupt. There is no provision for automatic determination here as there is when the contractor becomes bankrupt, since the contractor will in his own interest stop work. However, since the employer will default in payment, the contractor can then determine under 1 above.

The following are the respective rights resulting from the determination of employment by the contractor.

1. The contractor must, within a reasonable period of time, remove all the items belonging to him. He should also issue comparable

instruction to all subcontractors. He must, however, ensure that the removal of temporary works is not done unreasonably, or cause future damage to persons and property for which he is responsible under clause 20. The courts would probably extend this clause to cover malicious damage that might be caused to an existing structure for which the contractor is not responsible under clause 22C. The reasonableness of the contractor's action would be viewed accordingly.

2. The effect of determination by the contractor results in the following sums being paid by the employer:

   (a) the value of any work already completed;
   (b) the value of any work currently under construction, that has been properly authorized by the architect;
   (c) any sum resulting from direct loss and expense under clause 26;
   (d) the costs of any materials or goods already provided for this project;
   (e) the reasonable costs of the removal of plant and equipment;
   (f) any direct loss or expense that has occurred as a result of this termination.

The respective procedure, therefore, after determination by the contractor, is as follows. The contractor will clear the site, and the employer will pay for any work carried out, the materials already available and a sum in the form of damages for this premature action.

Determination by employer or contractor (clause 28A)

This new clause results from the Tribunal's decision that those grounds in clause 28.1.3, under which the contractor could give notice to determine his employment and which were not acts or defaults of the employer but were neutral events, should be withdrawn from clause 28.1.3 and should instead be given as grounds for determination by either the employer or the contractor under a new determination clause. These were:

(a) *force majeure*;
(b) loss or damage of the works resulting from one of the specified perils. These are specified in clause 1.3;
(c) civil commotion.

The Tribunal further decided that if determination has been affected, the payments by the employer to the contractor under this new clause should be the same as under clause 28, but omitting the payment by the employer for any direct loss and/or damage caused to the contractor or his subcontractors by the determination.

Chapter 15

Works by other persons

The following group of clauses relate to those parts of the works that are done by firms other than the main contractor. In some examples the main contractor has no choice in the matter, other than a reasonable objection to such firms or persons on the works.

Clause 19   Assignment and subcontracts.
Clause 29   Works by employer or persons employed or engaged by
              employer.
Clause 35   Nominated subcontractors.
Clause 36   Nominated suppliers.

The first of these clauses allows the main contractor to appoint his domestic subcontractors. The number of subcontractors employed will depend on the overall facilities provided by the main contractor. On some projects the contractor may work in a co-ordinating and organizing role only, after subcontracting the whole of the work. The architect must approve all these subcontractors, and in any event the main contractor's responsibilities within the terms of the contract are not diminished. The assignment of these responsibilities to another firm is generally not acceptable to the architect or building owner.

Clause 29 provides the right to allow the employer's own contractors to be engaged upon the works during the normal contract period. These firms may be of a very specialized nature, such as sculptors, and the employer may wish, therefore, to retain a more direct control over their work.

Clause 35 is one of the longer clauses of JCT 80, and deals with the provision for nominated subcontractors. The clause is subdivided into 26 subclauses, as follows:

35.1	Definitions.
35.2	Provision for main contractor to tender for nominated subcontractors' work.
35.3	Documents.
35.4–35.12	Procedure for nomination.
35.13	Payment of nominated subcontractors.
35.14	Extension of period for completion of nominated subcontract works.
35.15	Failure to complete nominated subcontract works.
35.16	Practical completion of nominated subcontract works.
35.17–35.19	Final payment of nominated subcontractors.
35.20	Position of employer in relation to nominated subcontractors.
35.21	Position of main contractor.
35.22	Limitation of liability of nominated subcontractors.
35.23	Position where nomination does not proceed further.
35.24	Circumstances where re-nomination is necessary.
35.25–35.26	Determination of employment of nominated subcontractors.

Nominated subcontractors include statutory undertakings, although these are special subcontractors since neither the client, the architect nor the main contractor has any choice in their appointment.

The work to be executed covered by classes 35 and 36 are written into the bill of quantities as prime cost sums, and are subject to adjustments under the terms of the contract.

Assignment and subcontracts (clause 19)

Neither the employer nor the contractor shall, without the written consent of the other, assign the contract. The contractor must also, prior to subletting any portion of the works, obtain the written consent of the architect. The consent must not be unreasonably withheld. The terms of the contract accept that the main contractor will probably not undertake all the trades, but that some of the work will be done by subcontracting firms. The subcontractors whom the main contractor chooses to employ are known as domestic subcontractors. In order that the architect can have some influence over domestic subcontractors, he needs to know who they will be in order that he can approve them. This approval would only be withheld where the architect considered them to be unreliable or where they performed a poor standard of workmanship. He may have previously worked with them on other contracts or be dissatisfied with their standards of sample work.

Subletting occurs where the contractor chooses to enter into a subcontract with other firms for some part or even the whole of the contract, while still maintaining his existing relationship to the employer in all respects. Assignment occurs where another firm takes over the contractual rights of the contractor, and for all purposes the contractor to whom the project was contracted ceases to exist. Although subletting occurs, to some degree, on all construction projects, assignment is extremely unusual.

Where the main contractor intends to sublet some of the work, the names of the firms together with work to be sublet should be annexed to the contract bills. The architect must list at least three suitable firms for each section that may be sublet. The architect and the contractor are also entitled, with the consent of each other, to add additional firms to these lists at any time prior to the execution of a binding subcontract agreement.

If for any reason the main contractor's employment is determined under the contract, then the employment of all his domestic subcontractors will also cease.

Where subletting occurs, then all the conditions in the contract between the main contractor and the employer must apply equally to the subcontract. The main contractor will, of course, have to ensure that these arrangements are written into the subcontract agreement otherwise he will be under conditions that he will be unable to enforce on the subcontractor.

When tendering he will base his prices on these subcontract quotations. He does this at his own risk, because approval to sublet may be refused by the architect at some later date. The contractor should therefore attempt to seek the approval of the architect to these subcontractors prior to signing the contract.

Works by employer or persons employed or engaged by employer (clause 29)

This clause in the previous editions of the *Standard Form of Building Contract* was described as 'Artists and Tradesmen'. It envisages that the employer may choose to employ some trades directly. This work may be of a relatively minor nature or concerning items which are only loosely related to the building industry. The clause is required to secure the right to the site for such persons or firms. The contractor, knowing that these will require entry to the site, can organize and allow for any possible inconvenience or disruption. This knowledge will also give the opportunity to the contractor of including for any expense that may thus be incurred. If there is any delay on the part of their work the contractor has some redress by an extension of time (clause 25), or loss and expense (clause 26) or determination (clause 28).

If the execution of work under this heading is an afterthought on the part of the employer, the contractor must be prepared to give the same reasonable access to the works. It should be noted that the employer is responsible for their proper organization and control, because they will not fall within the jurisdiction of a subcontractor.

Nominated subcontractors (clause 35)

Works which are required to be carried out by nominated subcontractors should be included in the bills of quantities as a prime cost sum. These subcontractors may supply and fix materials or goods or execute work. The *Standard Method of Measurement of Building Works*, seventh edition, provides for the inclusion of such items. In addition, works undertaken by nomininated subcontractors may arise from the following situations:

1. The expenditure of provisional sums.
2. An instruction from the architect requiring a variation. This is providing that such work is an extra to the contract, and that it is similar in content to other work already being carried out by nominated subcontractors.
3. By agreement between the contractor and architect on behalf of the employer. It should be noted, however, that the architect does not have the power under the contract to omit contractor's work and award this to a nominated subcontractor (clause 13.1.3). The creation of prime cost sums can only generally be formed with the agreement of the main contractor.

It is the architect's prerogative to nominate firms to undertake the above work. The firms selected should meet the approval of the contractor. The nomination, however, may still proceed in certain cases where the main contractor believes that he has reasonable grounds for refusing such an approval. In these circumstances it may be unwise on the part of the architect to proceed with the nomination of such a firm. If the contractor has a reasonable objection to a proposed nominated subcontractor he should inform the architect, preferably in writing, as soon as possible. This obviously needs to be done prior to actual nomination, but also in sufficient time to enable the architect to nominate others without any delay occurring in the contract programme.

The main contractor may also wish to carry out work, for which a prime cost sum has been included in the contract documents. It is sometimes usual to supply, with the tender form, both a list of the main contractor's domestic subcontractors and also a list of prime cost sums for which the contractor desires to tender. Both of these forms are often required to be returned with the contractor's tender. The following conditions from clause 35 will generally apply regarding such prime cost sums:

1. The contractor, during the ordinary course of his business, must directly carry out this work. This does not preclude subletting if agreed by the architect.
2. The contractor must give notice of this intention as soon as possible. This is in order to pre-empt a contract being awarded to another firm. The architect may at the tender stage have already received quotations for this work.
3. The architect must be willing to allow the contractor to tender. Refusal to tender, or to accept the contractor's lowest tender should this be the case, will usually mean that the architect prefers a specialist firm to do the work.

If the main contractor is allowed to submit a tender for this work, then the invitation to submit a price must make it absolutely clear on items such as the contractor's discounts, profit and attendances. Where the price is submitted in competition, then the importance of these items may influence the choice of the successful tender. An obvious way is to treat the main contractor's quotation in the same way as each of the other subcontractors. Problems in practice may, however, favour a composite price from the main contractor inclusive of all these items.

The following are the documents which relate to nominated subcontractors:

NSC/1   *Standard Form of Nominated Subcontract — Tender and Agreement.*
NSC/2   *Standard Form of Employer/Nominated Subcontractor Agreement.*
NSC/2a The form of agreement as NSC/2, but adapted for use where the tender NSC/1 has not been used.
NSC/3   *Standard Form for Nomination of a Subcontractor,* where NSC/1 has been used.
NSC/4   *Standard Form of Nominated Subcontract.*
NSC/4a The standard form of subcontract, adapted for use where the tender NSC/1 has not been used.

Procedure for nomination of a subcontractor

The tender NSC/1 and agreement NSC/2 should be used wherever possible. In those circumstances where they are not used the contractor may make a reasonable objection to the architect. This needs to be done within seven days of the receipt of the instruction from the architect nominating the subcontractor using the alternative procedures. It is expected that NSC/1 and NSC/2 will be used in the majority of instances, but situations do occur where a streamlined process needs to be adopted. The absence of NSC/1 and NSC/2 therefore usually occurs where insufficient time is available for the full nomination process. In other circumstances, where negotiations have broken down with a subcontractor, the shortened process of NSC/2a may need to be applied.

The full process of nomination using tender NSC/1 and agreement NSC/2 is as follows:

1. The subcontractor is invited to submit a tender using form NSC/1.
2. If this is acceptable by the architect the subcontractor then enters into the agreement NSC/2 with the employer.
3. The architect must then forward to the contractor copies of these forms for his agreement to issuing the formal notice for nomination. The contractor and subcontractor must then agree to all the conditions in schedule 2 of NSC/1 after amending them where necessary. There may be items in this schedule on which the parties cannot agree. If after 10 days from the receipt of the preliminary notice of nomination they still fail to agree, the contractor must inform the architect of the reasons why they cannot agree.
4. The architect must then issue appropriate instructions to the contractor to remedy the disagreement.
5. Even at this stage the subcontractor can inform the contractor that he is withdrawing the offer set out in his tender.
6. When the subcontractor and the contractor agree with the contents of the tender NSC/1, this should be forwarded, duly completed, to the architect.
7. The architect must then issue to the contractor instructions on the nomination form NSC/3, nominating the proposed subcontractor to carry out this work. A copy of this should be sent to the said subcontractor.

Payment of a nominated subcontractor

Before any nominated subcontractor's work can be included in a valuation, invoices must be made available for inspection by the quantity surveyor. The invoice signifies that the subcontractor concerned requires payment. The quantity surveyor should check the invoice against the quotation and tender NSC/1 as may be appropriate. The rates, the prices, and the arithmetic should be checked; and a check should also be made to ensure that the quantity of work has been properly executed. Although it is not the quantity surveyor's duty to inspect the quality of the materials and workmanship, he should nevertheless not include work that is obviously defective. If he has any doubts he should bring the matter to the attention of the architect. The approved invoices are then included in the quantity surveyor's valuation of the work as per clause 30.2, and subsequently in the architect's certificate.

Upon the issue of each interim certificate, the architect must inform the contractor of the amount that has been included for each nominated subcontractor. It must also be clearly stated whether these amounts are interim or final payments due to the subcontractors. The architect will also inform the individual subcontractors accordingly. The main contractor must then make these payments as directed. He cannot make any deductions for contra charges unless these are agreed by the subcontractor concerned. Before the issue of each certificate, the contractor must provide some evidence that he has paid the appropriate amounts shown on previous certificates. Such evidence for example, might include a receipt for the amount listed. The absence of this evidence will not automatically assume that the subcontractor has not been paid, but before proceeding to issue another certificate the architect must be reasonably satisfied that this is not the case.

The form of contract provides a remedy for paying the subcontractor direct, in those cases where the main contractor defaults in payment. In circumstances where he is unable to provide adequate proof to the satisfaction of the architect, the architect shall issue a certificate accordingly together with a copy to the nominated subcontractor. The employer is now able to pay the subcontractor direct and to deduct these amounts from future payments to the contractor. If, however, it is known that the main contractor is shortly due to enter into liquidation, such a direct payment will not be made by the employer. In no circumstances does the employer want to be placed in a position of having to pay a subcontractor twice. Unfortunately situations do, however, occur where this may be necessary in order to secure the services of a particular subcontractor, without which, the project would not be completed. There are also provisions in the Form of Contract (clause 35.13) to allow an employer to pay a nominated subcontractor for design work, materials and goods prior to the issue of an instruction of nomination. Such direct payments are ignored in computing interim and final certificate payments.

Time

The main contractor is not able to give a nominated subcontractor an extension of time (this being an extension of the period in which the subcontract works are to be carried out) without the written consent of the architect. It is up to the architect to operate the relevant provisions of the subcontract, namely clause 11 in this respect.

If any nominated subcontractor fails to complete the subcontract works within the period allocated on the contract programme, or any revision thereof, then the contractor should inform the architect of this event. The architect should then send a certificate to the contractor accordingly. A duplicate copy of the certificate should be forwarded to the nominated subcontractor concerned. The certificate must be sent within two months of the date of notification to the architect.

When, in the opinion of the architect, a nominated subcontractor achieves practical completion of the works, a certificate should be sent to the contractor to this effect, with a duplicate copy to the nominated subcontractor.

If either NSC/2 or NSC/2a has been entered into by the two parties to the contract, and providing clause 5 has not been changed, then final payment can be made to the nominated subcontractor prior to that of the main contract. Twelve months must elapse before this payment can be made from the date of the subcontractor's certificate of practical completion. The subcontractor concerned must, however, have remedied any defects for which he is responsible, and sent through the contractor to the quantity surveyor the necessary documents for the final adjustment of the contract sum.

If upon discharge by the contractor to the nominated subcontractor, the subcontractor fails to rectify those items for which he is responsible, then, in accordance with the contract, the architect will issue an instruction to others to rectify the work. The employer in these circumstances will take the necessary steps to recover the amounts of this remedial work. If the employer is unable to recover these sums from the subcontractor, then the main contractor must provide for the necessary payments.

The main contractor will, however, be responsible for any defects to the nominated subcontractor's work from the date of the subcontractor's completion up to the issue of the final certificate for the project as a whole. Before the subcontractor is therefore released from his contract, the main contractor will require some form of indemnity against the possibility of defects occurring and the costs of their making good.

The existence of clause 35, or even other clauses within the conditions of contract, will not render the employer liable in any way to a nominated subcontractor. The only exception to this rule may be by way of the terms and agreement set out in clause NSC/2 or NSC/2a. Bills of quantities often state that once the formal process of nomination has been completed such subcontractors are not dissimilar to the domestic subcontractors in contractual terms.

The main contractor is not liable to the employer in any way regarding the nominated subcontract works covered by clause 2 of NSC/2 or clause 1 of NSC/2a. The main contractor is thus excluded from any design responsibility that may be undertaken by the nominated subcontractor. The main contractor in general undertakes no design responsibility. He is, however, responsible for the carrying out of the work in order to ensure that it complies with the design and that the materials and workmanship are in accordance with the specification.

The liability of the main contractor to the employer cannot exceed the liability of the subcontractor to the main contractor in respect of subcontract works.

If the nomination of a particular subcontractor does not proceed, then the architect must either omit the work from the contract or nominate another firm to do the work. This situation can occur if:

(a) the contractor under clause 35.4 sustains a reasonable objection to the proposed nominated subcontractor;
(b) the subcontractor does not settle the outstanding conditions of schedule 2 (NSC/1) within a reasonable time;
(c) the shortened form of nomination is used and the nominated subcontractor fails to enter into NSC/4a within a reasonable time and for good cause.

Renomination of a nominated subcontractor is necessary if the following conditions arise:

1. If the architect is of the opinion that the nominated subcontractor has made a default regarding items in NSC/4 or NSC/4a (clauses 20.1.1−29.1.4 of the subcontract). The main contractor must have informed the architect of the alleged default together with any observations. The architect must be of the opinion that the subcontractor has made the default.
2. If the nominated subcontractor becomes bankrupt or makes an arrangement with his creditors for the winding up of the company, voluntary or otherwise. This is with the exception of amalgamation or reconstruction.
3. If the nominated subcontractor has determined his employment under clause 30 of the subcontract.

Where any of the above three events occurs, then the following are to apply:

1. The architect must issue an instruction to the main contractor to give to the nominated subcontractor the notice specifying the default. The instruction may also require the contractor to obtain a further instruction prior to determining the employment of the nominated subcontractor.
2. The contractor must inform the architect, following the issue of the notice, if the employment of the nominated subcontractor has been determined. If the second instruction under this clause has been given, then the contractor must confirm the determination to the architect.
3. Once the architect has been finally informed of the determination of the nominated subcontractor, he must renominate as necessary. Where such determination has occurred because of the failure of the subcontractor to remedy the defects, the main contractor must be given the opportunity to agree the price to be charged by the substituted nominated subcontractor.

The architect must renominate as necessary in the case of the subcontractor's bankruptcy. If, however, the architect reasonably believes

185

that the appointed receiver is prepared to continue to completion, then the architect may postpone a renomination. This is as long as the relevant subcontract does not detrimentally affect any other person involved in the works.

If the subcontractor has reasonably determined his contract (clause 30, form of subcontract), then the architect must renominate as necessary. Any excess price of the substituted nominated subcontractor over that of the originally nominated subcontractor may be recovered by the employer from the contractor. The reasonableness of this charge against the contractor is because, in this case, determination is a result of the contractor's default.

All amounts payable to the renominated subcontractors must be included in the interim certificates and added to the contract sum.

The contractor cannot determine the contract of any nominated subcontractor without an appropriate instruction from the architect. If the determination is made under clause 29 of NSC/4 or NSC/4a, the architect must direct the contractor with regards to any amounts due in an interim certificate.

Nominated suppliers (clause 36)

Goods and materials which are required to be obtained from a nominated supplier, are to be included in the contract bills as a prime cost sum. Where the architect knows the name of the supplier, this should be stated in the description. The fixing of these items will be undertaken by the main contractor or his own subcontractor where this is approved. The costs associated with fixing generally include all those items from the point of delivery to the site. The right of nomination is solely that of the architect. The nomination of firms to supply materials or goods may arise in the following ways:

(a) by the inclusion of a prime cost sum in the contract bills for the supply of goods or materials;
(b) where a provisional sum is included in the contract bills, and an architect's instruction names the supplier of any goods or materials involved;
(c) where a provisional sum results in an architect's instructions to a sole source of supply of such goods or materials;
(d) where a variation made by the architect specifies goods or materials for which there is only a single source of supply.

In the conditions of contract a nominated supplier must be covered by a prime cost sum. The naming of a supplier as part of the contractor's work — even where this is a sole supplier of goods and materials — will not therefore always result in a prime cost sum. Work can therefore be measured in the contract bills as supply and fix, even where only one supplier is known. The architect must issue instructions for the purpose of nominating a supplier, for the works that are covered by a prime cost sum in a bill of quantities.

The amounts properly chargeable to the employer in respect of nominated suppliers' accounts, include the following items as appropriate:

1. A cash discount to the contractor of 5 per cent, where the contractor makes the necessary payment within 30 days of the end of the month during which delivery of the materials or goods are made. Any discount offered in excess of this must be passed on for the benefit of the employer. Where no discount has been included, the main contractor is allowed to add one-nineteenth to the nett cost of the invoice. Quotations should be checked with regard to the discount offered prior to their acceptance.

2. Any tax or duty that is recoverable under this contract. This excludes value added tax which is capable of being treated as an input tax by the contractor (see clause 15).

3. The nett cost of appropriate packaging, carriage and delivery charges. The main contractor should return the empty packing to the supplier for any credit that may be available. The credit is for the benefit of the employer. The cost of such carriage should be identified on the quotation.

4. The charges incurred for any adjustment in price, in accordance with clauses 38—40.

5. If, in the opinion of the architect, the contractor incurs additional expense for which he is not being properly reimbursed, then such an amount may be added to the contract sum. Such an amount may arise as a direct charge made to the contractor by the supplier.

The architect should only nominate firms as suppliers of goods and materials where the following conditions apply. The contractor can refuse to enter into a contract of sale, where they do not.

1. The quality of the materials and goods must conform to the standards specified. This is largely a matter for the architect to determine, but they may affect the overall quality of the works and the method of fixing undertaken by the contractor.

2. The nominated supplier must make good any defects, in the materials or goods, which appear before the end of the defects liability period. The supplier should also reimburse the contractor for any costs that he may incur — for example, in refixing or returning the defective materials to the suppliers. Any extra costs might also presumably include loss and expense caused by delays. Reimbursement of the contractor's costs will only be paid in the following circumstances:

   (a) where a reasonable examination of the goods by the contractor would not have revealed their defects;

   (b) where the goods have not been improperly stored and misused before, during or after their incorporation in the works.

3. The delivery of the materials or goods, including unloading, is done in accordance with the instructions of the supplier, or agreed between the supplier and the contractor, or undertaken in a reasonable manner by the contractor. The supplier must also be prepared to accept the contractor's programme as far as delivery is concerned. If he is unable to meet this, then the contractor can reasonably expect the architect to nominate an alternative supplier, because they may be crucial to the overall programme.

4. The nominated supplier must make the appropriate allowance for the discount of 5 per cent.

5. The nominated supplier will not usually deliver goods to the site after the contractor's determination, unless they have already been paid for by the employer.

6. The main contractor must pay the required amount within 30 days of the end of the month during which delivery is made.

7. The ownership of the materials or goods will pass to the contractor upon delivery to site by the nominated supplier, regardless of whether payment has been made. This may be a difficult clause to substantiate in practice, particularly if some of the components or materials supplied have a defective title.

8. If differences in opinion exist between the supplier and the contractor, they must first agree to take their differences to arbitration.

9. The conditions of sale, often printed on the reverse side of suppliers' quotations and invoices, will not override the conditions as described above.

Of course, in practice, if the supplier can persuade the architect or the contractor to waive any of these conditions, this can be done by agreement. Good advice, recommended elsewhere, is that the standard clauses should not be tampered with except in extreme circumstances. If, however, the architect wishes to appoint a firm whose contract of sale excludes a condition listed above, then the architect must also be prepared to relieve the contractor of this same obligation towards the employer.

Chapter 16

Injury and insurance of the works

The definition of 'insurance' is that one party (the insurer) undertakes to make payments to or for the benefit of the other party (the assured) upon the occurrence of certain specified events. The insurance contract between these parties is generally contained in a document called a policy. The consideration, which is necessary to make such a contract binding, is provided by the assured in the way of a premium.

An insurance contract is said to be *uberrimae fidei*: that is, it is based upon good faith between the parties. The assured must therefore make a full disclosure of every material fact known to him. A material fact is information which, if disclosed, would influence the judgment of the insurer. Filling in the proposal form incorrectly can make the policy voidable by the insurer, even where an innocent mistake occurs. The insurance policies are usually printed on standard forms by the company issuing its own terms. Each policy must, however, be clear on the terms of insurance, and be accompanied by certain exclusions of liability.

If a situation occurs that may result in a claim by the assured, this must be notified to the company within a reasonable time of the event. The claim is often forwarded by the insurance company to a loss adjuster. This is the general procedure involving sums of even a relatively minor amount. The loss adjuster will then assess the amount of damage and the sum payable in respect of the insurance policy. Although the loss adjuster works on behalf of the insurance company, he will try to achieve an equitable settlement between the parties. In some circumstances the employer or contractor may employ a loss adjuster on their behalf in order to negotiate with the insurance company's loss adjuster.

The clauses examined in this section are as follows:

Clause 20	Injury to persons and property and indemnity to the employer.
Clause 21	Insurance against injury to persons and property.
Clause 22	Insurance of the works.
Clause 22A	Erection of new buildings. All-risks insurance of the works by the contractor.
Clause 22B	Erection of new buildings. All-risks insurance of the works by the employer.
Clause 22C	Insurance of existing structures. Insurance of the works in or extensions to existing structures.
Clause 22D	Insurance for employer's loss of liquidated damages.

Injury to persons and property and indemnity to the employer (clause 20)

The contractor is liable for, and must indemnify the employer against, any expense, liability, loss, claim or proceedings of any nature. These may arise because of statute legislation or at common law. They are in respect of personal injury to, or the death of, anyone caused by the carrying out of the works by the contractor or anyone employed by him, such as subcontractors. The contractor's liability does not extend to any act of negligence either by the employer or persons directly under the employer's control, such as his directly employed contractors. Indemnity in this circumstance means the protection that one party gives to another in respect of claims by a third party. Mainly because the contractor may be forced into liquidation, the contract provides for insurance under clauses 21 and 22 of these conditions. If, however, for some reason the insurance fails, this does not relieve the contractor of his indemnity.

The contractor is also liable for, and must indemnify the employer against, injury to property. The injury applies to any type of property and must be as a result of the carrying out of the works. The two exceptions to this liability are the same as for personal injury, viz. employer's negligence and the employer's own directly employed contractors.

The employer does, however, have the option of accepting some of the risks himself where he chooses one of the alternatives of clauses 22B or 22C. Also, the contractor will not be responsible should damage occur because of an inappropriate or false design, but he must ensure that even in these circumstances he has taken all reasonable precautions during the execution of the works. Where loss or damage does occur the contractor's main area of defence is to point any negligence in the direction of the employer and his agents.

Insurance against injury to persons and property (clause 21)

The main contractor under clause 20 has a liability to indemnify the employer against injury to persons and property. The main contractor is responsible for the whole works, including that of subcontractors. He should therefore seek to ensure that all subcontractors maintain insurances to cover the liability of the contractor in respect of all of those items in clause 20. If, however, a subcontractor fails to provide the appropriate insurance cover, this will not remove the overall liability of the main contractor to the employer. The contractor is only exempt in the case of negligence caused by the employer or persons for whom the employer is directly responsible.

Insurance is required against claims submitted by third parties for injury to persons and property. These third parties will include the owners and the occupiers of adjoining properties and the general public. It will also include all those who visit the site or who have lawful entry to the works. A public liability policy will protect the contractor against claims arising through negligence or mistake. There may also be occasions when a third party will be able to substantiate a claim even when negligence cannot be proved. The policy must therefore include clauses to guard against such claims. A major risk with constructional work is the danger of subsidence to adjoining property. It is equally important to ensure that the contractor's public liability policy also covers this event.

The contractor will also be required to provide an employer's liability insurance for his own workmen. Although the National Insurance provides for compensation of employees for injury, the employer will still be liable at common law to compensate the employee for injury due to negligence, whether through his own or that of another employee. The premiums paid are often calculated on the basis of the annual wage bill.

The employer can at any time request the contractor, or any subcontractor, to produce for inspection by the employer, documentary evidence that the insurances are properly maintained. This will usually require the appropriate policies being produced at least some time during the early stages of the contract. The employer can, however, require them to be produced at other reasonable times, as long as this is not done simply to irritate the contractor.

If the contractor or a subcontractor fails to insure properly or continue to insure the works as requested, then the employer may insure on their behalf. He will pay the necessary premiums and deduct these amounts from sums due to the contractor. The amounts recoverable from the contractor are those amounts that the employer actually pays, rather than any amount inserted by the contractor in the bills. Because this problem is more likely to occur at the beginning of the contract, the employer can deduct the appropriate amounts from interim certificates.

In some circumstances a provisional sum may be included in the bills of quantities for insurances. The contractor should then maintain in the joint names of the employer and contractor, insurances to the appropriate amount as stated in the contract bills. Such indemnity shall cover damage to property other than the works caused by collapse, subsidence, vibration, weakening or removal of support, or lowering of ground water, unless the damage occurs because of:

(a) contractor's liability under clause 20.2;
(b) errors in the design of the works;
(c) damage that is likely to be inevitable having regard to the nature of the works, which is almost an uninsurable item;
(d) where the employer has accepted responsibility for the insurance of the works;
(e) war risks or excepted risks.

Any insurance required for the above should be placed with insurers approved by the employer. The contractor must also provide proof of the policy and that the premiums have been paid. The inclusion of a provisional sum may mean that some of these items are difficult to insure.

In no circumstances will the contractor be liable to insure or indemnify the employer against:

(a) the effects of ionizing radiations;
(b) the contamination by radioactivity from any nuclear fuel or from any nuclear waste from the combusion of nuclear fuel;
(c) radioactive toxic explosive;
(d) other hazardous properties of any nuclear assembly or component;
(e) pressure waves caused by aircraft;
(f) other aerial devices travelling at sonic or supersonic speeds.

The amount of insurance cover required for any one occurrence or series of occurrences arising out of one event, in respect of injury to persons and property, is to be stated in the appendix to the form of contract. The employer may need to seek expert advice in connection with this sum, but in any event the contractor may well wish to maintain his third party policies at a much higher level.

Insurance of the works (clause 22)

The responsibility for the cost of making good any damage to the works, during the period of construction under JCT 80 allows for one of three choices to be made by the employer. Two of these should therefore be deleted. The conditions do not envisage, in any circumstances, the contractor being responsible for insurance beyond the period of practical completion of the works. They assume that the date of handover of the project will become the entire responsibility of the employer as far as the insurance items are concerned.

The three choices available for the insurance of the works are as follows:

22A Erection of new buildings. All-risks insurance of the works by the contractor.
22B Erection of new buildings. All-risks insurance of the works by the employer.
22C Insurance of existing structures. Insurance of the works in or extensions to existing structures.

Where the project is comprised of two separate parts, one being new works and the other being alterations, it is possible to use both clauses 22A and 22C. Confusion might occur regarding the common stock of materials and the apportionment of the preliminaries costs. From a procedural point of view, the events would be governed by the alternative invoked when a particular incident occurred. A further clause 22D has also been added, to cover the insurance for employer's loss of liquidated damages under clause 25.4.3.

Essentially two kinds of policy are available for property insurance. The first type is known as an indemnity policy. 'To indemnify' means not only to protect against harm or loss and make financial compensations, but also to secure legal responsibility. The payments made by the insurance company are based upon the damage that occurs less any depreciation in the value of the property. The alternative policy has a reinstatement clause which commits the insurers to paying the full cost of replacement, no account being taken of depreciation. If property is insured for less than its true value, the policy holder then will be paid an average sum based upon a ratio of insured to true value. For example, if the property is only insured at half the true amount then whatever the size of the claim only half of it will be reimbursed. Some property owners choose to carry a part of the risk themselves, and in these circumstances the insurance company will then only be responsible for a proportion of the loss. In other circumstances an excess clause may be included to avoid claims for trivial amounts of damage. In addition to the cost of reinstatement the insured could be put to further expense as a result of the incident, such as the provision of alternative accommodation. This is known as consequential loss and a clause to cover this should be included in the policy.

Clause 22 is largely concerned with definitions, for example, all-risks insurance — defined as insurance which provides cover against any physical loss or damage to work executed and site materials but excluding the cost necessary to repair, replace or rectify:

1. Property which is defective due to wear and tear, obsolescence, deterioration, rust or mildew.
2. Materials or workmanship which are defective in terms of their design or executed work which relied upon the support or stability or work which was defective.
3. Loss or damage caused or arising from events such as war, invasion, rebellion, revolution, etc., but not riot or civil commotion.
4. An excepted risk as defined in clause 1.3, e.g., radiation and nuclear activities and pressure waves caused by aircraft or other aerial devices.
5. Other exclusions also refer to Northern Ireland and the Northern Ireland (Emergency Provisions) Act 1973.

The contractor where clause 22A applies and the employer where either clause 22B or 22C applies, shall insure the works in the joint names of both the employer and the contractor. The joint names policy must provide for either recognition of each nominated subcontractor or include a waiver by the relevant insurers of any right of subrogation which they might have against any such nominated subcontractor in respect of loss or damage by the specified perils where applicable. The specified perils are defined in clause 1.3 and include fire, lightning, explosion, storm, tempest, flood, bursting or overflowing of water tanks, apparatus or pipes, earthquake, aircraft or other aerial devices or articles dropped therefrom, riot and civil commotion, but excluding the excepted risks defined above.

Erection of new buildings — all-risks insurance of the works by the contractor (clause 22A)

The contractor must take out and maintain a joint names policy for all-risks insurance as defined in clause 22. The insurance to be provided by the contractor is to be for the full reinstatement value including professional fees, the percentage for which is as stated in the appendix. The policy shall be maintained up to the issue of the certificate of practical completion or up to any date of determination under clauses 27 or 28. The insurance to be provided by the contractor is to be for the full reinstatement value.

The joint names policy must be taken out with insurers approved by the employer. The contractor must send to the architect, for deposit by the employer, a copy of the policy and the receipt for the premiums paid. Where the contractor fails to provide adequate insurance cover in respect of the contract, the employer may insure against the risks described. He cannot extend the policy to cover other risks, but he can deduct the premiums from amounts owed to the contractor under interim payments. If, however, the contractor maintains an all-risks policy as the normal pattern of business efficiency, then this may be accepted as an alternative to the joint names policy outlined above. It will be subject to the endorsement of the employer's interest on the policy, and evidence that it is appropriate and being maintained and that the necessary premiums have been paid. The architect, on rare occasions, may also wish to inspect the policy and the contract provides for this possibility. The annual renewal date, as supplied by the contractor, of this insurance is stated on the appendix. The provisions outlined previously in regard to any default by the contractor in taking out and maintaining insurances apply equally in this case.

If the necessity for an insurance claim arises then the contractor shall proceed as follows:

1. Inform both the architect and employer in writing of the nature, extent and location of the claim.
2. Allow for inspection by the insurers.
3. Diligently restore any work which has been damaged, replace or repair any site materials which have been lost or damaged, remove and dispose of any debris and proceed with the carrying out and completion of the works.

The insurance monies received for this work will be paid to the employer. The contractor will be paid for the rectification of this work by instalments under certificates of the architect on a similar basis to that of interim certificates. The sums received for professional fees will be paid to parties concerned. The contractor will not be paid anything extra to cover the restoration of the damaged work other than that received from the insurers. Before proceeding 'with due diligence' the contractor should make sure that the insurers have accepted the claim. Unless it is necessary for safety reasons this part of the works should not be disturbed until the company's loss adjusters have inspected the damage. The final amount received by the contractor and the employer for professional fees may be inadequate since the nature of the damages may not be pro-rata in either situation.

Erection of new buildings — all-risks insurance of the works by the employer (clause 22B)

Under this clause the employer is responsible for insuring the works and a similar procedure to the above is adopted. The insured roles of the two parties are reversed and the principles of providing documentary evidence by the employer, or a subsequent failure to insure the works by him can be rectified by the contractor. In this case the amount of the premiums are added to the contract sum. The procedure to be followed by the contractor in the event of an insured claim also follows the pattern outlined above. The value of rectifying the damaged work may be on the basis of bill rates, but agreement with the insurance company's loss adjusters will be necessary to determine the actual amount to be paid to the employer. Whether the insurer's basis of payment is the same as the contract basis is a matter which must remain at the employer's risk.

Insurance of existing structures — insurance of the works in or extensions to existing structures (clause 22C)

The employer is responsible for insuring the existing works under this clause in a joint names policy, with the same contractual risks occurring as with clause 22B. The procedure for notifying both the architect and the employer follows that of clause 22A. A similar pattern of reinstatement by the contractor and payment by the insurance company occurs as under clause 22B. One assumes that in this case, the contractor will be paid the full cost of reinstatement, in accordance with the contract and valuation rules. Any shortfall between that received by the employer from the insurance company and that paid to the contractor would thus be borne entirely by the employer. The insurer may, however, pay for reinstatement on the basis of the contractor's estimate for making good. Under this section, however, the occurrence of loss or damage by a specified peril may result in determination of the contract by the employer or the contractor. Presumably the damage could be so extensive as to make reinstatement of the existing building unwise as far as the employer is concerned. The contractor may also wish to terminate because the damage could result in a project that is now too complex to contemplate.

Insurance for the employer's loss of liquidated damages (clause 22D)

The appendix to the form of contract identifies to the contractor whether or not this clause will be applied. Once the contract has been signed then the contractor may be requested to obtain a quotation for such insurance. This will be on an agreed basis of a genuine pre-estimate of the damages which may occur as the result of any delay and at the rate stated for liquidated and ascertained damages included in the appendix. The amounts expended by the contractor to take out and maintain this insurance shall be added to the contract sum.

Chapter 17

Fluctuations in costs

Contracts are often described as either fixed price or fluctuating price contracts, the essential difference being that the former expects the contractor to have allowed for any changes to the contract sum for items such as inflation, etc., and the latter does not. The relevant provisions are contained in the following clauses:

Clause 37 Fluctuations,
Clause 38 Contributions, levy and tax fluctuations.
Clause 39 Labour and materials costs and tax fluctuations.
Clause 40 Use of price adjustment formulae.

Fluctuations (clause 37)

Fluctuations can be dealt with in the conditions of contract in one of three ways.

1. *Clause 38*. This allows only for the adjustments in price of contributions, levies or taxes. This technically is therefore described as the 'firm price' contract.
2. *Clause 39*. The assessment of labour and materials costs and tax fluctuations, using the traditional method of calculation.
3. *Clause 40*. The calcuation of price fluctuations by the formulae method.

Only one of these clauses may apply and this clause should be stated in the appendix. If this has been omitted then it is presumed that clause 38 will be used. The three fluctuation clauses are contained in a separate booklet detailing the various provisions of each clause. In the approximate quantities version, clause 38 cannot apply. The formulae method, therefore, cannot be used without the quantities version. It should be noted that a strictly firm price version is not now available, since each of the choices allow for fluctuations in cost, caused by government legislation.

Contributions, levy and tax fluctuations (clause 38)

The contract sum is deemed to have been calculated as detailed by this clause. The adjustments that may therefore be necessary will occur where differences eventually arise because of the following provisions.

Clause 38.6 includes the following definitions that are appropriate both to this clause and to clause 39.

1. *Base date.* In the first edition of JCT 80 this was described as the date of tender which was defined as ten days before the date fixed for the receipt of tenders. Representation to the Tribunal suggested that this did not provide a firm enough date because employers infrequently revised the tender date so necessitating recalculation and causing uncertainty. A firm date is now written into the appendix and called the base date, which brings the terminology in line with the *Formula Rules for Price Adjustment.* The necessity for the date is to avoid contractors having to make last-minute adjustments to their tenders.

2. *Materials and goods.* This excludes consumable stores, plant and machinery, but can include timber used in formwork, electricity, and fuels if this has been specifically stated in the bills.

3. *Workpeople.* Persons whose rate of wages are governed by rules, decisions or agreements of the National Joint Council for the Building Industry or some other wage-fixing body. Foremen, for example, who work as tradesmen will be assumed to be tradesmen for the purpose and application of this clause. It should be noted that workpeople not only include those employed by the contractor on the project, but also those who may work off site in the contractor's workshops, e.g. joinery shop.

4. *Wage-fixing body.* A body which lays down recognized terms and conditions of workers as under the Employment Protection Act 1975.

The prices in the contract bills are based upon those contributions that are current at the base date. Should these change or the contractor's status be revised, then adjustment will become necessary. Although this clause is one of the trio of increased cost provisions, money may need to be repaid to the employer where the contributions decrease. It should be noted, however, that levies payable under the Industrial Training Act 1964 are expressly excluded from any adjustment.

To enable the contractor to claim fluctuations in the costs of labour, the following provisions must apply. Each employee must have worked on the project for a minimum of two working days in any week for which the claim is applicable. The aggregation of days and parts of a day do not therefore apply. The highest properly fixed tradesman's rate must be used, provided that such a tradesman is employed by either the contractor or one of his domestic subcontractors. The clause is applied in the context of the Income Tax (Employment) Regulations 1973 (the PAYE regulations) under s. 204 of the Income and Corporation Taxes Act 1970.

Where any of the tender types or tender rates change, then the nett actual amount of an adjustment must be calculated. This sum is then paid to or allowed by the contractor. The change is measured as the difference between monies actually expended and those that were appropriate at the base date. It has already been noted that some changes are based upon a theoretical adjustment. For example, where a foreman works as a craftsman any adjustments that may be due are based upon the craftsmen rate adjustment. In other circumstances where the workpeople are contracted out within the meaning of the Social Security Pensions Act 1975, the method of adjustment is on the basis that they are not contracted out employees.

The contributions, levies and taxes which are subject to adjustment are those which result because of an Act of Parliament or because of a change in an Act of Parliament. They are the amounts that a contractor must pay as a result of being an employer of labour, and therefore include sums such as the statutory insurances against personal injury or death. Originally the *Standard Form of Building Contract* (1963 edition) allowed only for fixed price and fluctuation price contracts. Either the contractor was eligible to claim for increased costs because of, for example, pay rises, or these were deemed to be included in the fixed price tender. The mid-1960s saw the introduction of taxes such as Selective Employment Tax, and strictly in the way the fixed price contract was calculated this sum could not be recovered. Because of the expected further intervention by future governments the clause was changed so that all contracts would not include the minimum provision of dealing with these items.

The contract sum is deemed to have been calculated in the following manner in respect of materials, goods and fuels.

1. The prices contained in the contract bills are based upon the types and rates of duty and tax applicable at the base date (other than VAT). These include amounts payable on the import, purchase, sale appropriation, processing or use of the materials, goods, electricity and, where specifically mentioned in the bills, fuels.
2. If any types or rates of duty, in the context of the above, are altered, then the nett difference between that actually paid by the contractor

and what he was presumed to have allowed in his bills must be calculated. This sum will then be either paid to the contractor or allowed by him to the employer.

Where the main contractor has chosen to subcontract some of the works to domestic subcontractors the following should apply. The subcontract must incorporate provisions to provide the same effect as clause 38 of the main contract, together with any percentage that may be appropriate (clause 38.7). These adjustments will be paid to the contractor or allowed by him to the employer.

The contractor must give a written notice to the architect of the occurrence of any of the events regarding the following provisions, for the purposes of this contract.

Clause 38.1.2   Tender types and rates, and workpeople.
Clause 38.1.6   Tender types and rates, and refunds.
Clause 38.2.2   Tender types and rates, and materials.
Clause 38.3.2   Domestic subcontractors' fluctuations.

The written notice is a condition with which the contractor must comply if he wishes to recoup any increased costs. The notice must be sent within a reasonable time, so that the architect is aware that further expenditure is likely. Presumably this also gives the architect the opportunity of rejecting a spurious claim that is outside the scope of these conditions. The quantity surveyor and the contractor will calculate and agree the amount of fluctuation appropriate to each notified event. Any amounts that have been agreed are then added to or deducted from the contract sum. They will also be taken into account when calculating the contractor's determination payments under clause 28. The contractor must provide the quantity surveyor with the necessary evidence, in order that he may calculate the amounts of fluctuations. This must be done within a reasonable time. The incentive necessary for the contractor to do this is that he will receive payment within the interim certificates once they are agreed (clause 30.2). When a fluctuation is claimed in respect of employees other than workpeople, the necessary evidence must include a certificate signed on behalf of the contractor each week, certifying the validity of the evidence. Fluctuations are always nett under this clause, exclusive of any profit to the contractor.

Where the contractor is in default over completion, the fluctuations will not be adjusted in line with actual expenditure. The amount of fluctuations will be technically frozen at the level applicable at completion date. The contractor will therefore still be eligible for increases, but not at the true level of expenditure. If the architect has already awarded an extension of time in accordance with clause 25, or subsequently does so, then the actual increases will be reimbursed to the contractor.

These fluctuation provisions are not applicable in respect of:

(a) Dayworks, because these will have been valued at current rates and therefore take into account the appropriate adjustments (clause 13.5.4);

(b) specialist works carried out by nominated suppliers or nominated subcontractors as all fluctuations will be dealt with by their invoices;
(c) a contractor acting as a nominated subcontractor, where the above provision will apply;
(d) changes in VAT, because these are exempt under this clause.

The percentage stated in the appendix must be added to fluctuations paid or allowed by the contractor. The percentage stated can only be recovered on certain defined fluctuations covered by clauses 38.1.2, 38.1.3, 38.1.6, or 38.2.2. The tendering documents will stipulate the percentage to be added. Although JCT discussed a figure of 20 per cent, the typical amount inserted is nil.

Labour and materials costs and tax fluctuations (clause 39)

This is the traditional full fluctuation clause, and therefore the provisions of clause 38 are included. The contractor is thus able to claim for increases in the costs of employing labour and the costs of purchasing materials in addition to the other statutory increases. The definitions of clause 39.7 are identical to those described in clause 38.6.

Labour

The contract sum is deemed to have been calculated as follows. The prices in the bills are based upon the rates of wages, and any changes will result in an adjustment to the contract sum.

1. The adjustment is in respect of workpeople on site and of those employed directly upon the works in the contractor's workshops.
2. The rules or decisions of the National Joint Council for the building industry or other appropriate wage-fixing body as applicable to the works will be used.
3. The rates of wages also include other emoluments and expenses, such as holiday credits and insurances.
4. Only wage changes unknown at the base date are eligible for adjustment. Promulgated changes are those that have already been agreed, and must therefore have been allowed for in the tender, even though they may not come into operation until some time after the contract has started. The actual amount of the changes must, however, be known. Proposed unagreed rates are therefore not promulgated within this definition.
5. Incentive schemes or productivity agreements under the rules of the NJCBI are subject to adjustment. For example, changes in the amount of the guaranteed bonus payment would be eligible. Independent incentive schemes operated by the contractor on site —

for example, where a contractor agrees to pay his men an arbitrary increase — are not allowed to be reclaimed under this clause.

6. If the terms of the public holiday agreements change during the duration of the project, then the appropriate costs of these can also be included under the heading of fluctuations. If such changes were promulgated at the time of tender, then these are assumed to have been covered by the contractor.

7. The contributions and levies of the CITB, for example, are excluded from adjustment and the contractor must therefore bear the costs of all increases. In practice, considerable time is generally notified in respect of the future increases in these payments.

8. Promulgated wage rate increases known before the base date would also mean that the contractor should have allowed for increases in his liability insurance. He can only claim for increases that are unknown at the base date. Because the employer's liability insurance is often based upon the wages bill of the firm, this would be an accepted adjustable item in other circumstances. However, should the employer choose to provide a more expensive insurance this claim would not be valid. Increases because of changes in the wages bill or because of inflation are therefore allowable where they were unknown at the time of tender.

9. Increases in the cost of productivity bonuses resulting from increases in standard rates of wages are recoverable. Thus, where the appropriate wage-fixing body agree upon an increase in the basic rate, the contractor would be able to reclaim this similar proportion paid by way of his productivity agreement.

10. The contractor's employees, who are outside the scope of workpeople but who are engaged on the works, are subject to fluctuations as if they were craft operatives. A foreman working as a bricklayer would be reimbursed accordingly.

11. The prices in the bills are based upon basic transport charges as submitted by the contractor and attached to the contract bills. Provision is therefore made for increases in travel allowances payable to workpeople under a joint agreement, including increased costs of employer's transport where used, or public transport fares.

12. Clause 39.2 is largely a reproduction of the appropriate parts of clause 38, applicable to contributions, levies and taxes.

Materials

The contract sum is deemed to have been calculated in the following manner:

1. The prices contained in the contract bills are based upon the market prices of materials, goods, electricity and, where specifically stated in the bills, fuels which were current at the base date.

2. The above market prices are referred to as basic prices, and are included on a basic price list for these items. In practice, only the

202

major cost items are listed. This may be done by the quantity
surveyor in which case he selects the list, or alternatively, the
contractor is asked to prepare a list together with his prices.
3. Any changes in the market prices of these items are then subject to
fluctuations and adjustments of the nett changes. Only the items
included on the basic price are subject to adjustment.
4. Market price changes include any changes in duty or tax (other than
VAT) on the import, purchase, sale appropriation, processing or use
of goods, materials, electricity or fuels as specified.
5. In order to avoid contention later, the quantity surveyor must approve
of the basic prices shown on the list. These are usually supported by
invoices from a single supplier. It is usual then for the contractor to
obtain the actual materials from this supplier. Any changes,
therefore, between quotation and invoice can be easily calculated.
Where it is necessary for the contractor to use an alternative
supplier, the change in price may be calculated between the invoice
and the price on the basic price list and adjusted for any changes due
to the use of a different supplier.

Domestic subcontractors

The provisions relating to domestic subcontractors correspond generally
to the provisions of clause 38.3, but of increased scope to cover wage
fluctuations.

The remaining clauses 39.5−39.8 generally also correspond to the
similar provisions included under clause 38. The following briefly are
those provisions:

Clause 38.5.1	Written notice of fluctuations required from the contractor.
Clause 39.5.2	Notice must be provided within a reasonable time after the occurrence of any price change.
Clause 39.5.3.	Agreement of amount payable to be determined between the contractor and the quantity surveyor.
Clause 39.5.4	Amount of fluctuations to be added to the contract sum.
Clause 39.5.5	The contractor must provide the evidence for the computations.
Clause 39.5.6	Fluctuations must not result in any alteration to the contractor's profit.
Clause 39.5.7	Increased costs occurring after completion will only be paid for on the basis of those prevailing at the completion date. This may result in those circumstances where the contractor has defaulted over completion.
Clause 39.5.8	Percentage addition to be included in the appendix where appropriate.

Use of price adjustment formulae (clause 40)

The traditional method of calculating fluctuations has many drawbacks. These may be summarized as:

(a) disagreements over what is allowable;
(b) shortfall in recovery;
(c) delays in payment;
(d) extensive work in documenting and checking claims.

An alternative procedure has therefore been developed, based upon the idea of using index numbers. This method is known as the Formulae Method of Price Adjustment and is based upon rules published by the Joint Contracts Tribunal. The indices which are used are those provided by the National Economic Development Office and the method has thus become known as the NEDO formulae. The rules are given contractual effect by incorporation in the main contract or subcontract. Two series have been devised:

1. 34 work category indices, dated March 1975.
2. 48 work category indices, dated April 1977 and with 1980 amendments.

The series 2 formulae rates are in three sections:

1. Definitions, exclusions, correction of errors.
2. Operation of work category and work group methods.
3. Application of formulae to main contractor's specialist work.

In addition there are formulae rules for subcontracts.

The use of clause 40 prescribes that the contract sum will be adjusted by use of the formulae rules. The date of tender is chosen as the base date to which the indices will apply. Since the contract sum is exclusive of VAT, the operation of this clause will in no way affect the VAT agreement and clause 15.

The following definitions from rule 3 of the formulae rules are to apply to clause 40:

1. *Base date.* This is defined in the same way as clause 38.
2. *Index numbers.* Obtained from the monthly Bulletin of Construction Indices published by the Property Services Agency through HMSO.
3. *Base month.* Normally the calendar month prior to the date when the tenders are returned.
4. *Valuation period.* The date of the valuation and the mid-point of the period when the fluctuations are calculated.
5. *Work categories.* The 34 (series 1) or 48 (series 2) classifications of the contract work.
6. *Work groups.* The less detailed classification which may be used in preference to item 5 above. It operates by aggregating work categories into larger units. It reduces the number of calculations but may make the results untypical of the work being measured.

7. *Balance of adjustable work.* Some sections of the bills, e.g. preliminaries, are excluded from the work categories and are valued on the basis of averaging the index numbers which are used.

8. *Non-adjustable element.* A proportion of the value of work may be excluded from the operation of the formulae under the local authorities edition of the JCT form.

The formula calculation adjustment is added to each valuation on the basis of the work carried out that month. Unlike the calculation of increased costs in clause 39, the amount determined under this clause is subject to retention. Initially the amount will be calculated using provisional indices, and eventually three to four months later these will be firmed up, when the final indices can be determined.

Some articles may be manufactured outside the United Kingdom, and it would therefore not be realistic to apply the formulae rules in such cases. If any variation in the market price occurs, then they will be subject to fluctuation adjustment using similar provisions to those of clause 39.

The method of adjustment to nominated subcontracts depends upon the instructions, tender and agreement reached between the subcontractor and the architect. The available methods using a formula calculation are as follows:

1. Electrical, heating and ventilating, air-conditioning, lifts, structural steelwork and catering. The relevant specialist formula, rules 50, 54, 58, 63 and 69.
2. Where none of the specialist formulae applies, the formulae in part 1 of section 2 of the formulae rules and one or more of the work categories set out in appendix A to the formulae rules.
3. Some other appropriate method.

If the contractor decides to sublet any portion of the works he must incorporate the provisions into the subcontract as appropriate.

The quantity surveyor and the contractor have the power to agree any alteration to the methods and procedures for the formula fluctuations recovery. This is presumably to help to reduce the number of tedious calculations where an agreeable amount can be ascertained. The amounts calculated are then deemed to be the formula adjustment amounts. This is provided that such sums are a reasonable approximation to those that would have been calculated by the operation of the formulae rules.

Where the contractor does not complete the works by the completion date, the following procedure is to be adopted. The value of work completed after that date is subject to formulae adjustment on the basis of the indices applicable at the relevant completion date. Where a contract is therefore running behind schedule, the employer will consistently month by month be paying higher amounts than would otherwise be the case. If the architect has, however, granted an extension of time and fixed a later completion date, then formulae adjustment will continue to run at the current dates.

Chapter 18

Financial matters

Two clauses have been included under this heading dealing with matters relating to financial legislation.

Clause 15   Valued added tax — supplemental provisions.
Clause 31   Finance (No. 2) Act 1975 — statutory tax deduction scheme.

Value added tax — supplemental provisions (clause 15)

From April 1989 the supply in respect of a building designed for a relevant residential purpose or for a relevant charitable purpose (as defined in the legislation which gives statutory effect to the VAT changes) is only zero rated if the person to whom the supply is made has given to the contractor a certificate in statutory form (see VAT leaflet 708 revised 1989). Where a contract supply is zero rated by certificate only the person holding the certificates (usually the contractor) may zero rate his supply.

The current legislation was introduced in the Finance Act 1972. It is, however, subject to alteration and amendment by the Chancellor of the Exchequer, usually in his annual budget proposals. The management of VAT is under the jurisdiction of HM Customs and Excise.

The contract sum referred to in article 2 and clause 14 of the conditions is exclusive of value added tax. Adjustments to the contract sum will also be exclusive of the tax, since the conditions specifically state that VAT will not be dealt with under the terms of the contract. If after the date of tender the goods and services become exempt from VAT, then the employer must pay to the contractor an equal amount to the loss of the contractor's input tax. This will equate with the sum that the contractor would otherwise have recovered.

The supplemental provisions are included into the contract by clause 15.1. The employer agrees to pay the appropriate tax to the contractor that is chargeable by the Customs and Excise office. The employer must therefore pay to the contractor the appropriate amount in respect of any positively rated items in the contract. The procedure for this payment is as follows:

1. The contractor gives to the employer a written provisional assessment of the respective values of any goods and materials which have been included in a payment, and are subject to VAT.
2. This should be done not later than the date for the issue of each interim certificate.
3. The contractor must specify the rate of tax chargeable on these items. The rate is fixed by the Customs and Excise but it could change, and several different rates could be introduced.
4. The employer, on receipt of the provisional assessment from the contractor, must calculate the amount of tax due.
5. This amount is then included with the amount of the interim certificate and paid to the contractor.
6. If the employer has reasonable grounds for objection to the provisional assessment, he must write to the contractor within three working days of receipt.
7. The contractor must then either withdraw the assessment, and thereby release the employer from the obligations, or confirm the assessment.
8. When the certificate of making good defects has been issued, the contractor must then prepare a written final statement of the respective values of all the supplies of goods and materials. The contractor must specify the respective rates of tax on these items.
9. This final statement can be issued either prior to or after the issue of the final certificate. For practical purposes it is advantageous to issue the statement after the final certificate has been accepted.
10. The employer, on receipt of the final statement, must calculate the tax that is due. He must then pay the balance to the contractor within 28 days of receipt of the statement. In those circumstances where the employer may have overpaid the contractor in respect of VAT, a refund of the appropriate amount will be due to the employer.
11. The contractor must issue to the employer receipts under the certificates for the appropriate amount of tax that has been paid. These receipts must comply with Regulations 2(2) of the VAT regulations (1972), including the particulars as required by Regulation 9(1), taking into account any of the amendments or re-enactments.

12. The employer must disregard any set-off in respect of liquidated damages when calculating and paying the amounts of VAT due to the contractor. The contractor in a similar manner must ignore contra-charges of liquidated damages by the employer.
13. If the employer disagrees with the contractor's statement, he may require the contractor to obtain the decision of the VAT commissioners. This should be done before the payment becomes due. The employer can also request the contractor to appeal further to the commissioners, should he still disagree with their findings. In these circumstances the contractor would be able to claim any costs or expenses involved from the employer. Before the appeal can proceed, the employer must pay to the contractor the full amount of the tax that has been charged.
14. The commissioners' appeal decision is final and binding, unless they subsequently introduce a correction to the tax that has been charged.
15. Arbitration is not applicable to VAT assessments by the commissioners.
16. If the contractor fails to provide a receipt for the tax paid by the employer, then the employer is not obliged to make any further payments. This applies only if the employer requires a validated receipt for his own tax purposes, or where the employer has paid tax in accordance with the provisional assessments.
17. If the employer has determined the contractor's employment, any additional tax which the employer may have to pay as a result of the determination may be set-off by him against any payments to be made to the contractor.

Finance (No. 2) Act 1975 — statutory tax deduction scheme (clause 31)

The purpose of this legislation is to deal with the problems of tax evasion by subcontractors, particularly the labour only 'lump' subcontractors. Machinery is established whereby the main contractor collects tax on behalf of the Inland Revenue from those subcontractors who do not hold a tax certificate. Those subcontractors who hold the 217 certificate are eligible for full payment on the basis that they deal with the Inland Revenue direct.

The following definitions are included within this clause:

Act — Finance (No. 2) Act 1975.
Regulations — Income Tax (Subcontractors in the Construction Industry) Regulations 1975, SI No. 1960.
Contractor — A person who is a contractor for the purpose of the Act.
Evidence — That required by the regulations to be produced for the verification of a subcontractor's tax certificate.

Statutory deduction — Referred to in s. 69(4) of the Act.

Subcontractor — Any person who is a subcontractor for the purposes of the Act and Regulations.

Tax certificate — A certificate issuable under s. 70 of the Act.

In the appendix to the form of contract the employer needs to be stated as either 'a contractor' or 'not a contractor'. Where the former applies, the employer is responsible for making the statutory deduction. Where the employer is 'not a contractor', the appropriate deductions must be made by the main contractor. If the responsible party fails to make the necessary deduction they may find themselves liable to the authorities for the tax. The status of the employer for tax deduction purposes is also referred to in the fourth recital. An employer may automatically be a 'contractor' because of his wider statutory position, for example, in the case of local authorities. In the case of private employers it will largely depend upon whether he is engaged in 'construction operations'. These are defined very broadly in the legislation.

At least 21 days before the issue of the first certificate the main contractor must either:

(a) provide the employer with the evidence that the contractor is eligible to be paid without deduction; or

(b) inform the employer in writing and also send a duplicate copy to the architect that such a deduction should be made.

The onus is on the contractor to provide this information and presumably until he does condition (b) will apply. The employer, however, needs to be extremely careful, since if he fails to make the necessary deduction he will be liable for tax. Alternatively, if he deducts monies without the necessary authority to do so he may find himself in breach of contract. The employer must also attempt to make sure that the evidence is valid, and where he has any doubts he will continue to make the appropriate deduction. If the status of the contractor changes within the terms of this clause during the progress of the works, then it is up to the contractor to inform the employer accordingly in order that the alternative arrangement can be made. The contractor must immediately inform the employer in writing if his current tax certificate is cancelled, and also give the date of such cancellation. If the employer is of the opinion that the contractor's tax status has changed and he is now responsible for the statutory deduction, he must notify the contractor accordingly. The contractor must inform the employer if this is not the correct situation.

When the employer is required to make the statutory deduction, this amount must exclude the cost of any materials. The clause is only concerned with income tax deductions for labour. The contractor must provide the employer with this information, but should he fail to do so then the employer will make a reasonable estimate of the amount. If errors or omissions do occur in the calculation there is provision for their correction.

The importance of this clause is illustrated in clause 31.8. Clause 31 takes precedence over the other clauses of the conditions of contract to such an extent that non-compliance with another clause may be envisaged. The interpretation of this clause may cause differences of opinion to occur, and these should be dealt with at arbitration. If, however, a particular Act suggests a method of resolving the difficulty, then this will override any arbitration proceedings.

Chapter 19

Clauses of a general nature

The following clauses from JCT 80 have been grouped together because they appertain to matters of a general nature.

Clause 1   Interpretations, definitions, etc.
Clause 2   Contractor's obligations.
Clause 4   Architect's instructions.
Clause 5   Contract documents.
(Clause 19A   Fair wages.)
Clause 32   Outbreak of hostilities.
Clause 33   War damage.
Clause 34   Antiquities.
Clause 41   Settlement of disputes — arbitration.

Clauses 1, 2, 4 and 5 deal with matters of a broad nature that set the scene for the contract in general. Clause 1, for example, provides a considerable list of definitions which are used throughout the contract. The inclusion of these avoids undue confusion both in the interpretation of the clauses and the use of the contract in practice. Clause 2 defines very briefly the contractor's obligation in connection with the works and clauses 4 and 5 together cover those matters established as contractual and the procedures and provisions for instructions from the architect.

Clause 19A is now deleted from the local authorities edition.

The following three clauses deal with events that may never happen. Clauses 32 and 33 are more likely to occur in today's society than 20 years ago. They detail the procedures to be followed in the event of such happenings that could occur. The discovery of antiquities (clause 34) may seem a more remote possibility, since a number of finds have been made in recent years. It may be every builder's dream to unearth a unique Roman vase in one piece, but the value of such stays strictly with the landowner. Clause 41 is a new clause which embraces arbitration good practice.

Interpretations, definitions, etc. (clause 1)

The articles of agreement, the conditions and the appendix are to be read as a whole, and together they form the *Standard Form of Building Contract*. They cannot therefore be used independently, and in many instances they have a bearing upon each other. For example, the details completed in the appendix will generally override the specific requirements indicated in each clause. The appendix will make recommendations for the contract, but the parties have some liberty on the amounts or times that they wish to insert against the appropriate clause.

A selection of definitions appertaining to the contract are included in clause 1.3. The definitions listed generally also refer to appropriate clause references, and these are discussed in detail where necessary.

A new clause 1.4 has been added to reinforce the responsibilities and obligations of the contractor under the terms of the contract. This states that regardless of any obligations that the architect may have towards the employer or whether or not the employer appoints a clerk of works, the contractor will nevertheless be responsible for carrying out and completing the works in accordance with clause 2.1. This is so irrespective of whether the architect or clerk of works inspects the works, workshops or any other place where work is being prepared. The architect is not made responsible under JCT 80 for the supervision of the works which the contractor is to carry out and complete. The contractor's responsibility for his work is in no way reduced by the conditions which allow for an architect or clerk of works' inspection.

Contractor's obligations (clause 2)

The contractor will carry out and complete the works in accordance with the:

(a) contract drawings;
(b) contract bills;
(c) articles of agreement;
(d) conditions of contract;

(e) appendix to the conditions of contract;
(f) numbered documents (subcontract agreements).

Collectively the above are known as the contract documents. The contractor must use the materials and workmanship that have been specified. The approval of the quality of materials or standards of workmanship will be decided by the architect. These are to be to his reasonable satisfaction. The architect can, however, only require that standard described in the contract documents. In the selection of materials and the assessment of workmanship the architect and the documents must be precise. Although objectivity may achieve the appropriate and desired standards, some subjective analysis by the architect will also be necessary.

The contract bills cannot override or modify either the application or the interpretation of these conditions of contract, with the exception of the rules for measurement. Unless it has been previously stated, JCT 80 assumes that SMM7 will have been used for the preparation of the bills. If other methods of measurement are preferred and have been used, this must be clearly stated in the contract bills. If the quantity surveyor chooses to measure items not in accordance with SMM7, this too must be stated. Any errors subsequently found in the contract bills resulting from their method of preparation must be corrected. The correction of these errors is automatic and does not require a variation instruction to be issued by the architect. The errors referred to cover descriptions, quantities or omission of items. They are errors made by the quantity surveyor. Errors in pricing resulting from mistakes made by the contractor do not come within this definition, and will therefore not be corrected once the contract has been signed. A procedure for their correction prior to the contractor's tender being accepted is described in Chapter 6, describing the code of procedure for selective tendering.

If the contractor finds any discrepancies or divergences between or within the following documents, he must write to the architect detailing the differences.

1. Contract drawings.
2. Contract bills.
3. Architect's instructions.
4. Additional drawings or documents.
5. Nominated sub-contracts NSC 4 and NSC 4a.

The architect must then give instructions to the contractor in order to clarify the discrepancy or divergence, so that the works can proceed. The contractor cannot assume, for example, that the drawing will automatically take preference over the bills. He can, however, reasonably assume that the conditions of contract will always take preference unless there is some clause to the contrary (clause 2.2.1). It should further be noted that the conditions of contract is not one of the documents capable of discrepancy, as listed above.

The conditions do not imply that the contractor must go looking for differences in the documents. If the compliance with the drawings later revealed that the bills were different but correct, then the architect would need to issue further instructions for the correction of this work, if that was so desired. The contractor should, however, take all reasonable steps to avoid the occurrence of this situation.

Architect's instructions (clause 4)

The contractor must comply with all instructions issued to him by the architect, unless he makes a reasonable objection in writing regarding his non-compliance. A reasonable objection may include the refusal to accept the nomination of a subcontractor, where an unsatisfactory relationship has existed on a previous contract. The contractor may also challenge the architect's authority to issue certain instructions. In these circumstances he may request the architect to specify in writing the provision in the contract which empowers the issue of the particular instruction. The architect must comply with this request. If the two parties cannot agree upon this point, the matter may be referred to arbitration for a decision. If the contractor complies with the instruction on the basis of the architect's reply, then this shall be assumed to be an instruction under the terms of the contract.

The architect may write to the contractor requesting him to comply with an instruction forthwith. If after seven days of receipt of this notice the contractor does not comply, the employer may employ other firms to execute the work. The costs involved with this will be deducted from monies due to the contractor, or they may be recoverable as a debt by the employer. In more severe cases, particularly where the contractor persistently fails to comply with a written instruction, the employer may terminate the contractor's employment under clause 27.

All architect's instructions must be in writing to have any contractual effect. If, however, oral instructions are given by the architect, the following procedure should be adopted:

1. Confirmation should be given in writing within seven days by the contractor to the architect.
2. Unless the architect dissents in writing within a further seven days the instruction shall be accepted as an architect's instruction within the terms of the contract.
3. Alternatively, if the architect confirms in writing the oral instruction within seven days, then the contractor needs only to accept this as an architect's instruction.
4. If neither the architect nor the contractor confirms the oral instruction, but the contractor executes the work accordingly, then it may be confirmed by the architect at any time prior to the issue of the final certificate.

Contract documents (clause 5)

The contract documents using the JCT 80 form of contract with quantities are as follows:

1. *Contract drawings.* These are the drawings which have been signed by or on behalf of the parties.
2. *Contract bills.* These are the bills of quantities which have been priced by the contractor and signed by or on behalf of the parties.
3. *Form of contract.* JCT 80 duly completed where required.

Where bills of quantities have not been prepared, either a specification or a schedule rates may become a contract document. In these circumstances the form of contract, without quantities, is used. When the contract has been signed the architect must provide the contractor with:

(a) a copy of the documents certified by the employer;
(b) two further copies of the contract drawings;
(c) two copies of the unpriced bills of quantities.

Within a reasonable period of time the architect should then supply the contractor with further information, which might include descriptive schedules and further drawings to amplify the contract drawings. These additional documents are not allowed to impose further obligations beyond those described in the contract documents.

The contract drawings and contract bills are to remain in the custody of the employer but must be available at all reasonable times for the inspection of the contractor. The contractor must also keep one copy of the contract drawings, one copy of the unpriced bills and other schedules, documents and drawings on the site for reference by the architect or his representative at all reasonable times. Copies of all the information provided by the architect for the construction of works should be retained on site by the contractor for use by the contractor and the architect.

It is the contractor's responsibility to provide the architect with two copies of his master programme. If this requires updating because of either an extension of time or war damage, then the contractor must supply a further copy of the revised master programme. A copy of the master programme should be retained on site for reference purposes. There is no requirement under the clause for the contractor to indicate his progress of the works.

When the contractor has received the final payment under the terms of the contract, he may be requested to return all drawings, details, schedules and other documents which bear the architect's name to the architect. The copyright of the design is vested in the architect. If the building owner or the contractor wish to repeat the design, then the architect can request a further fee. None of the documents mentioned must be used for any purpose other than this contract. The contractor's rates must not be divulged to others, or be used for any purpose other than this contract. Of course, where permission is sought from the architect or contractor, as appropriate, the contractual information may be re-used for other purposes.

Any certificates that the architect issues shall be sent to both the contractor and the employer concurrently.

Fair wages (clause 19A)

Clause 19A was a clause which was only included in the local authorities edition, hence its peculiar numbering system. It might have been preferable to have attached a separate clause to the standard form. There are, however, other matters which also differentiate the private and local authorities editions. This particular clause is now a matter for the history books, at least for the time being. Amendment 6 which was issued in July 1988 deleted this clause in its entirety from the local authorities edition. The provisions of the clause could no longer be operated in view of the provisions contained in the Local Government Act 1988. The clause was concerned with rates of wages, hours of work, conditions of employment, trade union representation and covered both operatives on site and those in workshops as well as those employed by subcontractors.

Outbreak of hostilities (clause 32)

If the United Kingdom is involved in a war, either the employer or the contractor may terminate their contract immediately. This clause includes certain provisions pertaining to the termination of the contract. First, it is not necessary that an outbreak of war has been declared. Second, the extent of the hostilities must include a general mobilization of the armed forces of the Crown. A few battalions sent to deal with a small local uprising would not represent a general mobilization. Third, the notice to terminate must be sent either by registered post or by recorded delivery to the other party. The matter is of such grave importance that there must be no mistake regarding the receipt of the notice.

The notice must not be given within 28 days from the date on which the order is given for the general mobilization. A notice should not be given once practical completion of works has been achieved, unless the project has suffered war damage as described in clause 33.

Within 14 days of the receipt of a notice under clause 32 the architect must issue appropriate instructions to the contractor. These instructions may require the contractor to bring the works up to a reasonable stage, due account being made of the time and resources available, or to execute protective work that the architect requires to be carried out. If, however, the contractor, after a period of three months, has been unable to comply with these instructions for reasons beyond his control, he may abandon the contract.

Within 14 days of the date of determination or when the architect's instructions have been complied with, or if the project is abandoned, the contractor must be paid for the value of these additional works by the employer.

In the event of an outbreak of hostilities the parties may at any time agree to make further arrangements as necessary. These may include some agreement with regard to completing the works when hostilities cease, on the basis of terms to suit the circumstances.

War damage (clause 33)

If the works or any unfixed materials or goods intended for the works and already on site sustain war damage, the following procedure will apply:

1. The occurrence of war damage will not affect or influence any payments to the contractor.
2. The architect may issue instructions requiring the contractor to remove and dispose of the debris arising from the damaged work, and to execute any protective work that he may specify.
3. The architect must in writing fix a later completion date that is fair and reasonable.
4. Any additional work required to be performed by the contractor arising from war damage will be treated in the same way as variations.

If there is an outbreak of hostilities together with war damage, there may already have been a determination under clause 32. In these circumstances the contractor's liability will already have ceased. The contractor must always be fully reimbursed by the employer for all the work that he carries out. The employer may be able to retrieve some of these amounts should the government of the country have a fund for the repair of war damaged properties on a compensation basis.

The definition of war damage used under this clause means damage defined in section 2 of the War Damage Act 1943.

Antiquities (clause 34)

Antiquities include fossils and other items of interest or value which may be found on the site or during the excavation part of the works. These items become the property of the employer, and if such finds occur:

1. The contractor shall use his best endeavours not to disturb the object and, if necessary, cease construction operations within the vicinity until he receives instructions from the architect. If he has any reasonable doubt about a discovered object he should adopt this precaution.
2. The contractor shall take all necessary precautions in order to preserve the condition of the objects from possible damage until they can be dealt with by experts if necessary.
3. The contractor shall inform either the architect or clerk of works of the discovery and its precise location on site.

The architect must issue instructions regarding the removal of antiquities. This may involve a third party, such as an archaeological society, examining, excavating or removing the object. Such a party will not be described as a subcontractor but as persons directly employed by the employer.

If in the opinion of the architect the above instructions involve the contractor in direct loss or expense, for which he will not be reimbursed elsewhere under the contract, the architect or quantity surveyor shall ascertain the amount of such loss or expense. This amount will then be added to the contract sum. If the architect considers that an extension of the contract is appropriate, then the removal of the antiquity becomes a relevant event under clause 25.

Settlement of disputes — arbitration (clause 41)

This is a new clause which was inserted into the Form of Contract in July 1987. It replaces much of what was included in Article 5 of the Form. If any of the following disputes or differences occur, as referred to in Article 5, then the matter shall be referred to arbitration:

(a) any matter or thing left by the contract to the discretion of the architect;
(b) withholding by the architect of any certificate due to the contractor;
(c) adjustment of the contract sum;
(d) rights and liabilities of the parties in respect of determination by the contractor or employer, outbreak of hostilities, and war damage;
(e) unreasonable withholding of consent or agreement by the employer or the architect on his behalf or by the contractor.

If the disputes or differences which are to be referred to arbitration raise issues which are substantially the same as, or connected with issues in a related dispute between the following, then the employer and contractor agree that the same arbitrator shall be used:

(a) employer and nominated subcontractor;

(b) contractor and nominated subcontractor;

(c) contractor and/or employer and nominated supplier so long as the contract of sale provides for such an arrangement.

Clearly if the employer or architect considers that the appointed arbitrator is not appropriately qualified to determine the dispute then a different arbitrator must then be appointed. These clauses will apply unless they have been deleted in the appendix.

Arbitration usually arises after the practical completion termination of the contractor's employment or the abandonment of the works. It may be commenced earlier as long as the employer, architect and contractor agree and put this consent in writing. There are, however, some circumstances which can be dealt with as and when the dispute occurs, such as the following:

(a) whether or not the issue of an instruction is empowered by the conditions;

(b) whether or not a certificate has been improperly withheld;

(c) whether a certificate is not in accordance with the conditions;

(d) whether a determination under clause 22C 4.3.1 will be just and equitable;

(e) any dispute or difference regarding the issue of architect's instructions in regard to a reasonable objection by the contractor in respect of partial possession by the employer or in regard to withholding of consent by the contractor;

(f) extension of time (clause 25);

(g) outbreak of hostilities (clause 32);

(h) war damage (clause 33).

The arbitrator has the power to direct such measurements and valuations which in his opinion are desirable in order to determine the rights of the respective parties who are in dispute. He can ascertain and award any sum which ought to have been included in any certificate. The arbitrator can open up works, review and revise certificates, opinions, decisions, requirements or notices in order to determine the matters that are in dispute. These are subject to the provisions of the following clauses:

Clause 4.2   Provision of architect to issue instructions.
Clause 30.9   Effect of final certificate.
Clause 38.4.3   Agreement of fluctuations by the contractor and the quantity surveyor.
Clause 39.5.3   Similar provisions to clause 38.4.3.
Clause 40.5   Similar provisions to clause 38.4.3.

The arbitrator's award is final and binding on both parties. Unless it is subsequently amended all arbitrations in England apply under the Arbitration Acts of 1950 and 1979. The parties may appeal to the High Court on any question of law arising out of an award or in the course of a reference, and the parties agree that the High Court should have jurisdiction to determine any such question of law.

The appendix to the Form of Contract allows for an appointer to be stated. This can be either the President or Vice-President of:

(a) Royal Institute of British Architects;
(b) Royal Institution of Chartered Surveyors;
(c) Chartered Institute of Arbitrators.

If none is stated then the appointer will come from the RIBA.

The following... (a) the ... (b) the ... (c) ...

(a) ...
(b) ...
(c) ...

Part 5

Subcontract conditions

Chapter 20

JCT standard forms of nominated subcontract

These documents comprise the following:

NSC/1   Tender, which comprises two schedules. Schedule 1 contains the particulars of the main contract and the subcontract.

NSC/2   Nominated subcontractor agreement in accordance with clauses 35.6 to 35.10 of the main contract conditions.

NSC/2a   Nominated subcontractor agreement, but in accordance with clauses 35.11 to 35.12 of the main contract conditions.

NSC/3   Form of nomination where tender NSC/1 has been used.

NSC/4   Form of subcontract (see Chapter 21).

The combination of these documents is described in clause 35.3 of the main contract conditions. NSC/1–4 are used with the basic method of nomination. The documents carrying the suffix 'a' are used with the alternative method of nomination.

Tender NSC/1

The two schedules provide the full details of subcontractors' offer. These agreed terms, together with NSC/4 and the drawings and bills where appropriate, will constitute the subcontract documents. The tender is the formal offer in response to an enquiry from the architect, after any preselection procedures have been completed. The subcontractor then agrees to carry out and complete the works in accordance with these documents for:

(a) a VAT exclusive subcontract sum (clause 15.1); or
(b) a VAT exclusive tender sum (clause 15.2) where the work will be completely remeasured upon completion.

In both cases a $2\frac{1}{2}$ per cent cash discount is allowed to the main contractor. The offer is subject to nomination and may be withdrawn within 14 days or if there is a failure to agree with the main contractor on the requirements of schedule 2. If this occurs the employer may be faced with paying for the subcontract design works or any materials already ordered under the terms of NSC/2.

NSC/1 — schedule 1

This provides the essential and general information relating to both the main contract and to the subcontract conditions. The details of the main contract appendix are provided, appropriately completed. This schedule includes:

(a) a description of the main contract works;
(b) the form of the main contract;
(c) where the documents can be inspected;
(d) whether the main contract has been executed under hand or seal;
(e) insurance provisions of the main contract;
(f) any changes to the standard main contract conditions (and if so they must be brought to the attention of the subcontractor);
(g) any special order required for carrying out and completing the works;
(h) location and access of the works;
(i) any obligations or restrictions imposed by the employer and included in the preliminaries bill;
(j) any other relevant information;
(k) fluctuation provisions, where appropriate.

NSC/2 — schedule 2

When the main contractor receives NSC/1 and the architect's preliminary notice of nomination, he must agree the terms of schedule 2 with the proposed subcontractor. The subcontractor sets out the details of his

preliminary programme for the works as indication for the contractor and
the architect. This will include dates for the preparation of design work,
shop drawings and any off-site manufacture that may be required. The
programme details are eventually agreed by both the main contractor and
the subcontractor. The preliminary programme is then deleted.

Schedule 2, item 3A, includes the details of any attendance, other
than general attendance, to be provided by the main contractor. The
general attendance is provided as a separate item in accordance with
SMM7 clause B9.2. Other attendance, will vary considerably from
subcontractor to subcontractor. The item in the bills should be in
sufficient detail to enable the main contractor to price it. Item 3A
describes the attendance proposals required by the nominated
subcontractor under each of seven headings. These are identical to the
description of other attendance in SMM7. This schedule allows the main
contractor and subcontractor to alter the provisions of other attendance in
order to come to some agreement between themselves.

Other matters to be included are insurances, special industrial labour
agreements, the name of the adjudicator and the trustee shareholder
(clause 24), information under the statutory tax deduction scheme, VAT
provisions and other matters such as limitations on working hours.

When the various matters are finally agreed they are signed by the
main contractor and the subcontractor. Tender NSC/1 is published in
pads of three in a set, with notes on the front entitled 'Notes on the use
of tender NSC/1 and agreement NSC/2'. The agreement NSC/1 is also
published separately.

Employer/nominated subcontractor agreement, NSC/2

In the JCT nominated subcontract form the above agreement is a separate
but integral part of the basic method of documentation. Whereas NSC/1
(tender) and NSC/4 (conditions of subcontract) are between the
subcontractor and the main contractor, NSC/2 is an agreement between
subcontractor and the employer. It is made in accordance with clauses
35.6 to 35.10 of the main contract.

When the architect has issued his preliminary notice of nomination,
and the conditions in schedule 2 of NSC/1 have been signed by the
parties, the agreement NSC/2 is issued. This is before the actual
nomination is achieved in NSC/3. In the form of agreement the
subcontractor warrants to the employer that reasonable skill and care will
be taken in:

(a) the design of the subcontract works, where these have been
undertaken by the subcontractor;
(b) the selection of goods or materials where selected by the
subcontractor;

(c) the satisfaction of any performance specification or requirement if appropriate.

The subcontractor may, prior to nomination, be requested by the architect to proceed within the agreement with any design work or the ordering of materials for the works. The employer will pay for this in advance of nomination, in which case the materials become his property and the design work is only to be used for the purpose of the works.

The obligations of the employer to the subcontractor are largely financial: he agrees to notify the subcontractor of the amount included in interim certificates; he agrees to early final payment under clause 35.17 of the main contract where this occurs; he also agrees to pay the subcontractor direct, where the main contractor has failed to do so. The employer must, however, be indemnified if he pays direct after bankruptcy or liquidation.

Agreement NSC/2a is similar to the above but with minor differences. It is made in accordance with clauses 35.6 to 35.10 of the main contract.

Nomination NSC/3

This is the standard form of nomination signed by the architect under clause 35.10.2 of the main contract. It is used where tender NSC/1 has been adopted. It is addressed to the main contractor and identifies the main and the subcontract works, referring to the appropriate page number of the bill of quantities or specification.

Subcontract conditions, NSC/4

These are described more fully in the next chapter.

Chapter 21

JCT Standard Form of Nominated Subcontract

This form of subcontract is intended to be used for the nomination of subcontractors when JCT 80 is the main contract. It supersedes the standard form of subcontract (the 'green' form) and this publication has ceased. (The blue form was used for non-nominated subcontracts.)

The *JCT Standard Form of Nominated Subcontract* is referred to as NSC/4 and contains many of the provisions of the main contract form. Indeed, the main contractor must seek to ensure that all the conditions that are imposed on him must also exist between him and the nominated subcontractor.

The layout of NSC/4 is indeed very similar to JCT 80, including articles and subcontract conditions. It is intended to be read in conjunction with the following documents:

NSC/1   *JCT Standard Form of Nominated Subcontract —
                 Tender and Agreement.*
NSC/2 or NSC/2a   *JCT Standard Form of Employer/Nominated
                 Subcontractor Agreement.*
NSC/3   *Standard Form for Nomination of a Subcontractor,*
                 which NSC/1 has not been used.

The combination of these NSC forms is as follows:

	Normal	*Short version*
Tender and agreement	NSC/1	
Employer/Subcontractor agreement	NSC/2	NSC/2a
Standard form of nomination		NSC/3
Form of subcontract	NSC/4	NSC/4a

Reference should also be made to clause 35 of the main contract conditions. These cover the nominated subcontractor provisions of the contract between the employer and the main contractor. NSC/4 are the contract conditions between the main contractor and the nominated subcontractor.

The recitals and articles of agreement of NSC/4 follow a very similar pattern to those included in the main contract. The only major difference is that reference to the subcontractor has now been included. The nominated subcontractor's obligation is to carry out and complete the subcontract works in return for the subcontract sum. The settlement of disputes is to be dealt with in the same way as the main contractor; by arbitration. In order for the subcontract to be binding, it must be properly signed by completing the attestation clauses.

The subcontract conditions are annexed to the articles of subcontract agreement and include the following clauses.

Clause 1: Interpretation, definitions, etc.

This clause very closely follows clause 1 of the main contract conditions. A large number of the definitions refer to tender NSC/1, but much of the information is the same as the main contract conditions. Variations are defined and the wording follows precisely that of clause 13 of the main contract conditions. It includes reference to clause 10 of SMM7 in the context of provisional sums for defined and undefined work.

Clause 2: Subcontract conditions

The subcontract documents comprise the tender (NSC/1) and the subcontract (NSC/4). Although other documents or schedules may be available and accepted, they cannot impose any obligation beyond that which is included in the subcontract documents. Where a conflict occurs between the subcontract documents, NSC/4 will be taken as the overriding document. If, however, discrepancies occur between the subcontract and main contract documents, then the terms of the main contract will prevail.

A subcontractor may be required to enter into a contract with a third party for the supply of goods and materials or for the execution of part of the subcontract. In these circumstances the subcontractor will only be responsible to the extent that this liability can be passed on to this third party. The architect's written approval must be obtained in respect of any restriction, limitation or exclusion of such liability that might occur.

Clause 3: Subcontract sum — additions or deductions — computation of ascertained final subcontract sum

This is the same provision as clause 3 of the main contract. Once any adjustment has been agreed, even if only in part, then it may be included in the computation of the following interim certificate. This is largely to aid the subcontractor's cash flow, recognizing that payment is the life-blood of the industry.

Clause 4: Execution of the subcontract works — instructions of the architect — directions of the contractor

The subcontractor's obligations under the contract are as follows:

(a) carrying out the subcontract works;
(b) operating in accordance with the subcontract documents;
(c) using materials and workmanship of the quality and standards specified;
(d) conforming with the reasonable directions and requirements of the contractor;
(e) ensuring that workmanship quality and standards are to the reasonable satisfaction of the architect.

The subcontractor must also keep on the works a person-in-charge to whom the contractor can give directions and instructions. The architect will deliver his instructions through the contractor to the subcontractor. The contractor must pass on these instructions efficiently to avoid the occurrence of possible misunderstandings or delays. The subcontractor must comply with these instructions unless he makes reasonable objection to such compliance. Reasonable objection may arise in connection with variations (clause 1.3); for example, the subcontractor may be in the process of fabricating a specialist component and a variation changing this may be accepted as a reasonable objection. If the subcontractor finds any discrepancies or divergencies in the documents he should immediately inform the contractor of such in writing. The contractor will then request the architect to issue instructions accordingly.

Instructions given to the subcontractor must be in writing or confirmed in writing within seven days. Confirmation may be given by the architect (through the contractor), contractor, or subcontractor. The provisions are the same as clause 4.3 of the main contract. Confirmation can also be provided at any time up to the issue of the final certificate. If the subcontractor fails to comply then the contractor, with the permission of the architect, may employ others to carry out this instruction and deduct these costs from any amounts due to the subcontractor.

The subcontractor may also require the contractor to request the architect to specify, in writing, the provisions of the main contract which allows him to issue such an instruction. This is similar to clause 4.2 of the main contract. It should be noted that the architect's powers, where they exist, are from the main contract rather than the subcontract.

Amendment 5 issued in January 1988 has two purposes:

1. To step down into the nominated subcontract the terms of the revised clause 8.4 regarding the powers of the architect for work which was not in accordance with the contract. (See also Chapter 12.) In addition to allowing the architect instructions for the removal of non-conforming work this clause now provides for a combination of the following alternatives:

   (a) allow any of the non-conforming work to remain;
   (b) issue instructions for a consequential variation;
   (c) issue instructions for opening up of the works for inspection or testing.

2. To deal with the effect of compliance by the contractor with instructions of the architect or a nominated subcontractor whose work is in accordance with the subcontract but which has to be taken down and re-executed as a direct consequence of such compliance.

Clause 5: Subcontractor's liability under incorporated provisions of the main contract

The nominated subcontractor must observe, perform and comply with all the provisions of the main contract, and the information contained in his tender, schedule 1. The following clauses of the main contract are explicitly referred to, although the generality of the previous provision is all embracing.

Clause 6	Statutory obligations, notices, fees and charges.
Clause 7	Levels and setting out the works.
Clause 9	Royalties and patent rights.
Clause 16	Materials and goods unfixed or off site.
Clause 32	Outbreak of hostilities.
Clause 33	War damage.
Clause 34	Antiquities.

The subcontractor must also fully indemnify the contractor against any breach of contract which might involve the contractor in any liability to the employer. The subcontractor will not, of course, be liable in respect of any act or omission on the part of the employer, contractor or subcontractor.

Clause 6: Injury to persons and property — indemnity to contractor

The subcontractor is responsible for injury that may be caused to persons or property by the carrying out of the subcontract works. He must indemnify the contractor accordingly. The indemnity excludes any act or neglect on the part of the contractor or another subcontractor.

The liability for loss or damage excludes the Specified Perils defined in clause 1.3 of the main contract and clause 1.3 NSC/4 and in Chapter 16. In other circumstances, as in the case of an existing building, the employer may have decided to accept the sole risk for any liability, and this is therefore excluded.

Clause 7: Insurance against injury to persons and property

The subcontractor is responsible for maintaining such insurances that are necessary to cover his liability in respect of personal injury that may be caused by carrying out subcontract works. These insurances should be detailed in schedule 2, item 4, of tender NSC/1. This should describe any limits of indemnity which are required. The amount of insurance must comply with the Employer's Liability (Compulsory Insurance) Act 1969, and any statutory orders that have been made.

The subcontractor is not liable to indemnify the contractor or to provide insurance in respect of personal injury or death or damage to the works, materials or property by the effect of an excepted risk. These are defined in clause 1.3 and include radioactivity, pressure waves from aircraft, etc.

Clause 8: Loss or damage to the main contract works and to the subcontract works

Three options for insurance are offered, in line with the provisions of the main contract and the one retained will be on the same basis.

Clause 8   New buildings — contractor arranges joint names policy
             (clause 22A of the main contract).
Clause 8B   New buildings — employer arranges joint names policy
             (clause 22B).
Clause 8C   Existing structures — employer arranges joint names policy
             (clause 22C).

Clause 8A: Subcontract works in new buildings — main contract conditions clause 22A

The main contractor is responsible for insuring the works and materials against the specified perils defined in clause 1. This responsibility runs until the issue of the certificate of practical completion, and includes the subcontractor's work and materials. Any loss or damage occurring after this date to the subcontract works, unless it is due to negligence, breach of statutory duty, omission or default, is not the subcontractor's responsibility. The subcontractor is not responsible for any loss or damage that occurs due to the occurrence of one of the specified perils. Neither will he be responsible for any loss or damage that might arise due to the fault of the main contractor or anyone for whom the main contractor or employer is directly responsible. The subcontractor is of course responsible for defects or damage caused by his own workmen. He is also responsible for his own temporary buildings, plant, tools and equipment and will need to insure these accordingly. The subcontractor should also consider whether any insurance should be provided, at his own expense, to cover any risks which are not covered under clause 8A, such as impact, subsidence, theft, vandalism, etc.

If any loss or damage occurs, either due to a specified peril or otherwise, then the subcontractor must inform the main contractor in writing of the extent, nature and location of the damage. The subcontractor on the instructions of the architect or contractor must restore any damaged subcontract works or materials and dispose of any debris that might have arisen. If the loss or damage is not the responsibility of the subcontractor, then it should be treated as if it were a variation. The sum is then recovered from the contractor as a debt but not added to the subcontract sum. The main contractor must then claim this amount from his insurers.

Clause 8B: Subcontract works in new buildings — main contract conditions clause 22B

Under these conditions it is the contractor's responsibility to ensure that the employer insures the works in a joint policy as referred to in clause

22B of the main contract works. The subcontractor is either recognized as an insured under the joint names policy or the insurers waive any rights of subrogation (i.e., the substitution of one person for another, in regard to a legal claim) they may have against the subcontractor. The same procedures apply as under clause 8A except that it is treated as if it were a variation and the amount added to the contract sum. The employer would then seek to recover this amount from his insurers. The subcontractor will continue to insure those things for which he is responsible such as temporary plant and equipment and risks not covered by clause 8B, such as impact, subsidence, theft, vandalism, etc.

Clause 8C: Subcontract works in existing structures — main contract conditions clause 22C

These are similar provisions to clause 8B above.

Clause 9: Policies of Insurance — production — payment of premiums

The main contractor and the subcontractors, respectively, are both required to have the necessary insurance in compliance with the contract. The provision of such insurance by one party may affect the other. There is, therefore, the provision to allow either party, at reasonable times, to inspect the policies or premium receipts of the other. If the subcontractor fails to properly insure then the main contractor may do this for him on his behalf and deduct the premiums from any amounts due to the subcontractor.

Clause 10: Subcontractor's plant, etc. — responsibility of contractor

Any plant, tools or equipment brought onto the site by a subcontractor are at the sole risk and responsibility of the subcontractor. If any negligence, omission or default by others (main contractor, other subcontractors) results in damage or loss to these items, the subcontractor can claim from the parties responsible. The subcontractor is, however, responsible for injury to persons or property resulting from the use of his plant or equipment. The main contractor will require to be indemnified by the subcontractor against all possible claims or proceedings in this respect. The subcontractor is also responsible for any insurance that may be required for his own plant and equipment.

Clause 11: Subcontractor's obligation — carrying out and completion of subcontract works — extension of subcontract time

The subcontractor's obligation is to:

(a) carry out and complete the works in accordance with the agreed programme details in the tender, schedule 2, item 1C;
(b) do this reasonably in accordance with the progress of the main contract works;
(c) commence work on site as detailed in the tender, schedule 2, item 1C upon receipt of notice and to the operation of clause 11.2.

Clause 11.2 deals with the provisions of an extension to the contract time. The procedure involved is similar to the main contract, with the exception that the subcontractor must give his written notice of the delay to the main contractor. The subcontractor must therefore estimate the likely delays and keep the contractor up to date regarding any changes in this information. The relevant events listed in clause 11.2.3 are an identical reproduction of the main contract, with one important addition: i.e. the right of the subcontractor to suspend the work under clause 21.8.

The subcontractor, although he may be granted an extension of his contract period, should attempt to do all that he can to reduce the delay to a minimum.

Where the architect fails to award an extension of the subcontract period, the subcontractor concerned may reasonably request the main contractor to join him in arbitration proceedings.

Clause 12: Failure of subcontractor to complete on time

If a subcontractor fails to complete his work within the period of time that has been agreed, or within an extended period of time described in clause 11, then the main contractor must notify the architect, and send a copy to the subcontractor. If the architect agrees that a delay has occurred he must then certify in writing, under clause 35.15 of the main contract, that the subcontractor has failed to complete within the allotted period of time. This he must do within two months. The subcontractor is then liable to the main contractor for the loss suffered by this breach.

Clause 13: Matters affecting regular progress — direct loss and/or expense — contractors' and subcontractors' rights

A subcontractor who feels that he will incur direct loss or expense for which he will not be reimbursed under the provisions of the subcontract must inform the contractor accordingly. This must be done in writing, listing one or more of the reasons offered in clause 13.1.2. The reasons listed are identical to those of clause 26.2 of the main contract. The subcontractor's application under this clause should be made as soon as he becomes aware that regular progress of the works is likely to be affected. The subcontractor must, as soon as possible, provide the contractor with the details of loss and expense incurred, in order that the architect or quantity surveyor can assess the likely amount of money involved. It is particularly important to the client that any extra amounts to the contract sum are known as soon as possible in order that he can become fully aware of his total financial commitment to the contract.

The regular progress of the works may become materially affected because of any act, omission or default of the contractor or any other subcontractor. In these circumstances the subcontractor must give written notice to the main contractor of a possible claim against him. Any amount agreed is therefore a debt recoverable from the main contractor.

Clause 13.3 is the opposite to the above. The subcontractor is at fault and a claim is now due to the main contractor. During the preparation of this claim, the main contractor should also take into account in his computations any liability towards other subcontractors working on the site.

All of the provisions of clause 13 are without prejudice to any other rights or remedies which the main contractor or subcontractor may possess.

Clause 14: Practical completion of subcontract works — liability for defects

The subcontractor must give to the main contractor a written notice when he considers that practical completion of the subcontract works has been achieved. This information is then passed to the architect who decides the date for the purpose of the contract, and issues a certificate of practical completion of the subcontract work accordingly.

Clause 14.3 deals with defects which must be made good at the expense of the subcontractor in accordance with the instructions of the architect, or on the directions of the main contractor. Clause 18 of the main contract sets out the liability of the main contractor in respect of defects. The subcontractor must be similarly liable for his own defects which occur before the end of the defects liability period, or for frost damage occurring before practical completion.

Defects in the design are a separate matter between the employer and subcontractor (clause 2 of agreement NSC/2).

Clause 14.4 covers a usual proviso that if the architect instructs that the cost of making good defects shall not fall upon the contractor, then the contractor must offer a similar benefit to the subcontractor.

Clause 14.5 makes the subcontractor responsible for clearing up the works and leaving them tidy to the satisfaction of the contractor. Reference should also be made to the general attendance requirements of the Standard Method of Measurement.

Clause 15: Price for subcontract works

The final price for the subcontract works may have been based upon a lump sum with or without complete remeasurement provisions. The distinction in the form of subcontract is that the former is described as a subcontract sum and the latter as a tender sum. Where a subcontract sum is used there is provision for variations, and these are to be valued in accordance with clause 16. Where complete remeasurement is originally envisaged, the valuation rules of clause 17 apply. The difference between these two clauses is, however, minor. In either case, the subcontractor's schedule of rates, or bill rates where applicable, are used as a basis.

Clause 16: Valuation of variations and provisional sum work

The rules for the valuation of subcontract works is the same as that for the main contract works, i.e.:

1. For work of similar character and similar conditions as work in the subcontract documents, the same rates apply (clause 16.3.1.1).
2. For work of similar character but different conditions, pro-rata rates are used (clause 16.3.1.2).
3. For work that is dissimilar to that included in the contract documents, a fair valuation shall be made (clause 16.3.1.3).
4. For work which cannot be properly measured or valued, daywork rates are to be used (clause 16.3.4).
5. Omissions are to be undertaken at the rates set out in the subcontract documents.
6. Approximate quantities in sub-contracts are valued on the same basis as in the main contract i.e. depending upon the accuracy of the quantities which were included in the contract.

The work is to be valued by the quantity surveyor in accordance with the above provisions. Where, however, the contractor, subcontractor and employer agree otherwise, other methods of valuation can be used. These might include a lump sum amount or a price agreed before the work is put in hand. The measurement of variations should, however, be on the same basis as the contract documents. If the variations affect the value of preliminary items, then the adjustment for these should also be made. The expenditure of appropriate provisional sums is treated in a similar way.

Where it is necessary to measure work for the purpose of a variation, the subcontractor and the main contractor should both be given the opportunity of being present.

Clause 17: Valuation of all work comprising the subcontract works

Where the alternative basis of pricing is used and complete remeasurement is required, the same rules of valuation are adopted as described previously in clause 16.

Clause 18: Bills of quantities — standard method of measurement

If bills of quantities have been prepared for the subcontract works, they should have been prepared in accordance with SMM7. Any departure from the method of preparation (unless clearly identified) or errors of whatever kind other than subcontractor's errors in pricing, must be corrected, and treated in the same manner as a variation to the contract.

The quality and quantity of works in the subcontract is that which has been described in the bills of quantities.

Where the description of a provisional sum for defined work does not provide the information required by general rule 10.3 in SMM7 (see Chapter 13) the correction should be made by correcting the description so that it does provide such information. Any correction will then be treated as if it were a variation required by the architect under clause 13.2 of the main contract conditions.

Clauses 19A/B: Value added tax

These clauses operate in a similar manner to clause 15 of the main contract. The clause therefore provides for the subcontract sum to be exclusive of the tax, and to be paid as an extra under the subcontract. The contractor will, in turn, recover any tax that he has to pay as an input tax.

Clauses 20A/B: Finance (No. 2) Act 1975 — tax deduction scheme

These two clauses relate to clause 31 of the main contract. They are alternatives to cover cases where the subcontractor has a current tax certificate and where he does not. They complement the procedures of the main contract.

Clause 21: Payment of the subcontractor

Interim payments and the final payment to nominated subcontractors are made in accordance with this clause. It incorporates the provisions of clause 30 of the main contract and, in addition, the appropriate sections from clause 35 regarding payment.

Clause 21.2 makes it clear that the subcontractor must apply for payment through the main contractor. It further emphasizes that this application must be in writing. A letter will be accepted, but in practice for accounting purposes an invoice is preferable. The invoice may include work completed, materials on site and materials off site, as long as the provisions of clause 30.3 of the main contract have been observed. There are also provisions in the JCT 80 main form of contract (clause 35.13) and this is repeated in NSC/4 (clause 21.3.3) to allow an employer to pay a nominated subcontractor for design work, materials and goods prior to the instruction of nomination.

Notification by the main contractor to the subcontractor of the amount included in the valuation must be made within 17 days from the date of the interim payment. This notification should also include the appropriate payment due, less $2\frac{1}{2}$ per cent cash discount. This envisages a cheque being posted to the subcontractor, upon receipt of payment to the main contractor by the employer. In practice, should the employer default in payment, then this is likely to cause a chain reaction of non-payment by the main contractor to his subcontractors. The subcontractor must issue a receipt to the contractor which can be shown as reasonable proof of payment to the architect. Comparable provisions to those included in the main contract to allow the employer to pay the subcontractor direct, or for a final payment to be made to the subcontractor, are also included.

Where the value of any of the subcontractor's goods or materials have been included in an interim certificate, and the employer has paid the main contractor for them then such goods become the property of the employer. The architect must inform the subcontractor of the amount of payment in this respect, in the usual way. This is to avoid the employer having to pay twice for these items in the case of any default by the main contractor.

The ascertainment of the amounts due to the subcontractor are as follows:

1. Subject to retention:
   (a) total value of work properly executed including the formulae adjustment where applicable but excluding any restoration, replacement or repair or loss of damage and removal and disposal of debris which in clauses 8B and 8C are treated as if they were a variation;

(b) materials on site that have been properly delivered at the relevant time, and are also adequately protected;

(c) materials off site, at the discretion of the architect.

2. Not subject to retention:

(a) defects not chargeable under clause 14.4, and payments under clause 6 (statutory obligations, notices, fees and charges) and clause 7 (levels and setting out of the works) of the main contract;

(b) reimbursement of loss and expense;

(c) fluctuations calculated in accordance with clauses 35 and 36;

(d) any amounts in respect of the cash discount to the main contractor.

Previous forms of contract have been unclear on this last point. To enable the subcontractor to allow the main contractor his discount on fluctuations, 1/39th is first added.

Where the subcontractor is dissatisfied with the amount of interim payment or the failure on the part of the architect to certify any amount, then both he and the main contractor can instigate arbitration proceedings. These may result because:

(a) the main contractor has withheld payments under the set-off provision of clause 24, and these have been contested by the subcontractor;

(b) the employer has failed to operate the provisions for payment directly to the subcontractor, when the main contractor has defaulted in this respect.

The subcontractor can also choose to suspend his works until the matter is properly resolved, provided that he first gives the contractor and the employer notice of this intention.

The main contractor's interest in the subcontractor's retention is fiduciary as trustee for the subcontractor. This relationship is the same as that between the employer and the main contractor.

The subcontract sum, where clause 15.1 applies, shall be adjusted as follows:

1. Deductions from the contract sum:

(a) provisional sums;

(b) provisional work;

(c) omissions resulting from variations;

(d) fluctuations plus 1/39th;

(e) any other amounts which should be deducted.

2. Additions to the contract sum:

(a) amounts payable under clauses 6 and 7 of the main contract or clause 14.1 of the subcontract;

(b) additions resulting from variations;

(c) expenditure on provisional sums;

(d) direct loss and expense under clause 13.1;

(e) fluctuations;

(f) any other amount which should be added;

(g) 1/39th of (a), (d) and (e).

The subcontractor should be supplied with a copy of the above adjustment before he receives the final payment.

If clause 15.2 applies and a complete remeasurement of the subcontract works apply, then the ascertained final subcontract sum shall be the aggregate of:

(a) amounts payable under clauses 6 and 7 of the main contract, or clause 14.1 of the subcontract;
(b) the amount of valuation under clause 17;
(c) direct loss and expense under clause 13;
(d) fluctuations;
(e) any other amount which should be added;
(f) 1/39th of (a), (c) and (d).

The effects of the final certificate issued under clause 30.8 of the main contract conditions are conclusive evidence in respect of the subcontracts which have been included. These are in respect of the following:

(a) quality of materials and goods and standards of workmanship are to the reasonable satisfaction of the architect;
(b) contract sum has been properly adjusted within the terms of the contract (other than accidental inclusions or exclusions or arithmetical errors);
(c) extensions of time have been given;
(d) final settlement in respect of loss and expense.

If arbitration proceedings have been commenced by either party (or by the employer) within 21 days after the final certificate has been issued, then the final certificate shall remain as conclusive evidence in those matters other than those to which the proceedings relate.

Clause 22: Benefits under the main contract

The rights and benefits enjoyed by the main contractor are to be made available to the subcontractor wherever possible. If this involves any additional cost or payment on behalf of the main contractor, then such sums will be borne by the subcontractor.

Clause 23: Contractor's right to set-off

The main contractor is entitled to deduct from money due to nominated subcontractors if:

(a) the subcontractor agrees that the amount is owing to the main contractor; or

(b) the sum has been finally awarded in arbitration or litigation in favour of the main contractor.

The main contractor is also entitled to set-off against any money due to the nominated subcontractor for loss or expense because of a failure on the part of the subcontractor to observe the provisions of the subcontract. The main contractor must be able to prove an actual loss or expense because of the subcontractor's breach of contract. Any amount ascertained in this respect can only be deduced from the subcontractor's outstanding payment if any of the following applies:

1. The architect has issued a certificate for 'failure of subcontractor to complete on time' in accordance with clause 12. This certificate should have been sent to the main contractor, with a duplicate copy to the subcontractor concerned.

2. The amount of set-off deducted by the main contractor has been accurately calculated by him.

3. The main contractor has already written to the subcontractor of his intention to deduct the amount calculated in item 2. The main contractors must have written to the subcontractor at least 20 days before the money becomes due to the subcontractor.

The contractor has the option of amending such a notice where arbitration proceedings are contemplated. This may result in a lower amount being accepted by the main contractor in settlement of his loss, or even a higher sum by taking other factors into account which were excluded from the previous notice.

Clause 24: Contractor's claims not agreed by the subcontractor — appointment of adjudicator

Where a subcontractor disagrees with the amount of payment to be made by the main contractor because of set-off deductions, he may take the following action:

1. Within 14 days of receiving the notice from the contractor, send a registered or recorded statement to the contractor. This must set out reasons for the disagreement and the particulars of any counterclaim.

2. The counterclaim cannot simply be the subcontractor's whim, since it needs to provide details and also be reasonably accurate.

3. At the same time the subcontractor should give the contractor notice of arbitration.

4. Request the appointment of the adjudicator named in the tender, schedule 2. The adjudicator's decision on the matter of disagreement shall be immediately binding upon both the contractor and

242

subcontractor. The purpose of this process is to obtain a decision very speedily, rather than to wait months as in the case of other disputes.

5. The final decision on the matter may eventually be solved independently by the parties by an agreement, or determined by an arbitrator or by the courts.
6. The contractor has 14 days in which to formulate his own reply to the adjudicator, setting out his own point of view.
7. The adjudicator must, within 7 days of the above statement, decide on how the amount shall be dealt with. It may be:
   (a) retained by the contractor;
   (b) deposited with the trustee-stakeholder, pending arbitration;
   (c) paid to the subcontractor;
   (d) a combination of the above.
8. The adjudicator's decision shall be fair and reasonable, taking into account the known facts. This shall be notified to both the subcontractor and the contractor.
9. The trustee-stakeholder may be a bank and shall retain the amount until the two parties reach their final decision on the dispute. Any normal interest which may accrue, less the trustee's charges, shall be paid when a final decision has been reached.

Clause 25: Right of access of contractor and architect

The contractor and the architect, and any other persons authorized by either of them, can at any reasonable time have access to work that is being prepared for the subcontract works. Only if the architect has previously certified in writing to the contrary will the subcontractor have reasonable grounds for refusing access, such as to protect any proprietory right of the subcontractor.

Clause 26: Assignment — subletting

The provisions of this clause are identical to clause 19 of the main contract.

Clause 27: General attendance, other attendance, etc.

Attendance provided by the main contractor is classified under one of two headings.

General attendance

These are facilities that are normally provided by the main contractor and are extended for the general use of all nominated subcontractors. The definition of 'general attendance' is given in clause 27.1.

Other attendance

These facilities have been specifically requested by the individual subcontractors in tender, schedule 2, item 3 and should therefore be properly described in the bill of quantities.

If the subcontractor requires workshops, etc., on the site, he must provide them. The main contractor agrees to provide adequate space, and allow reasonable facilities to the subcontractor for such erection.

Any nominated subcontractor is allowed the free use of standing scaffolding (a provision of general attendance). If such a subcontractor requires scaffolding to be erected in another location by the main contractor, then this must be described under other attendance to allow the main contractor to price such an item. In other circumstances the subcontractor may choose to provide and erect his own scaffolding. Once erected any scaffolding can be used by anyone working on the site. Any warranty on fitness, condition or suitability of use, however, is expressly excluded.

Clause 28: Contractor and subcontractor not to make wrongful use of or interfere with the property of the other

The various parties to the contract must not misuse or interfere with each other's property. In addition, they must not contravene any Act, byelaw, regulation, order or rule made by a competent authority.

Clause 29: Determination of the employment of the subcontractor by the contractor

One of the remedies which the main contractor may request, if a subcontractor defaults in one of the following ways, is the determination of the employment of the subcontractor. This may occur if the subcontractor:

(a) suspends his work without reasonable cause;
(b) fails to proceed with the work in a regular manner, as set out in clause 11.1;

(c) neglects to remove defective work after receiving a written notice from the main contractor;

(d) fails to comply with the provisions of clause 26 (Assignment — subletting).

It is the contractor's responsibility to first inform the architect that one of the above has occurred, and to supply the architect with the appropriate details. The architect may then instruct the main contractor to issue a notice of the subcontractor's impending determination. The notice should be issued by way of either registered post or recorded delivery to ensure that the subcontractor receives it. The subcontractor now has 14 days in which to remedy his default, otherwise his employment is forthwith determined.

In the event of a subcontractor becoming bankrupt or making arrangements to enter into liquidation in accordance with the Insolvency Act 1986, the subcontract shall be automatically terminated.

If the subcontractor or any person employed by him, even without his knowledge, offers an inducement or reward in relation to the obtaining or execution of the subcontract, then the employer may determine the subcontract. This clause on corruption can also be extended to subcontracts on any of the employer's other projects.

Once the subcontract has been terminated, the following are the respective rights and duties of the contractor and subcontractor:

1. The subcontractor's temporary buildings, plant and equipment may be used freely by the firm appointed to complete these works. Any materials or goods intended for the works may also be purchased by this firm.

2. The subcontractor must assign to the main contractor, without payment, any benefit of any agreement for the supply of materials or goods or for the execution of any of the subcontract works.

3. The contractor may be directed by the architect to pay for any goods or materials that have been delivered to the site, but not paid for by the subcontractor.

4. The subcontractor must remove his temporary buildings, plant and equipment when requested to do so by the architect. If the subcontractor ignores this instruction, then the main contractor may, within a reasonable time, remove and sell them. The main contractor will then hold the proceeds of such a sale to the credit of the subcontractor.

5. The subcontractor shall pay the main contractor for any direct loss or expense that has resulted because of his determination.

Clause 30: Determination of employment under the subcontract by the subcontractor

If the main contractor makes a default for one of the following reasons, the subcontractor can determine his employment under the subcontract:

1. The contractor wholly suspends the main contract works, without reasonable cause. Note that the whole of the project must come to a standstill for no apparent reason.
2. The contractor fails to make reasonable progress with the main contract work, and this affects the progress of the subcontract works.

The subcontractor may then take the following action:

1. He may issue a notice to the contractor specifying the default. This must be sent by registered post or recorded delivery, with a copy to the architect.
2. If, for 14 days after the notice for default has been given, the contractor has not rectified the situation, then the subcontractor may terminate his employment under the subcontract.

The rights and remedies, without prejudice to other accrued rights, or to the subcontractor's liability to the contractor under clause 6 for injury to persons or property, are as follows:

1. The subcontractor must promptly remove his temporary buildings and equipment. He must take the necessary precautions to prevent injury or damage to those items for which he is already responsible under clause 6.
2. The contractor must then pay to the subcontractor:
    (a) the total value of work completed, ascertained in accordance with clause 21;
    (b) the total value of any work already in progress;
    (c) any sum ascertained in respect of direct loss or expense under clause 13;
    (d) the costs of any goods or materials already provided for the works, which include items ordered but not delivered;
    (e) the reasonable cost of removal of the items in (a) above;
    (f) any direct loss or expense resulting from the determination.

Clause 31: Determination of the main contractor's employment under the main contract

If the employment of the main contractor is terminated under clause 27 of the main contract, then the employment of every subcontractor is automatically terminated. The provisions of clause 30.2 will then apply, regarding the rights of the main contractor and the subcontractor.

If the main contractor decides to terminate the contract because of one of the reasons listed in clause 28 of the main contract, then the subcontract is also automatically terminated. The main difference is, however, that the subcontractor will receive a share of any payments that become due because of the termination of the contract. These amounts in respect of subcontractors are calculated under clause 28.2.2.6 of the main contract. The subcontractor, of course, will necessarily have suffered direct loss or expense, and will need to substantiate this to the main contractor. Sums agreed and due to the subcontractor under interim certificates are not affected because of the main contractor's determination under clause 28.

Clause 32

This clause, previously on fair wages, has been deleted from the contract.

Clause 33: Strikes — loss or expense

If either the main contractor or a subcontractor is affected by a local strike or lockout, neither party will be able to claim off the other for any loss or expense. These strikes or lockouts may involve trades employed upon the site, or they may involve trades engaged in the preparation, manufacture or transport of materials. The main contractor must take all reasonable practicable steps to keep the site open. The subcontractor, should the strike or lockout particularly affect him, endeavour to continue with the subcontract works. The provision of clause 33 does not affect any other rights that the parties may have under the contract.

Clauses 34–37: Choice of fluctuation provisions

This group of clauses follow a very similar pattern to the main contract conditions. Clause 35 will apply if no mention is made of either clause 36 or 37. Clause 36 is the traditional price fluctuation clause, whereas clause 37 deals with the formulae method of price adjustment. The use of the latter may depend upon a suitable analysis of the original contract sum.

Clause 38: Settlement of disputes — Arbitration

This clause incorporates the provisions of the main contract and gives the arbitrator specific powers to rectify a subcontract. The JCT Arbitration Rules published in July 1988 are to apply.

Chapter 22

Domestic
subcontract
conditions

A main contractor tendering for a proposed construction project is unlikely to intend to carry out all of the works himself. The contracting situation in the early 1980s is such that more work than ever is being offered and undertaken by trade subcontractors on the main contractor's behalf. The conditions of the contract do not generally recognize the existence of such firms contractually. The work that they carry out is therefore deemed to be work undertaken by the main contractor.

The contractor at tender stage will decide which work he intends to carry out himself, and the remainder will therefore be done by his subcontractors. In order to incorporate their prices within the tender sum, he will extract from the bills of quantities the appropriate sections of their work. He will usually supply this to several firms in order to obtain a competitive price for the tender.

The main provisions regarding these types of firms in JCT 80, is that the main contractor must first obtain the approval from the architect before placing the contract with them (clause 19.2). Unless the architect has a reasonable objection, his consent to their approval must not be withheld. If the main contractor is successful with his tender, a firm order can then be placed with the appropriate subcontractors. He must, of course, be satisfied with their previous performance, the price that they have quoted, and that they can carry out the work at the required time.

The terms of subletting will be agreed between the main contractor and the subcontractor. The main contractor may have his own preprinted conditions for this purpose. He may, however, choose to use one of the non-nominated subcontractor forms which are available in these circumstances. These forms seek to provide fair and reasonable conditions to both parties and their use is therefore encouraged. They can avoid friction occurring between the main contractor and a subcontractor by giving a clear interpretation of the contract's terms. Subcontracting of this type can result in more *ad hoc* arrangements being made, and these are unlikely to result in the smooth running of the project. The use of a standard non-nominated form of subcontract is therefore recommended. The following notes refer to the domestic form of contract that was brought into use in 1980 to be used with JCT 80. This form has now largely replaced what came to be known as the 'blue' form which had been approved by the NFBTE, FASS and CASEC. The main contractor is, of course, still at liberty to use this form where he considers it to be more appropriate.

The JCT 80 non-nominated forms of subcontract are as follows:

1. Domestic subcontract DOM/1 articles of agreement. This is appropriate for use where the form of main contract is one of the usual JCT 80 forms.
2. The subcontract conditions for use with the above.
3. Domestic subcontract DOM/2 articles of agreement, for use with the JCT standard form with contractor's design.

DOM/1 was published in 1980 and DOM/2 in 1981 when the contractor's design form was first issued. The following notes apply only to DOM/1 and its subcontract conditions unless otherwise stated.

The articles of agreement are in line with the articles of agreement to be found in other JCT documents. This agreement is, of course, between the main contractor and the domestic subcontractor. The name of the employer is given for the subcontractor's information only. He is not a party to this contract and cannot therefore either sue or be sued under these conditions of contract.

Article 1 describes the subcontractor's obligation to familiarize himself with the provisions of the main contract and the requirements, therefore, of the employer. He will only, of course, be bound by the contract conditions which are written into the subcontract agreement. In familiarizing himself with the main contract he will, however, be more aware of any implications that may affect his tender price and his proposed method of working.

Article 2 states that the subcontract price will be exclusive of VAT, in line with the main contract conditions. The agreed subcontract sum is entered here in the contract. This sum will include a $2\frac{1}{2}$ per cent cash discount to the main contractor, unless an alternative percentage has been inserted in Part 7 of these conditions. Article 2.1 refers to a subcontract sum where the subcontractor's tender sum is unlikely to be different from his final account. Where the work is to be remeasured, the subcontractor's tender sum will be inserted into the conditions. Only one of these alternatives is applicable, the other being deleted from the articles of agreement.

Article 3 refers to the settlement of disputes, and the requirement that all matters will be first referred to arbitration and not to the courts. The dispute will arise in the first instance because of a difference that may arise between the contractor and the subcontractor. This may, of course, result in arbitration proceedings being instigated by the contractor against the employer. This will occur where the dispute is more a matter to be resolved by the employer than a dispute directly with the contractor.

Appendix to DOM/1

The appendix to DOM/1 provides information relevant to the subcontract conditions in 14 parts.

Part 1

This contains information which is extracted from the main contract conditions, but which is relevant to the subcontract.

Part 1, section A

This includes the following information:

(a) description of the works;
(b) form of main contract;
(c) the main contract documents and where they can be inspected;
(d) whether the main contract has been executed under hand or under seal;
(e) which of the main contract conditions are to apply where an alternative is available, e.g. architect or supervising officer, type of insurance for the works;
(f) any of the standard main contract conditions which have been amended or revised.

Part 1, section B

This contains a copy of the completed appendix applicable to the main contract.

Part 1, section C

This is subdivided into three separate sections; the first of which deals with any obligations or restrictions that have been imposed by the employers on the project. These will therefore have been covered in the preliminaries section of the bill of quantities. It may include restrictions on working hours, the use of non-union labour, etc. Such matters will, of course, appertain to the contractor's domestic subcontractors. The second section outlines the employer's requirements affecting the order of the works where this is required. The third section covers a description of the location of the site and the mode of access.

Part 2

This describes briefly the particulars of the subcontract works that will be undertaken by this subcontractor. Any relevant documents — such as detailed drawings, specifications, or bills of quantities — should be listed for identification and contractual purposes.

Part 3

This requires the subcontractor to insure for personal injury, damage to property and liability. The amount of insurance is to be specified in accordance with clause 7.2 of the subcontract conditions.

Part 4

This includes reference to clause 11.1 of the subcontract conditions regarding the time factor of the subcontract works, and provides for:

(a) the date for commencement of the subcontract works, which is designated between two calendar dates;
(b) the subcontract period for this work;
(c) the period required for notice to commence work on site;
(d) the period for subcontract works off site and prior to commencement on site;
(e) any further details that may be appropriate to the time factor.

Part 5

Clauses 16.2 and 17.2 refer to daywork undertaken by the subcontractor. The provisions of the main contract will apply in respect of the definition of prime cost of daywork regarding the analysis of the work. The appropriate RICS schedule will be used depending upon the nature of the subcontractor. The subcontractor does have the option of including his own percentage additions for the daywork sections. The main contractor will, however, only be eligible to reclaim from the employer, where this is appropriate, at the rates which he has inserted in the contract bills. He will therefore endeavour to make sure that they are no higher than those rates.

Part 6

Clauses 19A and 19B deal with the alternative VAT arrangements, one of which should be deleted.

Part 7

This part covers the main contractor's cash discount on the subcontract invoices. The recommended discount is $2\frac{1}{2}$ per cent. Also listed is the retention percentage to be deducted from interim payments. This is normally in accordance with the provisions of the main contract, and 5 per cent is therefore considered to be the maximum.

Part 8

Clause 24 considers the contractor's claims against the subcontractor and the arrangement for set-off. This includes the same requirements as for nominated subcontractors. The name and address of the adjudicator and the trustee-stakeholder should be provided in accordance with this clause.

Part 9

Particulars of the subcontract's other attendance requirements should be described separately, initialled by the parties and attached to the appendix. The domestic subcontractor, in common with the nominated subcontractor, is entitled to the free provision of general attendance facilities. The main contractor may, however, make an allowance in his rates inserted in the bills for the appropriate costs associated with such items.

Parts 10–13

These relate to the fluctuation provisions and follow a similar pattern to the main form. Clause 35 will apply if there is nothing to the contrary. Clause 34 expects, however, that one of the alternatives will be clearly identified. Where the formula rules are used the base month appropriate to the subcontractor must be clearly indicated.

Part 14

If the main contractor desires to insist upon other stipulations in connection with a subcontractor, then this should be stated.

The subcontract conditions

These follow a similar pattern and content to the nominated subcontract conditions NSC/4. The domestic subcontractor, however, is not generally recognized by the employer in the same way as the nominated subcontractor. For example, there is no provision for direct payment by the employer should the contractor default in payment, nor for the early release of retention. If the nominated firm considers that he is receiving unfair treatment from the contractor he can appeal to the architect, since it was he who initially nominated him. The direct subcontractor does not have this redress. The architect will, however, require through the main contractor that the work is completed to his reasonable satisfaction, and that the subcontractor obeys his instructions, makes good defective work and allows him access to workshops if this is required.

Part 6

Other contract conditions

Chapter 23

Agreement for minor building works

The first edition of the *JCT Agreement for Minor Building Works* was published in 1968. This was subsequently extensively revised in January 1980, to bring it in line with the JCT 80. It is a simplified version of that form of contract and does not envisage the same contractual problems arising from the carrying out of construction works. The simplification inevitably, however, produces a less precise set of conditions. Since its publication in 1980 there have been a number of revisions and reprints of the form, the latest to date being in June 1990.

The major changes have incorporated an additional clause 9 covering the settlement of disputes through arbitration, the abolition of the fair wages clause which coincided with its deletion from JCT 80 and the change in title from supervising officer to contract administrator. This latter amendment is the most significant. Architects have always been unhappy with the title of supervisor, since they claim that this is not a fair description of their activities. Inspector of works would be a preference. Contract Administrator is perhaps better terminology since this represents more or less any profession's role within the scope of the contract. Where the term architect is used in this chapter it must also be interpreted to mean contract administrator.

The Minor Works Form is not for use under the following circumstances:

(a) in Scotland;

(b) where bills of quantities have been provided;
(c) where the employer wishes to nominate subcontractors or suppliers;
(d) on contracts of a duration that require the full labour and materials fluctuations;
(e) for works of a complex nature;
(f) for works which involve complex services;
(g) for works which require more than a short period of time for their execution.

It is intended to be used only on minor building works, although no value has been stated. One supposes, however, that in practice it is used on much larger projects. This is due to the reluctance of architects to get involved with the complexities of JCT 80. Its use is restricted to where an employer appoints an architect or any other professional such as a surveyor or engineer, but not the contractor as in the case of design and build. The contract is carried out on an agreed lump sum on the basis of drawings and specifications. It can be an appropriate form for maintenance works where these can be readily defined.

The form of contract follows a similar pattern to JCT 80, but comprises a form of agreement and conditions of contract only. The agreement, which needs to be completed by the parties, describes the works, who the contract is between, the contract sum, the name of the architect/contract administrator, provisions for arbitration, and the contract documents. A schedule of rates may be included should the project require remeasurement or the agreement of variations. A quantity surveyor may therefore still be used (he may hold the title of contract administrator) to prepare the specification or schedule of rates and to agree the final account.

The conditions of contract include the clauses under a group of nine headings:

Clause 1	Intention of the parties.
Clause 2	Commencement and completion.
Clause 3	Control of the works.
Clause 4	Payment.
Clause 5	Statutory obligations.
Clause 6	Injury, damage and insurance.
Clause 7	Determination.
Clause 8	Supplementary memorandum.
Clause 9	Settlement of disputes — arbitration.

The contents of these nine main sections are described below.

Clause 1: Intention of the parties

Clause 1.1 states that the contractor's obligations are to carry out the works:

(a) with due diligence and to complete the works;
(b) in a good and workmanlike manner;
(c) in accordance with the contract documents;
(d) using materials and workmanship of the quality and standard specified;
(e) to the reasonable satisfaction of the architect or supervising officer.

Clause 1.2 states that the architect/contract administrator's duties include the provision of the necessary information to the contractor; issuing certificates; and confirming all instructions in writing.

Clause 2: Commencement and completion

These clauses state when the works will start on site and when they must be completed. The clauses also cover matters relating to the defects liability period, which is normally three months. In the event of the project not being completed on time separate provisions for an extension of time, or damages for non-completion are included. The damages are assessed on a liquidated basis and the rate per week should therefore be included in the contract.

Clause 3: Control of the works

These matters deal with assignment and subcontracting, with the general provision that written permission must first be obtained from the architect. The contractor must at all reasonable times keep a competent person-in-charge on site to whom the architect can issue instructions. This is a less onerous position than JCT 80. Any person may be reasonably excluded from the site by the architect.

The architect's instructions to the contractor must be in writing, or confirmed in writing within two days. The provisions for covering non-compliance with an instruction are similar to JCT 80. The confirmation within two days is the period of time quoted for the confirmation of clerks of works' instructions under JCT 80. There is no provision for a clerk of works under this form of contract.

There are also provisions for variations to the contract. These are to be valued on a fair basis by the architect. Where a quantity surveyor is named in the agreement he will carry out this duty on behalf of the architect. Alternatively, a price can be agreed before the work is carried out, and this seems a sensible course of action. Provisional sums are valued in the same way, nomination being specifically excluded.

Clause 4: Payment

These clauses deal with payment to the contractor.

1. Provision is made for the correction of any inconsistencies in the documents.
2. Interim payments are to be issued every four weeks and include materials only upon the site. Retention is generally 5 per cent unless otherwise stated and payment should be made within 14 days.
3. This form of contract includes a penultimate certificate which is issued 14 days after the date of completion as stated in clause 2. The next certificate is issued subject to making good defects and within 28 days of the receipt of the necessary documentation from the contractor.
4. Generally, work undertaken on this form of contract will be such that a fixed price contract is always envisaged. Fluctuations in price are not, therefore, normally considered.

Clause 5: Statutory obligations

Clause 5.1 requires the contractor to comply with all the statutory obligations, notices, fees or charges.

Clauses 5.2 and 5.3 deal with the provisions of VAT and the statutory tax deduction scheme respectively, and these are identical to the provisions of JCT 80.

Clause 5.5 covers corruption, and although this may be incorporated into any contract it usually only applies where the employer is a local authority.

Clause 6: Injury, damage and insurance

These clauses deal with matters of injury and damage and the requirements for appropriate insurance on the part of the contractor. The employer needs to be sure in the first place that if injury or damage occurs the blame and responsibility is that of the contractor and not himself. This presumes, of course, that the injury or damage results because of the contractor's negligence, and not because of a fault in the design. The latter may not necessarily provide the contractor with an adequate defence. The employer will therefore need to satisfy himself that the contractor is properly insured (clause 6.4). As far as the works are concerned, alternative insurance provisions are available in the case of new works or existing structures. These are similar to clause 22 of JCT 80 and one of the alternatives therefore needs deleting.

Clause 7: Determination

These clauses cover determination of the contract by either the employer or the contractor. The employer may determine if the contractor:

(a) fails to proceed diligently with the works;
(b) suspends the works;
(c) becomes bankrupt.

The contractor has the option of determining the contract where the employer defaults in respect of:

(a) progress payments;
(b) interference or obstruction of works;
(c) failure to make the premises available;
(d) continuous suspension of the works for one month;
(e) bankruptcy or liquidation.

The procedures for determination are described and this act by either party should be considered as a last resort. This act often requires damages to be paid from one party to the other. Determination must be without prejudice to any other rights or remedies which the parties may possess.

Clause 8: Supplementary memorandum

The supplementary memorandum referred to in this clause is in three parts. The JCT's intention is that it should be used for reference and does not therefore need to be bound in with the executed agreement. The three parts are very similar to the provisions of JCT 80:

Part A   Fluctuations (clause 4.5).
Part B   VAT (clause 5.2).
Part C   Statutory tax deduction scheme (clause 5.3).

Clause 9: Settlement of disputes — arbitration

This clause provides for disputes or differences which may occur between the contractor and the employer to be referred to arbitration. The provisions are similar to JCT 80 and are to be conducted in accordance with the JCT Arbitration Rules. It should be noted that these rules contain stricter time limits than those prescribed by some arbitration rules which are frequently observed in practice. The parties to the contract should note that a failure to comply with the limits incorporated in the JCT Rules may have adverse consequences.

Comparison with JCT 80

Minor works clause	*Clause description*	*JCT 80 clause*
1.1	Contractor's obligations	2, 8
1.2	Architect's/contract administrator's duties	5
2.1	Commencement and completion	17, 23
2.2	Extension of contract period	25
2.3	Damages for non-completion	24
2.4	Completion date	23
2.5	Defects liability	17
3.1	Assignment	19
3.2	Subcontracting	19
3.3	Contractor's representative	10
3.4	Exclusion from the works	8.5
3.5	Architect's/contract administrator's instructions	4
3.6	Variations	13
3.7	Provisional sums	13
4.1	Correction of inconsistencies	2.3
4.2	Progress payments and retention	16.1, 30
4.3	Penultimate certificate	30
4.4	Final certificate	30
4.5	Contribution, levy and tax charges	38
4.6	Fixed price	37
5.1	Statutory obligations, notices, fees and charges	8
5.2	Value added tax	15
5.3	Statutory tax deduction scheme	31
5.4	(Number not used)	
5.5	Prevention of corruption	27
6.1	Injury to or death of persons	20, 21
6.2	Injury or damage to property	20, 21
6.3A	Insurance of the works — fire, etc. — new works	22
6.3B	Insurance of the works — fire, etc. — existing works	22
6.4	Evidence of insurance	22
7.1	Determination by employer	27
7.2	Determination by contractor	28
8.1	Supplementary memorandum	15, 31, 37
9.0	Settlement of disputes — arbitration	41

The following conditions from JCT 80 are specifically excluded from the minor works form.

Minor works clause	Clause description	JCT 80 clause
—	Levels and setting out of the works	7
—	Royalties and patent rights	9
—	Clerk of works	12
—	Materials off site	16.2
—	Partial possession	18
—	Loss and expense	26
—	Works by or on behalf of the employer	29
—	Outbreak of hostilities	32
—	War damage	33
—	Antiquities	34
—	Nominated subcontractors	35
—	Nominated suppliers	36
—	Price adjustment formulae	40

Chapter 24

JCT Intermediate Form of Building Contract

Introduction

Many of the professionals who are employed in the construction industry regard the Standard Form of Building Contract (JCT 80) as too complex, at least for medium-sized projects. Others felt that the gap between this form and the Agreement for Minor Building Works was too great, and that some types of midway conditions were both desirable and essential for the efficient running of construction contracts. The *Intermediate Form* was thus conceived and its first edition was published in 1984. It soon became known as IFC 84.

Whilst it was envisaged that this form would be used on projects at that time worth up to £250,000 (now considerably more) it has been used for projects of much larger values. One of the main differences between IFC 84 and JCT 80 is that there is no provision for nominated subcontractors, as usually understood. There is provision, however, for the architect to name a subcontractor for whom the main contractor assumes a much greater responsibility. The main concept of naming is as follows. All of the contractors tendering are provided with detailed information regarding the named subcontractor's price and conditions, programme of work and the attendances which the main contractor must provide. The contractor then assumes the same responsibility for the named subcontractor as with any normal domestic subcontractor. If, however, the named subcontractor defaults then there are provisions in the contract to safeguard the main contractor's interest.

IFC 84 generally follows the layout of the Minor Works Form, as the clauses are grouped under similar section headings. The clause content is, however, more detailed and comprehensive although much less so than JCT 80. Unlike JCT 80, IFC 84 is published in only one edition which allows for the differences envisaged in the contractual arrangements. In addition to the drawings, for example, either bills of quantities, a specification or a schedule of works can be used. If the drawings are supported only by a specification then either a schedule of rates or a contract sum analysis must be provided in support of his tender.

The agreement, articles and recitals

Agreement

This is the page in the document which identifies the parties concerned with the contract.

Recitals

These include:

- brief description of the works to be constructed;
- documents which are to be included as contract documents;
- reference to the person under whose direction the works are to be carried out.

Articles

There are five articles as follows:

1. Contractor's obligations.
2. Contract sum.
3. Architect or supervising officer.
4. Quantity surveyor.
5. Settlement of disputes — arbitration.

Intention of the parties

1.1 Contractor's obligations. He is to carry out and complete the works in accordance with the contract documents which have been identified in the recital above.

1.2 Quality and quantity of work. The quality is as specified in the contract documents, quantities depend upon type of contract documentation which has been prepared.

1.3 Priority of contract documents. A specification, schedule of works or bills of quantities cannot override the conditions of contract.

1.4 Instructions as to inconsistencies, errors or omissions. The architect must issue instructions regarding any inconsistencies which may arise in the documents. If these affect the contract sum then they are to be revalued under clause 3.7 (valuation of variations).

1.5 Contract bills and SMM7. Contract bills are assumed to have been prepared under SMM7 unless otherwise stated.

1.6 Custody and copies of contract documents. The contract documents are to remain in the custody of the employer, with the contractor being given one copy of the contract documents certified on behalf of the employer, and two further copies of drawings and other contract documentation, e.g., bills of quantities.

1.7 Further drawings and details. Other drawings and information are likely to be prepared during the course of construction and two copies of these are also to be made available to the contractor.

1.8 Limits to use of documents. The contractor must not use any of these documents for any other purpose than this contract.

1.9 Issue of certificates by architect/supervising officer. Certificates are normally issued to the employer with duplicate copies to the contractor.

1.10 Unfixed materials or goods, passing of property, etc. Goods and materials delivered to the site are not to be removed without the written permission of the architect/supervision officer. Where such items have been paid for by the employer they become his property. The contractor, however, remains responsible for their protection from damage or theft.

1.11 Off-site materials and goods, passing of property. Materials or goods paid for by the employer which are stored off-site become the property of the employer. Such items must not be used for purposes other than the works. The contractor is again responsible for their safe keeping.

Possession and completion

2.1 Possession and completion dates. The date of possession is stated in the Appendix and the contractor shall begin and regularly and diligently proceed with the works and complete them before the date stated in the Appendix as the date for completion.

2.2 Deferment of possession. If this clause is to apply, i.e., it is stated in the Appendix as such, then the employer may defer giving possession of the site to the contractor by the period stated.

2.3 Extensions of time. These are clauses to be followed and interpreted in the event of the works being or likely to be delayed. The contractor must inform the architect/supervising officer that a delay is likely to occur and the cause of such. If the architect/supervising officer feels that there are reasonable grounds for granting the contractor an extension of time then he must estimate the amount of time that is appropriate and inform the contractor in writing of the decision.

2.4 Events referred to in 2.3. This includes the list of events which the contractor may refer to, to support a claim for an extension of time. The list includes similar items referred to in the other JCT contracts.

2.5 Further delay or extension of time. This clause allows for further extensions of time as may be appropriate.

2.6 Certificate of non-completion. The architect/supervising officer must issue a certificate where the contractor has failed to complete the works, either by the date for completion or within any date extended under the terms of the contract.

2.7 Liquidated damages for non-completion. These are stated in the Appendix as a rate of £X per week or month to be paid by the contractor to the employer for delays which are attributed to the fault of the contractor.

2.8 Repayment of liquidated damages. If it is felt at some later date that the delays were not entirely the fault of the contractor then the damages (or a part of them) can be repaid to the contractor.

2.9 Practical completion. When the architect/supervising officer decides that the works are complete he issues a certificate to that effect.

2.10 Defects liability. All defects, which are due to materials or workmanship which are not in accordance with the contract, which are notified to the contractor within fourteen days after the expiry of the defects liability periods are to be made good at the contractor's expense.

Control of the works

3.1 Assignment. Neither the employer nor the contractor shall without the written consent of the other party assign the contract to someone else.

3.2 Subcontracting. The contractor cannot subcontract any part of the works without the written consent of the architect/supervising officer. The employment of a subcontractor is automatically terminated upon the determination of the main contract. A subcontractor is effectively treated in the same way as if he were the main contractor, so, for example, any materials or goods of a subcontractor which are brought to the site cannot be removed

266

without written permission. If the value of a subcontractor's materials or goods are included in a certificate and this sum is paid by the employer to the main contractor then such items become the property of the employer.

3.3 Named persons as subcontractors. The contract documents may name a person or firm to undertake a section of the works as a subcontractor. Within 21 days of entering into the main contract, the contractor must communicate with the proposed subcontractor using the standard form of tender and agreement NAM/T. If the contractor is unable to enter into a subcontract in this way he must immediately inform the architect/supervising officer of the reasons which prevent this. If the architect/supervising officer is reasonably satisfied that the particulars have prevented a subcontract being made then an instruction is given which may:

1. Change the particulars so as to remove the impediment.
2. Omit the work.
3. Substitute the work with a provisional sum.

In an instruction as to the expenditure of a provisional sum the architect/supervising officer may require the work to be executed by a named subcontractor. This clause also deals with the situation where the employment of a named subcontractor is determined and the procedures that should then be followed.

IFC 84 is a work and materials contract. It is not a design contract and the contractor is thus not responsible for any design work which may be required. If a named subcontractor has a design element then the main contractor is not responsible for any failures in the design but his liability is limited only in respect of the goods, materials and workmanship.

3.4 Contractor's person in charge. The contractor has to keep on the works a competent person in charge.

3.5 Architect's/supervising officer's instructions. This clause deals with the provision of instructions to the contractor, which must be in writing. It covers matters of non-compliance and the action the contractor may wish to take in respect of challenging the validity of an instruction.

3.6 Variations. The architect/supervising officer may issue instructions requiring a variation and sanction in writing to those made by the contractor. The term variation is defined to include the alteration or modification of the design, quality or quantity of works as shown on the contract drawings. This may include the addition, omission or substitution of any work, the alteration of the kind or standard of materials or goods to be used, the removal from site of materials or work which are not in accordance with the contract and the addition, alteration or omission of any obligations or restrictions imposed by the employer.

3.7 Valuation of variations and provisional sum work. These broadly follow the provisions laid down in JCT 80 regarding similar work, using the priced schedules as a basis for valuation, fair valuations in the absence of any comparable items of work, dayworks and omitted work. The valuation where appropriate can include the adjustment to the values of preliminary items.

3.8 Instructions to expend provisional sums. The architect/supervising officer must issue instructions regarding the expenditure of provisional sums.

3.9 Levels and setting out. The architect provides the information required for setting out, the contractor is responsible for the actual setting out. Errors are amended in the same manner as JCT 80.

3.10 Clerk of works. The employer may choose to appoint a clerk of works whose sole responsibility is that of inspector.

3.11 Work not forming part of the contract. This allows the employer to employ persons or firms direct and concurrently with the main building work. The contractor must permit this work to be undertaken. Where the contract documents do not allow for this, the contractor must not unreasonably give the employer permission to arrange for the execution of such work.

3.12 Instructions as to inspections and tests. This allows the architect/supervising officer the authority to open up work for inspection. Where the work is in accordance with the contract then the costs of opening up are added to the contract sum. Where it is not then the costs together with the costs of rectification are borne entirely by the contractor. The sub-standard work may be allowed to remain, in which case an agreed reduction in cost is made to the contract.

3.13 Instructions following failure of work, etc. See above.

3.14 Instructions as to removal of work, etc. The architect/supervising officer may issue instructions in respect of the removal from site of any goods or work which do not conform with the contract.

3.15 Instructions as to postponement. The architect/supervising officer may issue instructions in regard to the postponement of any work executed under the provisions of the contract.

Payment

4.1 Contract sum. The contract sum is not to be altered in any way, other than within the terms of the contract. Any computation of errors are deemed to have been accepted by the parties.

4.2 Interim payments. Interim payments are to be made monthly unless the contract states otherwise. The employer must pay the contractor within fourteen days of the date of the certificate. The majority of the work is subject to 5 per cent retention i.e., work completed and materials and goods on or off site. Some items of work are not subject to any retention, e.g., tax, insurances, etc.

4.3 Interim payment on practical completion. One half of the retention fund is released at practical completion and the remainder with the issue of the final certificate.

4.4 Interest in percentage withheld. The employer acts as trustee of the retention fund but without any obligation to invest.

4.5 Computation of adjusted contract sum. Either before or within a reasonable time after practical completion the contractor should provide all the documents which are necessary to adjust the contract sum and to calculate the final account.

4.6 Issue of final certificate. When the contract sum has been agreed the architect/supervising officer must issue the final certificate within 28 days.

4.7 Effect of final certificate. Only the final certificate is conclusive except for matters which are the subject of proceedings.

4.8 Effect of certificates other than final. None of the interim certificates is conclusive evidence that any work, materials or goods included in them are in accordance with the contract.

4.9 Fluctuations. These allow for the possibility of fluctuations in cost on the main contract. The JCT Fluctuation Clauses and Formula Rules for use with JCT Intermediate Form of Building Contract IFC 84 should be referred to for the specific details.

4.10 Fluctuations, named persons. This allows for fluctuations in cost in respect of any amounts for named subcontractors.

4.11 Disturbance of regular progress. This clause deals with any direct loss or expense which the contractor may have suffered and for which he will not be reimbursed by a payment under any other provision of the contract.

4.12 Matters referred to in clause 4.11. This clause identifies the matters which may give rise to a claim for loss and expense. These include delay in receipt of drawings, details, etc., opening up of work for inspection that is found to be in accordance with the contract, execution of work by the employer's own subcontractors, supply by the employer of materials or goods or a failure to supply postponement of the works, failure to provide access to the site, and certain architect's/supervising officer's instructions.

Statutory obligations, etc.

5.1 Statutory obligations, notices, fees and charges. The contractor must comply with all notices which may be required by statute, statutory instrument, by-law, etc., and pay all the fees or charges which may be required. If such charges arise, for example, from a variation then they will be added to the contract sum.

5.2 Notices of divergence from statutory requirements. If the contractor finds any differences between the contract documents or that any of these documents are in conflict with any statutory requirement then a written notice of such divergence should be given to the architect. The contractor is not expected to search for discrepancies, but if they come to the contractor's notice then they should be notified to the architect.

5.3 Extent of contractor's liability for non-compliance. The contractor is not liable for work which does not comply with statutory requirements, if it has been carried out in accordance with the contract documents.

5.4 Emergency compliance. If the contractor is requested urgently to comply with a statutory obligation, before receiving appropriate instructions from the architect, then the minimum that is necessary should be carried out. The architect must then be informed and the work treated as a variation.

5.5 Value Added Tax, Supplement conditional A. The contract sum is exclusive of any Value Added Tax and this is dealt with in the same way as in JCT 80.

5.6 Statutory tax deduction scheme, Supplemental condition B. This clause is also comparable to the similar clause in JCT 80.

Injury, damage and insurance

6.1 Injury to persons and property and employer's indemnity. The contractor is liable for and must indemnify the employer, against any action including costs and damages, in respect of injury or death of anyone. The contractor's only real defence is to show that such an occurrence was due to the neglect of the employer or of someone for whom the employer was responsible. The employer does have the option of accepting some of these risks and there is provision for such in clause 6.3.

6.2 Insurance against injury to persons and property. The provisions are broadly the same as JCT 80 in this respect, i.e., the contractor is responsible for the works and that of all subcontractors, the contractor should therefore seek to ensure that these subcontractors maintain relevant insurance and if there is a default in this respect then the employer can insure on their behalf and deduct the premiums from the contract sum.

6.3 Insurance in the joint names of the employer and contractor. The insurance will be taken out in the joint names of the employer and the contractor. There are three mutually exclusive clauses 6.3A, 6.3B and 6.3C and the Appendix must indicate which is to apply. These provisions broadly follow the principles described in JCT 80.

Determination

7.1 Determination by employer. The employer may determine the contract if the contractor
1. Unreasonably suspends the works.
2. Fails to proceed regularly and diligently with the works.
3. Persistently refuses to comply with an architect's instruction to remove defective work, and this results in further damage to the works.
4. Fails to comply with the provisions of subcontracting and named persons.
7.2 Contractor becoming bankrupt. If the contractor becomes bankrupt or makes a composition or arrangement with creditors or has a winding up order made against him voluntary or otherwise, then the contract is automatically determined. This may be reinstated and continued where the employer and liquidator or receiver agree.
7.3 Corruption, determination by employer. Where the employer is a local authority then determination of the contractor's employment can occur where a gift or inducement to seek favours has been made by the contractor. Certain of these would no doubt cause any employer to determine a contract.
7.4 Consequences of determination under clauses 7.1–7.3. The consequences of determination can be summarized as follows:
1. The contractor relinquishes the possession of the site.
2. If the architect so instructs then the contractor must remove from the works goods, materials, plant, etc.
3. The employer may engage others to complete the works and to use the goods, materials and plant. The benefits of these in practice may be limited, e.g., the right does not apply to hired plant, the goods and materials may be the subject of a retention of title clause and materials or goods used will form a part of the final account.
7.5 Determination by contractor. The contractor under some circumstances is also able to determine the contract. These are as follows:
1. The employer does not honour a certificate.
2. The employer interferes with or obstructs the issue of a certificate.
3. If the works are suspended for a period of at least one month due to inconsistencies, variations, postponement, late instructions, delays or failure by the employer or those engaged direct by the employer or failure on the part of the employer in respect of site access.
7.6 Employer becoming bankrupt, etc. If the employer becomes bankrupt then the contractor can terminate the contract. This is similar to clause 7.2.

7.7   Consequences of determination under clause 7.5 or 7.6. These are
      as follows:
      1.   The contractor removes temporary buildings, plant, tools,
           equipment, goods and materials and gives the subcontractors the
           same facilities.
      2.   The contractor is paid in respect of the following:
           (a) value of work done but not yet paid;
           (b) loss and expense ascertained;
           (c) cost of goods and materials properly ordered and paid for;
           (d) reasonable costs of removal under (a) above;
           (e) Direct loss and expense caused by the determination.
7.8   Determination by employer or contractor. This clause is now the
      same as appears in JCT 80 as clause 28A.
7.9   Consequences of determination under clause 7.8. These are the
      same as where the contractor determines under clause 7.7.

Interpretation of the contract

8.1   References to clauses. These are the clauses of IFC 84.
8.2   Articles, etc., to be read as a whole. This makes it clear that
      articles, clauses and items in the Appendix are to be read as a
      whole.
8.3   Definitions. This clause contains a number of pertinent definitions,
      e.g., Appendix, Clause 6.3 perils, contract sum analysis, etc.
8.4   The architect/supervising officer. If the person identified in Article
      3 is ineligible to be described as an architect under the Architect's
      (Registration) Acts 1931 to 1969 then the term supervising officer is
      to be used.
8.5   Priced specification or priced schedules of work. This refers to the
      documentation in the 2nd Recital of the Conditions of Contract.

Chapter 25

ICE conditions of contract

These conditions of contract are used on projects that can broadly be described as civil engineering works. The sponsoring authorities for the sixth edition, which was revised in 1991, are:

1. The Institution of Civil Engineers.
2. The Association of Consulting Engineers.
3. The Federation of Civil Engineering Contractors.

A permanent joint committee of these bodies keeps the document under review, and will consider any suggestions or amendments.

Civil Engineering Procedure (published by the *Institution of Civil Engineers*) lists the following documents that are normally used in connection with a civil engineering contract:

1. Conditions of contract.
2. Form of tender.
3. Form of agreement.
4. Instructions to tenderers.
5. Drawings.
6. Bills of quantities.
7. Specification.

The last three of the above documents are similar to those used on a building contract, but with a distinctly engineering emphasis. The bills of quantities, for example, will have been prepared in accordance with the rules of the *Civil Engineering Standard Method of Measurement* (CESMM), or alternatively the *Method of Measurement for Roads and Bridgeworks* (MMRB). Civil engineering contracts on the basis of measurement include a bill and a specification. As the specification will not identify the work sufficiently for pricing purposes, it more aligns with the trade preambles found in a bill for a building project. The specification will include:

(a) character and quality of materials and workmanship;
(b) special responsibilities imposed upon the contractor that are not covered by the conditions of contract;
(c) order for executing the works where necessary;
(d) methods of construction to be adopted where required by the engineer;
(e) particulars of facilities afforded to other contractors on the site;
(f) requirement on the part of the contractor to submit a programme for the works;
(g) request the contractor to describe his proposed method of working and his temporary works.

The drawings for a civil engineering project are more likely to have been prepared within the procedures of engineering drawing, rather than the way an architect would produce his drawings for a building project.

The purpose of the instructions to tenderers is to assist the tenderers in the preparation of their tenders, and to ensure that they are presented in a form required by the promoter and the engineer.

The remaining three documents, along with the form of bond, are all included in the document known as the ICE conditions of contract.

Form of tender

The form of tender is the tenderer's written offer to execute the work in accordance with the other contract documents. The form of tender should state:

(a) the contractor's price;
(b) commencement date and time for completion;
(c) salient particulars of the offer.

The form of tender also includes the appendix to the form of contract, which includes:

(a) defects correction period;
(b) contract agreement;
(c) performance bond;
(d) insurance;

(e) liquidated damages;
(f) venting materials not on site;
(g) method of measurement;
(h) percentage of value of materials; to be included in interim certificates;
(j) minimum amount of interim certificates;
(k) rate and limit of retention;
(l) Bank base rate.

Form of agreement

This is the legal undertaking entered into between the promoter and the contractor, for the execution of the work in accordance with the contract documents and which each party signs.

Form of bond

A security bond may be required by the promoter, and this is executed by the contractor at the time of signing the contract. The amount of the bond is often in the order of 10 per cent of the contract sum. Clause 10 of the conditions of contract deals with sureties.

Conditions of contract

The conditions of contract are subdivided into 23 sections which contain in total 71 clauses. In addition, a separate clause on contract price fluctuations and arbitration procedure may be included where the contract is on that basis. The conditions also include a very useful index to the clauses. The clause contents are similar to the *JCT Standard Form of Building Contract*, but have been written with civil engineering projects in mind. Space does not permit a detailed treatment of these clauses. The major differences between this and JCT 80 are therefore only highlighted. Students who require a more detailed exposition should refer to a text dedicated to the engineering contract.

Definition and intepretation (clause 1)

This clause provides the reader with several important definitions in a like manner to JCT 80.

Engineer and Engineer's representative (clause 2)

The engineer is defined in clause 1 by name. The nature of civil engineering works is that they are often large and cumbersome, and may be constructed on extended sites such as roads and railway projects. The engineer may therefore be assisted by his representative on site, who in turn may require the assistance of several other engineers. Each of these is able to issue instructions to the contractor; the 'other engineers' largely on points of detail for the particular area of work for which they are responsible. There are restrictions over which only the engineer may issue instructions. These include delays, extension of time, certificates of completion, agreement of the final account, maintenance certificate, forfeiture and assignment and the settlement of disputes.

Assignment and subcontracting (clauses 3 and 4)

The interpretation of these clauses is similar to JCT 80.

Contract documents (clauses 5–7)

These clauses fail to identify precisely what the contract documents comprise. Clause 1 includes a definition of the contract, and this has a wider interpretation than might be expected under JCT 80. Clause 6 identifies those documents which the contractor will receive at the start of the project. In other respects there is a great deal of similarity with JCT 80 regarding matters such as copyright, return of documents, delay in the issue of drawings and the general availability of the documents on the site.

General obligations (clauses 8–35)

The general obligations contain a wide range of matters which are covered by this group of clauses. Many of the clauses are self-explanatory. Clause 8 describes the contractor's general responsibilities to 'construct and complete the works', which, although in different words, is in essence the same as the building contractor under JCT 80. A performance bond (clause 10) may be required, and although this is absent from JCT 80 it can be incorporated, resulting in basically the same requirement.

Among this group, clause 12 is an important clause that really does not have anything comparable in JCT 80. This clause covers adverse physical conditions and artificial obstructions that may be encountered during the execution of the works. It specifically excludes bad weather conditions or conditions which may be the direct result of bad weather. Where, however, bad weather makes these adverse difficulties worse, this would have to be taken into account in this clause. It is worth remembering that a large amount of civil engineering works is carried out at or below ground level, and the possibility of this clause being used is therefore quite common. Even where adequate boreholes and a site investigation has been carried out, such problems still occur.

When such a problem occurs the contractor must attempt as soon as possible to give details of the cause and the likely effect upon the works. He must also give details of the countermeasures he intends to take. The engineer may also:

(a) require an estimate of the contractor's costs and time;
(b) approve the proposed measures with or without modification;
(c) give instructions on how the physical conditions are to be dealt with;
(d) order a suspension of the works.

It should be noted that the contractor's estimate is a guide only for the engineer. The contractor will be paid for this work in accordance with the terms of the contract.

Clause 13 requires the work to be to the satisfaction of the engineer, and has its comparable equivalent in JCT 80. It should, however, be noted that the powers of the engineer are wider than those of the architect under JCT. The contractor's mode, manner and speed of construction are to be to the approval of the engineer.

Clause 14 requires the contractor to provide a programme for the works. This has only become a requirement in the latest issue of the JCT form. In addition, the contractor must also describe how he intends to carry out the works, and the methods he intends to use. This can be of particular significance on a civil engineering project where construction method is more varied than on building works. A variation to the permanent works may cause severe repercussions in the construction of the temporary works. The engineer may require details of the contractor's temporary works and the construction plant he intends to use. The safety of the permanent works may be affected by these, and the engineer will therefore need to establish that no detriment occurs to the finished project. If the engineer delays in his approval of the proposed methods to be used by the contractor, then this may provide the basis for an extension of time. It should be noted that all these approvals by the engineer will not relieve the contractor of any of his duties or responsibilities under the contract (clause 14.9).

Clause 18 includes a specific clause requiring the contractor to undertake any exploratory excavation work if directed to do so by the engineer. It must be remembered that civil engineering is often predominantly at or below ground level, so this could be a common instruction in practice. The contractor will, of course, be paid for this work as it is actually carried out, even if different quantities had been assumed for the bill of quantities.

Clause 20 deals with the contractor's care of the works. It should be noted that the contractor remains fully responsible for the project until the date of issue of the certificate of completion. This clause places the responsibility for making good defects with the contractor other than the usual excepted risk items.

Clause 21 is the clause describing the contractor's responsibility for insuring the works. There are no alternatives, or allowance for the fact that the employer may already have a current insurance in existence. The scope of this clause is also much wider than the JCT counterpart. The contractor must insure in the joint names of the employer and contractor to cover:

(a) the temporary and permanent works;
(b) the plant and equipment materials;
(c) an additional 10% to cover any additional costs that may arise including professional fees and demolition.

JCT 80, as far as the client is concerned, only relates to permanent works. The ICE conditions, therefore, take account of and make a greater allowance for the fact that it is often more plant intensive and can also incorporate substantial temporary works for which the employer may have already paid for in an interim certificate.

Clause 27 clarifies to the contractor the often complex position that can arise where the project involves a certain amount of street works. The relationship between the contractor, the Public Utilities Street Works Act 1950 and the project are described. For a detailed understanding of this clause a study of the appropriate Act is necessary.

Clause 29 is concerned with limiting the amount of interference to the public, access to other roads or properties by the public, reducing noise, disturbance and pollution.

Clause 30 covers the avoidance of damage to highways, and the possible claims that may arise where extraordinary traffic within the meaning of the Highway Act 1959 can occur. This clause further identifies the different nature between building and civil engineering works. The costs of any precautions or temporary works will be borne by the employer. Where the contractor fails to carry out the works with reasonable care, and where, because of this, damage occurs, then the responsibility for its repair is entirely that of the contractor.

Clause 31 requires the contractor to afford all reasonable facilities for other contractors or statutory bodies whom the employer has contracted within independently. Some of these firms, who may be working beyond the limits of the site, could be undertaking extensive projects. These activities should be identified precisely in the contract documents in order to allow for the contractor to price them adequately. Where such contractors, whether known or unknown, cause a delay to the works, the contractor is entitled to a delay and extra cost claim.

Workmanship and materials (clauses 36−40)

Clauses 36−39 are very similar in content to those used in JCT 80. They cover the quality of materials and the standard of workmanship and tests as defined by the engineer. They include matters relating to:

Quality of materials and workmanship and tests;
Cost of samples;
Cost of tests;
access to site;
examination of work before covering up;
Uncovering and making openings;
removal of unsatisfactory work and materials.

The effects regarding responsibility and costs is similar to JCT 80. The contractor can also not assume that the work is satisfactory until he has been informed accordingly. The engineer has the option at any time to disapprove of any workmanship or materials.

Clause 40, dealing with the suspension of the works, has a similar effect to the JCT clause of postponement.

Commencement time and delays (clauses 41−46)

Clause 41. The works commencement date, if known, is stated on the appendix. If unspecified then it is within 28 days of the award of the contract or such other date as agreed by the parties. The engineer will notify the contractor, after his tender has been accepted, of a start date, and the work should then proceed reasonably soon after that date.

Clause 42. Due to the nature of civil engineering works, particularly the extended sites, provision of the site may be made progressively. This clause does not afford to the contractor the exclusive possession of the site. If the employer fails to give possession of the site in accordance with the contract provisions then the contractor will be entitled to a delay and cost claim. The contractor is also responsible for any access (rights of way) that may be necessary in the execution of the works. He will have to provide, for example, for temporary access roads where these are required and pay the costs accordingly.

Clause 43. Sectional completion is an optional clause that can be incorporated into JCT 80. The ICE conditions, however, intend that phased completion would generally be considered as the norm (see appendix). The completion dates would need to be considered in respect of the somewhat flexible date for commencement.

Clause 44 refers to extension of time caused by: variations, increased quantities, delays refered to in the conditions, exceptionally adverse weather conditions and other special circumstances.

Clause 45. This clause deals with night and Sunday work, which are both generally forbidden unless one or other is either unavoidable or absolutely necessary in the context of saving life or property or for safety reasons. If the type of work envisaged is normally carried out beyond the usual working hours, then this clause will not apply. In any case the contractor should always inform the engineer of his specific intentions.

Clause 46. The engineer may serve a notice on the contractor where he feels that reasonable progress is not being maintained. Clause 23 of JCT 80 includes a similar provision. The engineer will be able to measure the progress against the contractor's intentions shown on his programme for the works. The contractor may request to be allowed to carry out work beyond the normal working hours. The engineer's permission on this matter is not to be reasonably refused. Night or Sunday work is entirely at the expense of the contractor. The engineer's refusal to this request, if the project was close to a hospital for example, would not necessarily imply that the contractor should be given an extension of time. He would have to support this claim by one of the reasons mentioned in clause 44, which was not known at the time of tender.

Liquidated damages for delay (clause 47)

This clause seeks in its overall aims the same achievements as the one used in JCT 80. If the contractor is late in completing the works for reasons that were within his control, then damages become due to the employer accordingly. The damages are determined on the basis of loss and cannot become a penalty for late completion. Since the project is expected to be completed in sections, the appropriate and individual liquidated damages appropriate to the section of the works concerned is stated (see appendix). The complex arrangement regarding this item could result in unfortunate consequences in practice. This might result in inadequate recovery by the employer or the claim that the sum is really a penalty (even though the contract explicitly states that it is not), by the contractor. It is not clear whether some of the delays could result in overlapping damages for the sections of work that must be somewhere related.

Certificate of substantial completion (clause 48)

The main difference between this clause and the certificate of practical completion, issued under JCT 80, is in the wording and its concept. When the contractor considers that the civil engineering works are substantially complete he may request the engineer to issue the completion certificate. Practical completion on JCT 80 means virtually complete with only very minor items remaining to be carried out. Substantially complete on civil engineering projects may mean that the largest amount of work to be done has been finished. In each contract, however, they probably both imply that this certificate will be issued at the handover date to the client.

Outstanding work and defects (clauses 49–50)

Clause 49 describes the term, 'defects correction period' which largely has the same meaning as the commonly named defects liability period under the JCT forms. The length of this period must be stated in the appendix, but no recommendation on the time scale is given. The defects liability period under JCT 80 is the time allowed to remedy any of the contractor's defective work. The period of maintenance mentioned here allows for the rectification of any defective work. The contractor will, of course, be suitably reimbursed for repair work, due to an inappropriate design. The engineer is also entitled to expect the contractor to search or carry out tests in order to discover the reason for any inspections or faults which may arise.

Alterations, additions and omissions (clauses 51–52)

These clauses represent the equivalent of clause 13 in the JCT 80 form. They do, however, offer the engineer a wider scope in the issue of variations, and in addition he does not have to justify the instruction. Variations are defined as:

additions/omissions/substitutions/alterations;
changes in quality/form/character/position/dimension/line/level;
changes in any specified sequence/method/timing.

They may be ordered during the Defects Correction Period. Although variations must be in writing to be of any monetary effect, the procedure for the confirmation of verbal instructions does not place the same time restraints on the contract. Since this type of contract is of a remeasurement type, no instructions are required to vary the quantities of work involved.

The valuation of variations follows a similar pattern to the JCT forms. If the contractor and engineer cannot agree upon the rate to be used, even after a 'fair' valuation has been made, then the engineer will have the final say. Where the contractor does not believe that the rate used is reasonable and proper, the opinion of an arbitrator can be sought. The engineer decides which work is to be for a daywork basis, and the 'Schedules of Daywork carried out Incidental to Contract Work' are then used. These have some similarity to those used on building projects.

Clause 52(4) describes the procedure to be followed where the contractor intends to claim a higher rate than one previously notified to the engineer. The contractor must notify the engineer in due time, keep appropriate records available and present the accounts at various stages. Where the contractor does not follow this procedure, he runs the risk of difficulties of getting his claim accepted by the engineer. Once the claim has been agreed it will be included as an interim payment.

Property in materials and contractor's equipment (clauses 53–54)

Clause 53 seeks to provide the same sort of position regarding the ownership of materials, but the case of *Dawber Williamson* v. *Humberside County Council* is also relevant here. The employer's title to the materials or goods must not be defective. It is, however, doubtful whether this clause gives any enforceable rights in respect of subcontractors. In the event of insolvency, the employer may use the contractor's plant and materials, but the plant must be returned when no longer required. Hired plant is generally excluded from this provision. The vesting of certain items of plant and goods are listed in the contract appendix.

Measurement (clauses 55–57)

The only basis of tendering considered under these conditions is based upon approximate quantities and remeasurement upon completion. The method of measurement envisaged on both occasions is the *Civil Engineering Standard Method of Measurement* Second Edition 1985. The appendix to the conditions does, however, allow the use of other methods of measurement, for example, the *Method of Measurement of Road and Bridgeworks* produced by the Ministry of Transport. Whichever method of measurement is used, this must be clear to those tendering for the

282

project. The use of two different methods on a single project has been heard of but this is not to be recommended.

Errors in the documents are treated in much the same way as JCT 80, and the rules for valuing variations, described in clause 52, allow for new rates to be used where the quantities of work actually carried out differ considerably from those in the bills.

Provisional and prime cost sums and nominated subcontracts (clauses 58–59)

The contents of these clauses follow, in principle, the relevant conditions of JCT 80. There is, however, a refreshing absence of the procedures required for nomination that has become so cumbersome on JCT 80. Nominated suppliers do not exist in name, but are included within the definition of nominated subcontractors. The clauses adequately define prime cost sum and a provisional sum, and when these should be used on a civil engineering contract. The contractor may object to the nomination of a subcontractor, although the reasons listed are very limited in scope. In practice, where a contractor was sufficiently forceful in his objection an engineer would be unwise to proceed along those lines. The procedure to be adopted by the engineer where a contractor does object to a particular nomination are fully detailed in clause 59. The main contractor's cash discount is limited to any amount that is obtainable by the contractor, and he must therefore carefully check the bills of quantities in this respect and price the work accordingly.

Certificates and payments (clauses 60–61)

The provisions relating to the above follow a similar pattern to JCT 80, on the basis of payments on account. Each month the contractor submits a detailed statement to the engineer which might include:

(a) value of permanent works;
(b) lists of goods and materials on site;
(c) list of identified goods and materials not yet on site;
(d) value of temporary works or contractor's equipment;
(e) amount of nominated subcontractors.

The engineer's certificate must be honoured within 28 days rather than the more customary 14 days used on other contracts. There is also a provision for a minimum amount of interim certificates, and this amount is stated in the appendix. This means that unless the valuation achieves this amount each month any payment is deferred for another month. The purpose is to offer added incentive for regular progress of the works. Retention is recommended at 5 per cent of the monthly valuation, but a limit of 3 per cent of the contract sum is also applied. This form recognizes, therefore, that once a sufficient amount in a retention fund has been achieved there is no necessity to continue to deduct retention monies. Release of retention follows a similar pattern to JCT 80. Deductions for liquidated damages or for direct payments to nominated subcontractors can also be made from interim certificates. Another important difference between these provisions and JCT 80 is that the contractor is automatically entitled to add interest charges at 2% per annum above the base lending rate specified in the appendix. This applies on both interim and final accounts. In connection with the latter, the onus of preparing the final account is on the contractor and should be done within 3 months of the Defects Correction Certificate. Once it has been prepared the engineer must, of course, be allowed a reasonable period of time to check it — in this case three months. It is now commonplace for the quantity surveyor to be employed on civil engineering works, and it is he who generally prepares certificates and accounts in a similar manner to building contracts.

Clause 61 deals with the maintenance certificate, and the engineer's satisfaction that the works are now free from any defects. The remainder of the retention is released 28 days after the issue of this certificate, and the contractor's obligation to remedy any defective work now ends.

Remedies and powers (clauses 62−63)

Clause 62 covers the carrying out of urgent works. If the contractor fails to do this, then the engineer may employ others to do so, and adjust the contractor's account accordingly.

Clause 63 covers the causes leading to determination of the contract. These are similar to those of determination in JCT 80.

Miscellaneous clauses (clauses 64−71)

Clause 64 deals with frustration of contracts and clause 65 war and its associated damages. Clause 66 is the arbitration clause, with the minor difference that, prior to arbitration, both parties should discuss the matter with the engineer. One presumes, however, that even on a building contract a similar process will be carried out with the architect, prior to instigating formal arbitration proceedings.

Clause 67 applies the contract to Scotland, noting that Scottish law is different from English law. The location of the site will determine which law prevails.

Clause 71 allows additional clauses to be written into the form of contract where this is considered to be desirable.

Where the contract is on the basis of fluctuations, an additional clause covering contract price fluctuations is added. This follows a similar pattern to the appropriate clauses of JCT 80. The Baxter indices are, of course, used where the formula method is applied.

Clause comparision between JCT 80 and ICE conditions of contract

JCT 80		ICE
1. Interpretation, definition	1.	Definitions and interpretation
2. Contractor's obligation	8/9.	Contractor's general responsibilities
	55/56.	Measurement
	57.	Method of measurement
3. Contract sum		
4. Architect's instructions	2.	Engineer and Engineer's representative
	68.	Notices
5. Contract documents	5−7.	Contract documents
	14.	Programme to be furnished
6. Statutory obligations, notices, fees and charges	26.	Giving notices and paying fees
7. Levels and setting out the works	17.	Setting out
8. Materials, goods and workmanship	13.	Work to be to the satisfaction of the engineer
	16.	Removal of contractor's employees
	33.	Clearance of site on completion
	36.	Quality of materials and workmanship and tests
	38.	Examination of work before covering up
	39.	Removal of unsatisfactory work and materials
9. Royalties and patent rights	28.	Patent rights, royalties
10. Person-in-charge	15.	Contractor's superintendence
11. Access for architect to works	37.	Access to site
12. Clerk of works		
13. Variations and provisional sums	51/52.	Alterations, additions and omissions
	58.	Provisional sums

14.	Contract sum		
15.	Value added tax	70.	Value added tax
16.	Materials and goods unfixed or off site	53/54.	Vesting of contractors, equipment, goods and materials
17.	Practical completion and defects liability	48.	Certificate of substantial completion
		49.	Outstanding work and defects
		61.	Defects Correction certificate
18.	Partial possession by employer		
19.	Assignment and subcontracts	3/4.	Assignment and subcontracting
20.	Injury to persons and property and employer's indemnity	19.	Safety and security
		20.	Care of the works
		22.	Damage to persons and property
21.	Insurance against injury to persons and property	23.	Third party insurance
		24.	Accident or injury to workmen
		25.	Evidence and terms of insurance
22.	Insurance of the works against clause 22 perils	21.	Insurance of works
23.	Date of possession, completion and postponement	40.	Suspension of works
		41.	Works commencement date
		42.	Possession of site and access
		43.	Time for completion
		46.	Rate of progress
24.	Damages for non-completion	47.	Liquidated damages
25.	Extension of time	44.	Extension of time for completion
26.	Loss and expense		
27.	Determination by employer	63.	Determination of the contractors employment
28.	Determination by contractor	64.	Frustration
29.	Works by employer or persons employed or engaged by employer	31.	Facilities for other contractors
30.	Certificates and payments	60.	Certificates and payments
31.	Finance — tax deduction scheme		
32.	Outbreak of hostilities		
33.	War damage	65.	War clause
34.	Antiquities	32.	Fossils
35.	Nominated subcontractors	59.	Nominated subcontractors
36.	Nominated suppliers	59.	Nominated subcontractors
37.	Fluctuations	69.	Tax fluctuations

Chapter 26

General conditions of contract for building and civil engineering

Public works projects represent a significant sector of the construction industry. The various types of projects are undertaken by a variety of organizations both locally and centrally. Local authorities still have a preference for JCT 80 for building works and the ICE conditions for civil engineering works. Construction projects administered by central government agencies, however, prefer to use their own forms of contract, i.e., *General Conditions of Contract for Building and Civil Engineering Works*. The forms which are currently in use are:

1. GC/Works/1 — third edition 1989 which is for use on major projects. There are different versions depending upon whether the quantities are firm, subject to remeasurement or without quantities.

2. GC/Works/2 — second edition 1980 which is for use on minor works.

In addition a further form is in use for the measured-term type contracts, which are an important feature of maintenance projects carried out for government establishments within a specified contract period. Central government pioneered this type of contractual arrangement which is now used by other types of client.

The forms are now prepared under the auspices of the Department of the Environment and published by Her Majesty's Stationery Office. The Conditions do not include a form of tender or agreement but these are provided for separately. This latest edition of the Conditions envisages the use of a PM or project manager replacing the term architect on JCT 80 (although on some JCT forms supervising officer may be used) and engineer on the ICE Form. The PM is defined as being the manager and superintendent of the works. If the works have been fully designed (the implication in most of the forms in use!) then there is no necessity for the PM to be restricted to a designer. The appointment to this key position during the construction phase can then be given to the individual who is most suited to such a role. The names of the various parties associated with the project are given in the Abstract of Particulars.

The clauses are numbered consecutively from 1 to 65 and are grouped together under eight major sections. Conditions, such as a variation of price condition, may be added to supplement the printed General Conditions according to circumstances. They are incorporated into the Contract Conditions by listing in the Abstract of Particulars which is included with the invitation to tender. The clauses, known as conditions, under this form of contract, contain the usual amalgam of items that are to be found in the other forms. It is generally accepted that they are, however, more legally precise than the other forms and that they include more matters of a procedural nature. Some of the conditions are similar in their effect to JCT clauses, e.g., setting out, patents, antiquities. Other conditions have no parallel in JCT 80. Some of these cover matters more to do with procedures and include, for example, the provision of daily returns by the contractor, passes which are now a standard security measure of all government agencies, racial discrimination, photographs and emergency powers. Some clauses included in JCT 80 have no equivalent in this form, for example, the war damage clause. This matter should it occur is dealt with independently by the government department concerned.

The following is a brief résumé of some of these contract conditions, from GC/Works/1.

Contract, documentation, information and staff

Condition 1 lists a number of definitions which are referred to throughout the form of contract. Many other forms of contract now adopt this approach in order to clarify matters which are relevant to the execution of the project.

Conditions 2 and 3 are concerned with the contract documents and their relationship with each other. The documents are listed in the definitions under 'contract' and include:

- Contract Conditions
- Abstract of Particulars
- specification
- drawings
- bills of quantities
- the tender
- Authority's written acceptance.

In common with the ICE Form both a specification and bills of quantities are contract documents. The conditions of the contract are the most important followed by the specification and then the drawings. The PM can reverse the importance of these last two documents should this be desired. Condition 3 refers to bills of quantities and deals with the method of measurement (which needs to be identified). It also describes how errors and omissions should be dealt with and the use of approximate quantities.

Conditions 4−6 deal with staff matters, and include the delegation and representation of the Authority's powers, the requirement of the contractor to keep a competent agent on site to supervise the execution of the works, and the removal from site of anyone whom the PM thinks is undesirable. On this last matter, there is little scope for negotiation since the PM's view is final and conclusive.

General obligations

Condition 7 requires the contractor to have satisfied himself fully on the following points regarding the site:

(a) communications and access to it;
(b) its contours and boundaries;
(c) the risks associated with adjacent property and its occupiers;
(d) the ground conditions;
(e) conditions under which the work will be executed and the precautions necessary to prevent nuisance and pollution;
(f) availability of labour;
(g) availability of goods, materials, etc.;
(h) any other factors which will influence the execution of the works or the tender price.

No claim for additional payments will be allowed if the contractor misunderstands or misinterprets any of the above. If, however the contractor encounters unforeseeable ground conditions during the execution of the works the PM may agree to the contract sum being increased or decreased accordingly.

Condition 8 covers matters of insurance and specifically:

(a) employers' liability insurance;
(b) insurance against loss or damage;
(c) insurance against personal injury and loss or damage to property.

Condition 9 outlines the various responsibilities in respect of setting out. The PM provides the information for setting out the works. It is the contractor's responsibility to do the setting out including providing all the necessary instruments, profiles, templates, etc.

Condition 10 allows for some of the design to be done by the contractor or subcontractor should this be required. The contractor's liability in this respect is the same as if the design work had been provided by an architect.

Conditions 11–12 describe the need to comply with statutory provisions and pay the charges involved and to make the necessary payments for royalties or patent rights.

Conditions 13–14 require the contractor to protect the works and goods and material on site from damage, and to protect his workmen and the public from any danger. The conditions also require the contractor to prevent nuisances and inconvenience to anyone from occurring.

Conditions 15–17 require the contractor to inform the PM of the number and type of workmen employed on the site each day, that the excavations are ready to receive the foundations and that work which should be inspected by the PM is ready for being covered up with earth or other materials.

Conditions 18 and 25 cover the joint meeting of the quantity surveyor and the contractor's representative to agree measurements on site, and the keeping of contract records which may be needed by the quantity surveyor for the preparation of the final account. In the absence of the contractor's representative then the quantity surveyor can proceed to take measurements and to use these as if they had been agreed.

Condition 19 is concerned with loss and damage to:

(a) property;
(b) personal injury to, or sickness or death of, any person;
(c) the works including materials on site;
(d) loss of profits or loss suffered because of any loss or damage.

The contractor must take steps at his own expense to reinstate, replace or make good to the satisfaction of the Authority any loss or damage to the works. If this also results in a claim against the Authority by third persons, then the contractor has to refund the Authority for any costs or expense that may be incurred. The contractor is able to be reimbursed if the loss or damage was the fault of the Authority, due to unforeseen ground conditions, an accepted risk or circumstances outside the control of the contractor.

Conditions 20, 22 and 23 are conditions not found in other forms of contract. Condition 20 outlines the contractor's position in respect of the loss, destruction, disclosure and access to 'personal data' as defined in the Data Protection Act 1984.

Condition 22 deals with contractors working within the boundaries of existing government premises and Condition 23 covers the scope of the Race Relations Act 1976.

Condition 21 deals with the making good of defects during the maintenance period, the contractor's responsibility to do these at his own expense and in the case of his default, the recovering of costs by the Authority.

Condition 24 deals with corruption and the receiving of gifts, considerations, inducements or rewards for doing nothing or for showing favour. The Authority need be only reasonably satisfied that a breach has occurred, rather than needing to rely on the provisions of the Prevention of Corruption Acts 1889–1916 in order to determine the contractor's employment.

Security

Conditions 26–29 cover matters of a government-security nature, which are naturally not to be found in the other forms of contract. These include unauthorized admittance to the site, the need for passes in some site locations, limitations on photographs of the site and a general awareness of the Official Secrets Act 1911 to 1939.

Materials and workmanship

Condition 30 deals with the vesting of 'things' which have been defined in Condition 1 of the Form of Contract. '*Things*' has two different meanings:

- 'Things for incorporation' means goods and materials intended to form part of the completed work.
- 'Things not for incorporation' means good or materials provided or used to facilitate execution of the works but not for incorporation in them.

The contractor is responsible for the protection, preservation, and replacement of things that are lost, stolen, damaged, destroyed or unfit or unsuitable for their intended purpose. Nothing shall be removed from the site without the written consent of the PM.

Condition 31 is the main condition which deals with quality. It states that the contractor shall execute the works:

(a) with diligence;

(b) in accordance with the programme;
(c) with all proper skill and care;
(d) in a workmanlike manner.

The contractor must use the necessary skill and care to ensure that the works and anything that is due for incorporation conforms to the requirements of the specification, bills of quantities and drawings. The PM has the power at any time to inspect, examine or test on site at a factory or in a workshop. The PM can arrange for an independent expert to do the testing in order to ensure that there is conformity with the contract requirements. In the event of a failure then the contractor has to bear the costs of the test and any retesting that may ensue.

Condition 32 refers to excavations, which in this context means antiquities such as fossils and other items of interest or value found on the site. Such findings remain the property of the employer.

Commencement, programme, delays and completion

Conditions 33 and 35 deal with the programme and progress of the works. The contractor must submit a programme to show the sequence of operations, details of temporary work, method of working, labour and plant requirements and the critical events which might influence the progress and completion of the works. Progress meetings are normally held once a month where the contractor is required to provide a written report showing any or all of the following:

(a) the relationship between progress of the works and the contract programme;
(b) information required by the contractor;
(c) delays and possible delays;
(d) requests for an extension of time;
(e) proposals to bring the project back on schedule.

The PM then within seven days of this meeting must provide a written statement in response to these points.

Conditions 34 and 36−38 describe commencement, completion, extensions of time, early possession and acceleration. The Authority will notify the contractor of when possession can be effected and completion is then calculated from this time in accordance with the contract. Condition 36 identifies the reasons for granting an extension of time to the contractor. This is only done after first receiving a request for such from the contractor. Early possession of the project is covered in Condition 37 and referred to as a completed part, where a section or a part of the works is completed to the PM's satisfaction and the Authority wishes to take possession. This has the effect of starting the maintenance period for that part of the works, restricting any further liquidated damages and releasing part of the reserve, i.e., one-half of the retention money which is held on that part of the project. Condition 38 allows for achieving an accelerated completion date. If this is required then the contractor is asked to price specified proposals and indicate how early completion might be achieved.

Condition 39 covers matters relating to the issue of certificates at completion and at the end of the maintenance period.

Instructions and payments

Condition 40 lists the procedures dealing with the PM's instructions. The provisions allow for the issue of further drawings, details, instructions, directions and explanations. Instructions must be in writing or confirmed in writing within seven days. Instructions which alter, add, omit or change the design, quality or quantity of works are known as variation instructions (VI). Instructions may be given in respect of the following:

(a) the variation/modification of the specification drawings, bills of quantities, or the design, quality or quantity of works;
(b) discrepancy between specification, drawings and bills of quantities;
(c) removal from site of any things for incorporation and their substitution with any other things;
(d) removal/re-execution of work;
(e) order of execution of the works;
(f) hours of work and overtime;
(g) suspension of the works;
(h) replacement of any person employed in connection with the contract;
(i) opening up for inspection;
(j) making good of defects;
(k) execution of emergency work;
(l) use/disposal of materials from the excavations;
(m) action to be followed on the discovery of fossils, etc.;
(n) measures to avoid nuisance/pollution;
(o) any other matter which the PM considers is expedient.

Conditions 41−43 cover matters dealing with the valuation of work. The valuation of a VI can be determined in one of two ways:

(a) the acceptance by the PM of a lump-sum quotation;
(b) valuation by the QS using the following principles:
    (i) use of bill rates;
    (ii) use of rates which are pro-rata to rates in the bills;
    (iii) fair valuation or agreement;
    (iv) daywork rates;
    (v) adjustment to these rates for any disruption.

If circumstances arise where as a result of an instruction, not being a VI, the contractor properly incurs expense beyond that provided for, or makes a saving in the cost of executing the works then such costs can also be adjusted.

Condition 44 covers labour tax, i.e., any tax, levy or contribution which by law has to be paid by the contractor. If these vary during the course of the contract then the appropriate sum is added to or deducted from the contract sum.

Condition 45 consists of the usual conditions describing VAT.

Condition 46 covers prolongation and disruption to the works and the associated costs which might be involved.

Condition 47 deals with the honouring of payments due to the contractor. If the Authority withholds payments then the contractor is allowed to add finance charges to those amounts at a rate of 1 per cent above the Bank of England's lending rate.

Condition 48 deals with interim monthly payments as follows:

(a) 95 per cent of the relevant amount from a stage payment chart assuming that the project is on schedule. The remaining 5 per cent is defined as a reserve;
(b) 100 per cent of variations;
(c) 100 per cent of prolongation and disruption;
(d) 100 per cent of finance charges.

Condition 49 covers the preparation of the final account. Upon completion of the works half of the reserve fund is paid to the contractor. The final account should normally be prepared within six months from this date, and any difference between this and the amount paid at completion will be paid to the contractor as soon as possible. The remainder of the reserve fund is paid at the end of the maintenance period.

Conditions 50−52 cover the issue of certificates by the PM and the ability to be able to recover sums owing by the contractor against these certificates, even from other projects. Condition 52 deals with suggestions which the contractor may have for effecting cost savings either of the works or in the costs of its future maintenance of the project.

Particular powers and remedies

Condition 53. If the main contractor fails within a reasonable period of time to comply with an instruction then the contract may be terminated.

Condition 54 provides for emergency work to be undertaken as required by the PM.

Condition 55 outlines the procedures to be adopted in the case of a delay in completing the works and the application of liquidated damages. These are included in the Abstract of Particulars, and the appropriate amounts may be deducted from advances paid under interim certificates.

Conditions 56−58 cover determination by the Authority (there is no comparable provision for determination by the contractor) and the procedures to be followed in terms of contract completion and financial arrangements. There are circumstances, however, where the contractor may suffer unavoidable loss due to the determination and the contract makes provision for reimbursement where this is thought to be reasonable.

Conditions 59 and 60 describe the procedures to be followed in response to disputes arising between the parties. Initially matters are referred to the adjudicator who has been named in the Abstract of Particulars. If the matter cannot be satisfactorily resolved at this stage then the dispute can be referred to arbitration.

Assignment, sub-letting, subcontracting, suppliers and others

Conditions 61—65. This range of conditions deals with those employed on the site other than the main contractor. Condition 61 forbids assigning the contract without authority. Condition 62 covers sub-letting and the need to obtain authority to do so and to ensure that the main contract conditions are fully covered in each subcontract. Condition 63 describes the procedure to be used in the case of nominated suppliers and subcontractors. These include the usual provisions of the Authority paying for the work direct and the reasonable objection that a main contractor may have in entering a contract with a particular firm. The conditions make no references to either any main contractor's attendance or to cash discounts. Condition 64 refers to provisional sums, the need for instructions from the PM prior to their execution and their subsequent valuation under condition 42. Condition 65 gives the Authority powers to execute other work on site at the same time that the works are being executed.

Chapter 27

Building with contractor's design

Anyone wishing to have a building constructed has the choice of either commissioning an architect to produce the design, or approaching a building contractor to carry out the design work in addition to the normal construction work. The latter refers to a design-and-build project, and the use of the *Standard Form of Building Contract with Contractor's Design*, 1981 edition, in preference to the usual JCT 80 *Standard Form of Building Contract*. The above form superseded the NFBTE *Design and Building Form of Contract*, which had been in use since 1970. The contractor's duties under these forms are wider than usual, since he has to take responsibility for a much wider service.

The JCT form with contractor's design is based upon JCT 80, but incorporates significant differences due to the nature of the work envisaged. There are 38 clauses in this form compared with 41 in JCT 80. Some of the clauses are a direct reproduction of JCT 80, whereas others incorporate minor amendments or a completely new clause. All references to 'the architect' have been deleted, and these now become 'the employer'. There is no specific provision for a clerk of works, although such a person may well come within the definition of one of the employer's agents. The intention is, however, broadly the same. The following are some of the significant differences from the standard form.

Articles of agreement

The employer in the first recital in lieu of supplying the contractor with drawings and bills of quantities has issued him with his requirements. These requirements will broadly be the same as the information that would have been provided to the architect. In the second recital the contractor's proposals are identified. These include details of the contract sum analysis that will be required for the execution of these proposals. The third recital states that the employer has accepted these proposals and the contract sum analysis and that he is satisfied that they meet his requirements. The employer's requirements, contractor's proposals and the contract sum analysis are described in detail in appendix 3 to the conditions. Article 3 names the employer's agent. Since there is no independent designer or supervisor for the works envisaged, provision is made for someone to act on behalf of the employer. His duties may include:

(a) receiving or issuing applications, consents, instructions, notices, requests or statements;
(b) acting on behalf of the employer.

The conditions

Clause 2

Clause 2 includes the provisions of the counterpart clause of the standard form, but in addition covers matters appropriate to the contractor's design and his liability for it. The contractor in clause 2.1 shall carry out and complete the works, including the selection of any specifications of materials and workmanship in order to meet the employer's requirements. Clause 2.5 indicates that the contractor must carry out the design work in an equal manner to that of an independent architect or professional designer. The contractor's responsibility to the employer for any inadequacy of the design work includes the exclusion of defects or any insufficiency in the design work. Where the work includes the design and construction of dwellings, reference is made to the liability under the Defective Premises Act 1972. If the Act does not apply, the contractor's design liability for loss of use or profit or consequential loss is limited to the amount, if any, set out in appendix 1. The contractor's design under this clause includes that which may have been prepared by others on behalf of the contractor.

Clause 4

The contractor must comply with all instructions issued to him by the employer, as long as the employer has the contractual power to issue such an instruction. Variations are referred to as change instructions in clause 12, and where the contractor makes a reasonable objection in writing to a change instruction he does not need to comply with it. The provisions relating to employer's instructions generally are similar to those dealing with architect's instructions under the standard form.

Clause 5

This clause requires that both the employer's requirements and the contractor's proposals are to remain in the custody of the employer. The contractor is to be allowed access to them at all reasonable times. When the contract has been signed by the parties the employer will provide the contractor, free of charge, with:

(a) a copy of the certified articles of agreement, conditions and appendices;
(b) a copy of the employer's requirements;
(c) a copy of the contractor's proposals which includes the contract sum analysis.

The contractor must then provide the employer with two copies of the drawings, specifications, details, levels and setting out dimensions which he proposes to use on the works. All this information largely represents the equivalent of the contract documents of the standard form, but is not described as such in this form. A copy of all the above information is to be kept on site and available to the employer's agent at all reasonable times.
Prior to the commencement of the defects liability period the employer is to be provided with copies of the 'as built' drawings and other relevant information. This information may include details of the maintenance and operation of the the works, including any installations comprised in the works. The information provided by either party is for the use of this contract only. It would appear, therefore, that copyright of the documents is vested in the party who actually prepared them.

Clause 7

The employer is required to define the boundaries of the site, and this information is to be written into the conditions of contract at this point.

Clause 12

Variations are referred to as changes in the employer's requirements. The alteration in wording from the standard form may lead one to suspect that changes are intended to be of a minor nature only. The employer's requirements in the first instance being comprehensive and complete. A change in the contractor's proposals is not envisaged, but where the contractor considers these to be necessary he will need to obtain the employer's permission and possibly incur any extra cost where this occurs. In other respects this clause is very similar to clause 13 of the standard form which deals with variations and provisional sums.

Clause 16

Upon practical completion of the works, the contractor will receive a written statement from the employer to that effect. The defects liability will operate from that date, and the employer must provide the contractor with a schedule of defects within 14 days. Practical completion marks the end of the contract, and no further new instructions from the employer are permissible. A notice of completion of making good defects is issued when the work has been properly rectified.

Clause 26

Clause 26.2 includes the normal grounds for claiming loss and expense. In addition, it also includes the provision for dealing with a delay in receipt of any permission or approval for the purposes of development control requirements necessary for the works to proceed. The contractor must have taken all practicable steps to avoid or reduce this delay. This can also give rise to an extension of time under clause 25.4.7 as a relevant event. It is also considered to be an important factor that could result in the determination by the contractor under clause 28.1.2.8.

Clause 27

The employer may terminate the employment of the contractor for one of the reasons suggested under clause 27.1. In the event of this occurring, the contractor must provide the employer with two copies of all the current drawings, details, schedules, etc., in order that he may engage another contractor to complete the works. A similar condition will still apply where the contractor has terminated the contract for one of the reasons listed in clause 28.1.

Clause 30

The processes to be used for interim payments follow those of normal practice. Two alternatives are, however, specifically suggested, and these are described in appendix 2. Alternative A is on a stage payment basis. The stages are predetermined and the appropriate amounts set against them, the total of which adds up to the contract sum. Any adjustments to the employer's requirements or for fluctuations and claims must be properly documented. Alternative B describes the periodic payment basis which is the more usual method used with the standard form. Payment on this basis must be supported by the appropriate information. The other matters of retention, and when the payments are due to be paid by the employer, are in accordance with the standard form.

The final account must be presented to the employer within three months of practical completion of the works (clause 30.5.1). The employer must then agree to this within a maximum period of four months from the time of submission. Thereafter the account is conclusive evidence of the amount due. It is also conclusive evidence that the employer is fully satisfied that the project is in accordance with the terms of the contract and the employer's requirements.

Generally

The role of the building contractor in the design of any project is valid. Criticism has often been levelled at the absence of any contractor input, and the fragmentation of the design and construction process. There is no doubt, therefore, that this method of contracting plays a very vital role and function within the industry today. It does not include all the advantages over the more traditional methods, since if it did, these methods would now be moving nearer towards extinction. The more one can involve the contractor in both the constructional detailing and method, the more satisfactory buildings are likely to be. An employer, however, considering embarking upon this contractual option for a proposed project, is well advised to retain in some form his professional advisors of architect and quantity surveyor. The normal building employer is unlikely to be familiar with building contracts or the processes involved. An independent advisor is therefore likely to be able to offer both constructive comments on the contractor's proposals, and also assistance during the building's erection.

The JCT have produced a number of amendments (five up to 1989) to coincide generally with revisions to JCT 80. There are also three practice notes which are now available.

Part 7

Arbitration

Chapter 28

Arbitration

Arbitration is an alternative to legal action in the courts, in order to settle an unresolved dispute. No one is compelled to submit a dispute to arbitration unless he has agreed to do so within the terms of his contract. Once he has agreed to this method of settling his disagreement he cannot then take legal proceedings. If he attempts to do so the courts will stay such proceedings. All of the standard forms of contract used in the construction industry include an arbitration provision. It is, therefore, the procedure that is most commonly used for dealing with disputes that arise between the various parties concerned.

The arbitration agreement in the *JCT Standard Form of Building Contract* 1980 is covered in article 5 of the articles of agreement. The parties, under article 5.2 agree that proceedings will not take place until after practical completion has been achieved, or unless the contractor's termination of the contract has been made or if the project is abandoned. There are exceptions, however, to these rules where matters can be taken to arbitration during the progress of the works. Of course, where the two parties otherwise agree the guidelines can be amended as required. The following matters can therefore be dealt with prior to the issue of the certificate of practical completion:

Article 3	Contractor's objection to the appointment following the death of the architect
Article 4	Contractor's objection to the appointment following the death of the quantity surveyor
Clause 4	Dispute over the power to issue an instruction
Clause 3C	A certificate being improperly withheld or not being in accordance with the conditions

Clause 25   Dispute over the difference of an extension of time
Clauses 32/33 Disputes concerning outbreak of hostilities or war
             damage

The arbitrator's powers are very wide. He may review and revise certificates and valuations. He may also disregard opinions, decisions or notices that have already been given.

The essential features of a valid arbitration agreement are as follows:

1. The parties must be capable of entering into a legally binding contract.
2. The agreement should whenever possible be in writing.
3. It must be signed by the parties concerned.
4. It must state clearly those matters which will be submitted to arbitration, and when the proceedings will be initiated.
5. It must not contain anything that is illegal.

Arbitration Act 1979

This Act came into force on 4 April 1979, and extended the previous Act of 1950. The Act introduced a revised procedure of appeals, and reinforced the power of the arbitrator to proceed *ex parte* in some cases by adding the authority of the High Court. The Act consists of a number of provisions, some of which will apply to all arbitrations, and others to arbitrations provided by the parties in their agreement. The majority of arbitration agreements adopted by the construction industry accept the Act in its entirety.

Advantages of arbitration

1. Arbitration is generally less expensive than court proceedings.
2. Arbitration is a more speedy process than an action at law. A year awaiting a case to come before the courts is not uncommon.
3. Arbitration hearings are usually held in private. This, therefore, avoids any bad publicity that might be associated with a case in the courts.
4. The time and place of the hearing can be arranged to suit the parties concerned. Court proceedings take their place in turn among the other cases and at law courts concerned.
5. The arbitrator is selected for this expert technical knowledge in the matter of dispute. Judges do not generally have such knowledge.
6. In cases of dispute which involve a building site or property, it can be insisted that the arbitrator visit the site concerned. Although a

judge may decide upon a visit, this cannot be enforced by the parties concerned.

Disadvantage of arbitration

1. The courts will generally always be able to offer a sound opinion on a point of law. The arbitrator may, of course, seek the opinion of the courts, but this could easily be overlooked in which case a mistake could occur.
2. An arbitrator does not have the power to bring into an arbitration a third party against his wishes. The courts are always able to do this.

Terminology

The following terminology is associated with arbitrations.

Arbitrator — The person to whom the dispute is referred for settlement. He is often appointed by, for example, the President of the RIBA, CIArb or RICS. In practice he may be selected because of his expert technical knowledge regarding the subject matter in dispute.

Umpire — It may occasionally be preferable to appoint two arbitrators. In this event a third arbitrator, known as an umpire, is appointed to settle any dispute to which the two arbitrators cannot agree.

Reference — The actual hearing of the dispute by the arbitrator.

Award — The decision on the matter concerned made by the arbitrator.

Respondent — This is the equivalent of the defendant in a law court.

Claimant — The equivalent of the plaintiff.

Expert witness — This is a special type of witness who plays an important part in arbitrations. An ordinary witness must confine his evidence strictly to the statement of facts. The expert witness may, however, forward his opinion based upon his technical knowledge and practical experience. Prior to presenting his evidence, he must show by his experience and academic and professional qualifications that he can be recognized as an expert in the subject matter.

Appointment of the arbitrator

An arbitrator or umpire should be a disinterested person, who is quite independent from the parties that will be involved in the proceedings. The person appointed should, however, be someone who is sufficiently qualified and experienced in the matter of the dispute. It is, however, for the parties concerned to choose the arbitrator, and the courts will not generally interfere even where the person appointed is not really the most appropriate person to settle the dispute.

An arbitrator may, however, be disqualified if it can be shown that:

(a) he has a direct interest in the subject matter of the dispute (for example, where the decision may have direct repercussions on his own professional work);
(b) he may fail to do justice to the arbitration by showing a bias towards one of the parties concerned (for example, it could be argued that an architect might show favour to an employer since he is normally employed on this 'side' of the industry).

Each of the parties to the arbitration agreement must be satisfied that the arbitrator who is appointed will give an impartial judgment on the matter of the dispute. The remarks expressed by the arbitrator during the conduct of the case will probably show whether he favours one of the parties in preference to the other. This may lead to removal by the courts of the arbitrator on the grounds of misconduct.

Once the arbitrator has been appointed he will need to establish for himself the general matters relating to the dispute. He will also need to determine:

(a) the facilities available for inspecting the works;
(b) whether the parties will be represented by counsel;
(c) the matters the parties already agree upon;
(d) the time and place of the proposed hearing.

Outline of the procedure

The pleadings

These are the formal documents which may be prepared by counsel or solicitor. The arbitrator will first require the claimant to set out the basis of his case. These will be included in his document, termed the 'point of claim', which he then serves upon the respondent. The respondent then submits his reply in answer to the points of claim in his document, termed the 'points of defence'. The respondent may also submit his own points of counterclaim, which he will serve on the claimant at the same time. This may raise relevant matters that were not referred to in the points of claim. The claimant, in reply to the matters raised in the counterclaim, will submit his points of reply and defence to counterclaim.

The purpose of the above documents is very important, since they will make clear to the arbitrator the matters which are in dispute. Furthermore, the parties involved cannot stray beyond the scope of the pleadings without leave from the arbitrator.

Discovery

Once the pleadings have been completed, the precise issues which the arbitrator is to decide will be very clear. Every fact to be relied upon must be pleaded, but the manner in which it is to be proved need not be disclosed until the reference. 'Discovery' means the disclosure of all documents which are in the control of each party and which are in any way relevant to the issues of arbitration. Each party must allow the other to inspect and to take copies of all or any of the documents in his list, unless he can argue on the grounds that it is privileged. The most important of these types of documents are the communications between a party and his solicitors for the purpose of obtaining legal advice. A party who refuses to allow inspection may be ordered to do so by the arbitrator.

In fixing the date and place of the hearing the arbitrator has the sole discretion, subject to anything laid down in the arbitration agreement. He must, however, be seen to act in a reasonable manner. A refusal to attend the hearing by either party, after reasonable notice has been given, may empower the arbitrator to proceed without that party, i.e. *ex parte*.

The hearing

The procedure of the hearing follows the rules of evidence used in a normal court of law. The parties may or may not be represented by counsel or other representatives.

The claimant sets out his case, and calls each of the witnesses in turn. Once they have given their evidence they are cross-examined by the respondent (or his counsel/representative where appropriate). The claimant is then allowed to ask his witnesses further questions on matters which have been raised by the cross-examination.

A similar procedure is then adopted by the respondent who opens his case, and sets out the details of his counterclaim if this is necessary. He examines his own witnesses and these in turn are cross-examined by the claimant. The claimant then replies to the respondent's defence and counterclaim, and presents his own defence to the counterclaim. When this has been completed the respondent sums up his case in an address to the arbitrator known as his closing speech. The claimant then has the right of reply or the last word in the case.

The trial is now ended and both parties await the publication of the award. The arbitrator may now decide to inspect the works, if he has not already done so, or re-examine certain parts of the project in more detail. The arbitrator will usually make his decision in private, and will set the decision out in his award. This is served on the parties after the appropriate charges have been met. It is enforceable in much the same way as a judgment debt, where the successful party can reclaim such costs as the arbitrator has awarded.

Evidence

To enable the arbitrator to carry out justice between the parties, he must carefully consider the evidence which is submitted in turn by the claimant and the respondent. Evidence is the means by which the facts are proved. There are rules of evidence which the arbitrator must ensure are observed. These have been designed to determine four main problems.

1. Who is to assume the burden of proving facts? Generally speaking the person who sets forth a statement has the burden of determining its proof. The maxim, 'innocent until proved guilty' is appropriate in this context.

2. What facts must be proved? A party must give proof of all material facts upon which he relies to establish his case, although there can be exceptions to this rule. For example, the parties may agree on formal 'admissions' in order to dispense with the necessity of proving facts which are not in dispute.

3. What facts will be excluded from the cognizance of the court? In order to prevent a waste of time or to prevent certain facts from being put before juries, which might tend to lead them to unwarranted conclusions, English law permits proof of facts which are in issue and of facts which are relevant to the issue.

4. How proof is to be effected? The law recognizes three kinds of proof:
   (a) oral proof, which are statements made verbally by a witness in the witness box;
   (b) documentary proof, which is contained in the documents that are available;
   (c) real proof, which could include models or a visit to the site in order to view the subject matter.

It is usual in arbitration for the evidence to be given on oath. The giving of false evidence is perjury and is punishable accordingly by fine or imprisonment. The arbitrator has himself no right to call a witness, except with the consent of both parties. A witness will, however, usually answer favourably to the party by whom he is called, in order to further that party's case. He must not in general be asked leading questions which attempt to put the answer in the mouth of the witness. For example, 'Did you notice that the scaffold was inadequately fixed?' is a leading question. It must be rephrased: 'Did you notice anything about the scaffolding?' Leading questions can, however, be used to the opposing party's witnesses. The arbitrator must also never receive evidence from one party without the knowledge of the other. Where he receives, for example, communications from one party he must immediately inform the other.

An arbitrator must always refuse to admit evidence on the grounds that:

(a) the witness is incompetent, e.g., refuses to take the oath, too young, a lunatic;

(b) the evidence is irrelevant, e.g., evidence which has not real bearing upon the facts in the opinion of the arbitrator;

(c) the evidence is inadmissible, e.g., hearsay evidence since it is not made under oath and is not capable of cross-examination. (There are, however, exceptions to this rule such as statements made on behalf of one party against their own interests.)

Where documents are used as evidence it is the arbitrator's responsibility to ensure their authenticity. Where one party produces a document, this must be proved unless the other side accepts it as valid. Documents under seal must be stamped, and generally the original document must be produced wherever possible.

Stating a case

A question of law may arise during the proceedings, and the arbitrator may deal with this in one of three ways:

1. He may decide the matter himself.
2. He may consult counsel or a solicitor.
3. He may state a case to the courts.

Where he decides to take the latter course of action, he is required to prepare a statement outlining clearly all the facts in order that the courts may decide a point of law. Once the court has given its decision, the arbitration proceedings can continue. The arbitrator must then proceed in accordance with the court's decision. Failure to do so results in misconduct on the part of the arbitrator. The arbitrator may voluntarily take this course of action or be required to do so by one of the parties.

The arbitrator may also state a case to the courts upon the completion of the arbitration. In this case his award will be based upon the alternative findings to be resolved by the courts. The decision that the courts reach will depend upon which alternative is to be followed. For example, the arbitrator may state that a particular sum should be paid by one of the parties to the other if the courts approve the arbitrator's view of the law. Where the courts do not confirm this opinion, the arbitrator will have also indicated the course of action to be taken.

The award

The arbitrator's award is the equivalent of the judgment of the courts. The award must be made within the terms of reference, otherwise it will be invalid and therefore unenforceable. The essentials of a valid award can be summarized as follows:

1. It must be made within the prescribed time limit that has been set by the parties.
2. It should comply with any special agreements regarding its form or

method of publication that has been laid down in the arbitration agreement.

3. It must be legal and capable of enforcement at law.
4. It must cover all the matters which were referred to the proceedings.
5. It must be final in that it settles all the disputes which were referred under the arbitration.
6. It must be consistent and not contradictory or ambiguous. Its meaning must be clear.
7. It must be confined solely to the matters in question, and not matters which are outside the scope of dispute.
8. The award should generally be in writing, in order to overcome any problems of enforcing it in practice.

Publication of the award

The usual practice is for the arbitrator to notify both the parties that the award is ready for collection upon the payment of the appropriate fees to the arbitrator. If the successful party pays the fees then he is able to sue the other party for that amount, assuming that the costs follow the event. If the award is defective or bad, or it can be shown that there have been irregularities in the proceedings, application may be made to the courts to have it referred back for reconsideration or set aside altogether.

Referring back the award

The grounds on which the court are likely to refer back an award are:

(a) where the arbitrator makes a mistake so that it does not express his true intentions;
(b) where it can be shown that the arbitrator has misconducted the proceedings, for example, in hearing the evidence of one of the parties in the absence of the other;
(c) where new evidence, which was not known at the time of the hearing, comes to light and as such will affect the arbitrator's award.

The application to refer back an award should be made within six weeks after the award has been published. The courts have the full discretion regarding the costs of an abortive arbitration. There is, of course, the right of appeal against the court's decision. The arbitrator's duty in dealing with the referral will depend largely upon the order of the court. He will not, as a rule, hear fresh evidence unless new evidence has come to light. The amended award should normally be made within three months of the date of the court's order.

Setting aside the award

When the courts set aside an award it becomes null and void. The situations where the courts will do this — similar to those for referring back an award, but much more serious — are:

(a) where the award is void, for example, if the arbitrator directs an illegal action;
(b) the discovery of evidence that was not available at the time the arbitration proceedings were held;
(c) where the arbitrator has made an error on some point of law;
(d) misconduct on the part of the arbitrator by permitting irregularities in the proceedings;
(e) where the award has been obtained improperly, for example, through fraud or bribery;
(f) where the essentials of a valid award are lacking, for example, the award is inconsistent or impossible of performance.

Misconduct by the arbitrator

The arbitrator, in carrying out his duties, must do so in a professional manner. Where he is guilty of misconduct, the award can be referred back to him by the courts, and in a serious case the effects of setting aside an award are to make it null and void. Misconduct may be classified as 'actual' or 'technical'.

Actual misconduct would occur where the arbitrator has been inspired in his decision by some corrupt or improper motive or has shown bias to one of the parties involved.

Technical misconduct is when some irregularities in the proceedings occur, and may include:

(a) the hearing of evidence of one party in the absence of the other;
(b) the examination of witnesses in the absence of both parties;
(c) the refusal to state a case when requested to do so by one of the parties;
(d) exceeding his jurisdiction beyond the terms of the reference;
(e) failing to give adequate notice of the time of the proceedings;
(f) delegating his authority;
(g) an error of law.

Although an arbitrator may be removed because of misconduct, this will not terminate the arbitration proceedings in favour of, say, litigation. The courts, on the application of any party to the arbitration agreement, may appoint another person to act as arbitrator. The courts may also remove an arbitrator who has failed to commence the proceedings within a reasonable time or has delayed the publishing of his award.

If the arbitrator dies during the proceedings, the arbitration will not be revoked. The parties must agree upon his successor.

The parties may at any time, by mutual agreement, decide to terminate the arbitrator's appointment. Where he has commenced his duties he will, however, be entitled to some remuneration.

Costs

An important part of the arbitrator's award will be his directions
regarding the payment of costs. These costs, which include the
arbitrator's fees, can sometimes exceed the sum which is involved in the
dispute. The arbitrator must exercise his discretion regarding costs, but
should follow the principles adopted by the courts.

The agreement generally provides for the 'costs to follow the event',
which means that the loser will pay. Where an arbitration involves
several issues, and the claimant succeeds on some but fails on others, the
costs of the arbitration will be apportioned accordingly. If the award fails
to deal with the matter of costs, then any party to the reference may
apply to the arbitrator for an order directing by whom or to whom the
costs shall be paid. This must be done within 14 days of the publication
of the award. A provision in an arbitration agreement that a party shall
bear his own costs or any part of them is void.

The entire costs of the reference, which will include not only the
costs of the hearing but also the costs incurred in respect of preliminary
meetings and matters of preparation, are subject to taxation by the courts.
This involves the investigation of bills of costs with the objective of
reducing excessive amounts and removing improper items. For example,
if a party instructs an expensive counsel which the issues involved did not
justify, then the fees paid will be substantially reduced. If witnesses have
been placed in expensive hotels, then this may be struck from the claim
as an unnecessary expense. Such items are known as 'solicitor and client
charges' and have usually to be borne by the successful party.

JCT arbitration rules

In July 1988 the Joint Contracts Tribunal published a set of abitration
rules for use with all of its various forms of building contracts. The rules
contain stricter time limits than those prescribed by some arbitration rules
or those frequently used in practice, largely in an attempt to avoid
unnecessary costs.

The rules follow much of what has previously been described but
also seek to capitalize on what might be termed good practice. There are
twelve rules and these are as follows:

Rule 1   Arbitration agreements in each of the JCT Forms of Contract.
Rule 2   Interpretation and provisions as to time.
Rule 3   Service of statements, documents and notices — content of
         statements.
Rule 4   Conduct of the arbitration — application of Rule 5, Rule 6 or
         Rule 7.
Rule 5   Procedure without hearing.

Rule 6   Full procedure with hearing.
Rule 7   Short procedure with hearing.
Rule 8   Inspection by arbitrator.
Rule 9   Arbitrator's fees and expenses — costs.
Rule 10   Payment to trustee—stakeholder.
Rule 11   The award.
Rule 12   Powers of arbitrator.

Part 8

Appendices

Appendix A

Cases of interest

Case law relating to building

In some instances where the form of contract is thought to be either lacking or unclear, it is common practice to bring the matter before the courts for learned opinion. This may mean bringing the matter first to arbitration, then to the High Court, the Court of Appeal and finally the House of Lords, where leave to appeal along the way has been granted. The principles upon which these courts base their decisions are stated, and will then in future affect similar cases. This achieves a measure of consistency on matters on which the various parties to a contract may then rely. Where the higher courts reverse the decisions of lower courts, it is the higher opinions that will count in the future. The resulting body of opinion is then established as case law. It is published in the various law reports of the legal journals and, where relevant to the construction industry, in trade and professional journals.

The following cases represent just a sample of some of the disagreements that have reached the courts over a number of years. The complete list would probably form a book in its own right. Some of the cases described have become household names for the student of building contracts; others are perhaps a little less familiar.

Amalgamated Building Contractors v.
Waltham Holy Cross UDC — 1952
A contractor had applied for an extension of time because of labour and material difficulties. The architect acknowledged the request but did not at this time grant an extension to the contract period. Some time after the

completion of the works the architect granted the contractor an extension in retrospect. It was held that this was valid on the grounds that it was a continuing cause of delay. The architect was unable to determine the length of extension until after completion. The parties must therefore have envisaged the retrospective application of the extension clause. The granting of an extension of time after completion would therefore seem to be an explicit possibility.

AMF International Ltd v.
Magnet Bowling Ltd and Another — 1968

Bowling equipment had been installed for Magnet Bowling Ltd by AMF International Ltd. This equipment was damaged after a flood had been caused by exceptionally heavy rain. The bowling centre was only partially completed at this time. AMF therefore claimed £21,000 in damages against Magnet Bowling Ltd and the main contractor. The point at issue in this case was whether the indemnity clause included in the contract would protect the employer and enable him to claim successfully against the contractor. Held:

1. The employer was liable in tort due to his negligence in failing to check that the site had been made safe for AMF.
2. The contractor was liable under the Occupiers Liability Act for failing to take reasonable care.

The damages were apportioned on a 60/40 basis between the main contractor and the employer.
The question of whether the employer could recover from the contractor then arose. Held:

1. The employer, because he had been found guilty of negligence, could not therefore claim under the indemnity clause. This is based upon a legal principle that the indemnity clause will not protect negligence on the part of the one who relies upon it.
2. The employer was able to recover on contractual grounds since the contract included a clause requesting the contractor to protect the works from damage by water.

Bacal Construction v.
Northampton Development Corporation — 1975

This was a contract for a housing development. The development corporation had provided borehole data on which the contractor had based his substructure design. During the course of the work tufa was discovered in several area and this required a redesign of the foundation. It was held that there should be an implied term that the ground conditions would accord with the hypotheses upon which the contractor had been instructed to design the foundation. Because the client had provided the borehole data that were now shown to be inaccurate, the differing costs were to be borne by the employer.

Courtney v.
Fairbairn Ltd v.
Tolaini Brothers (Hotels) Ltd and Another — 1975

In 1969 Mr Tolaini, a hotel owner, decided to develop a site in Hertfordshire. He contacted Mr Courtney who was both a property developer and a building contractor. Mr Courtney wrote to Mr Tolaini stating that if he (Mr Courtney) found suitable sponsors for the scheme, he would undertake the building work. Mr Courtney found sponsors who were able to reach a satisfactory financial arrangement with Mr Tolaini. Mr Tolaini then instructed his quantity surveyor to negotiate a building contract for the project based upon cost plus 5 per cent. The financial aspects were quickly concluded, but negotiations between the quantity surveyor and the building contractor broke down. Mr Tolaini therefore decided to let the contract to another firm, and was promptly sued for breach of contract by Mr Courtney.

It was held, on appeal, that the exchange of letters did not constitute a contract. Because price was of such fundamental importance to the contract, no contract could be formulated until this was agreed, or there was an agreed method of ascertaining it.

Davies & Co. Shopfitters Ltd v.
William Old — 1969

A nominated subcontractor submitted a tender which was accepted by the architect. In placing the order for the work the main contractor added new terms that had been absent from the earlier documentation. One of those terms stated that no payment would be made to the subcontractor until the main contractor had been paid. In spite of this the nominated subcontractor started work. It was held that the order from the main contractor constituted a counter-offer which had been accepted by the subcontractor prior to starting work.

Davies Contractors Ltd v.
Fareham UDC — 1956

A contractor undertook to build 78 houses in eight months for a fixed price sum. He attached a letter to his tender with the proviso that the price was on the basis of adequate supplies of labour being available. The unexpected shortages of labour on a national scale increased the contract period to 22 months. The letter, however, failed to be incorporated into the contract. The courts held, therefore, that the employer must suffer the delay, but that the contractor must bear the expense.

Dawber Williamson Roofing v.
Humberside County Council — 1979

A main contractor had, with approval, sublet the roofing part of the project to a domestic subcontractor. The slates were delivered to the site and their value included in an interim certificate as materials on site. The certificate was honoured with the sum for these materials being paid to the main contractor. Prior to paying this domestic subcontractor the main contractor went into liquidation. The subcontractor therefore sought permission from the council to remove the slates, but this was refused. The subcontractor sued for the value of the slates on the grounds that they remained his property until fixed. It was held that the title rested with the subcontractor. This resulted in the employer paying twice for these materials.

Dawneys v.
F.G. Minter Ltd and Another — 1971

This case involved certified payments to a nominated subcontractor being withheld by the main contractor as set-off against damages. Lord Denning summed up this case as follows:

> When the main contractor has received sums due to the subcontractor — as certified or contained in the architect's certificate — the main contractor must pay those sums to the subcontractor. He cannot hold them up so as to satisfy his cross claims. Those must be dealt with separately in appropriate proceedings for the purpose. This is in accord with the needs of business. There must be a cash flow in the building trade. It is the very lifeblood of the enterprise. The subcontractor has to expend money on steel work and labour. He is out of pocket. He probably has an overdraft at the bank. He cannot go on unless he is paid for what he does as he does it. The main contractor is in a like position. He has to pay his men and buy his materials. He has to pay the subcontractors. He has to have cash from the employers, otherwise he will not be able to carry on. So, once the architect gives his certificates, they must be honoured all down the line. The employer must pay the main contractor; the main contractor must pay the subcontractor; and so forth. Cross claims must be settled later.

Dodd Properties v.
Canterbury City Council — 1980

Canterbury City Council built a multi-storey car park next to a building owned by Dodd Properties. Piling operations caused damage to the building and Dodd Properties claimed damages for both the cost of necessary repairs and for the loss of business during the carrying out of the repairs. When the case came to court the work had not been done, since they were awaiting the damages to pay for the repairs. Dodd Properties claimed current rates, whereas the council suggested that these should be based upon rates relevant at the time the damage was done. It was held that there had been no failure on the part of Dodd Properties to investigate the loss and their claim was therefore upheld.

Dutton v.
Bognor Regis UDC — 1971

The foundations of a house were built upon land that had been used as a refuse disposal tip. The foundations were passed and approved by the local authority building inspector. Some time later the plaintiff purchased the house from the original owner, and cracks that began to appear in the wall were discovered to be due to settlement. The builder settled the matter for an agreed sum. The local authority, however, were held to be liable for negligence, since they owed a duty of care and this had not been reasonably given. Lord Denning expressed the view that the cause of action arose when the defective foundations were laid.

East Ham Corporation v.
Bernard Sunley and Sons Ltd — 1965

The corporation claimed damages for defective work in the construction of a school in East Ham. The building contract was in the RIBA form (revision of 1950). The contractor had completed the work and the architect had issued his final certificate three years after practical completion. This final certificate issued by the architect at the end of the job was conclusive evidence of the adequacy of the works. Two years later some cladding panels fell down due to faults in the fixings. The courts had to consider two questions:

1. On the true construction of the contract, was the final certificate issued by the architect conclusive evidence as to the sufficiency of the works subject to the exceptions mentioned in clause 24(f)?
2. Did the words 'reasonable examination' mean that carried out during progress or at the end of the defect's liability period?

It was held by the courts that the final certificate was conclusive evidence that the works had been properly carried out, subject to the provisions of the final certificate clause.

The stone panels fell off as a result of the careless and incompetent fashion in which they had been attached. It was extremely fortunate that no one was killed or injured. Many contractors would have been not only too willing but anxious to remedy such defects. Not these contractors. They had relied on an escape clause in the contract and sought to throw the whole of their defective work onto the council. The Court of Appeal concluded that the contractors escaped liability under the contract provision. However, on leave to appeal to the House of Lords the decision was reversed. The employer was therefore awarded damages based upon the costs at the time of performing it.

English Industrial Estates Corporation v.
George Wimpey and Co. Ltd — 1972

This case was based upon the JCT conditions relevant at the time. In addition, a special condition allowed for the employer's tenant to install machinery and store materials during the construction of the works. The contractor was, however, to be responsible for insuring the works. During the construction period an extensive fire damaged the works with a loss of approximately £250,000. The issue then arose as to whether this loss should be borne by the contractor's insurers or by those of the employer. The contractor claimed that clause 12 of the conditions of contract excluded the possibility of special provisions, particularly where they were in conflict with standard conditions, in this instance clause 16 (clauses 18 and 2 of JCT 80, respectively).

The courts held in favour of the employer, because they were not satisfied that there had been a sufficient taking of possession for clause 16 to apply. It would appear that since, at the outset, both parties envisaged this early occupation by the employer, the insurance risk would remain with the employer.

A.E. Farr Ltd v.
Ministry of Transport — 1965

This was an appeal by A.E. Farr Ltd to the House of Lords which reversed a decision of the Court of Appeal. The case related to the payment of working space on a civil engineering contract using the relevant documents. The method of measurement at the time allowed for separate bill items to be measured for working space which would include their consequent refilling. Although the ICE conditions of contract at the time included a clause, 'The contractor shall be deemed to have satisfied himself before tendering as to the correctness and sufficiency of tender for the works', this could not be extended to include errors made by the client's advisors. The court therefore accepted that separate items should have been measured in accordance with the appropriate method of measurement. All bills of quantities are prepared in accordance with a method of measurement and strict compliance with this should be made, or specific amendments stated where necessary.

Re Fox ex parte Oundle & Thrapston RDC v.
Trustee — 1948

A building contractor became bankrupt and the question the courts had to decide was whether the materials not incorporated into the works, were vested in the contractor's trustee. The basis for this was the reputed ownership clause contained in the Bankruptcy Act. This stated, 'All goods being at the commencement of the bankruptcy in the possession, order or disposition of the bankrupt in his trade or business by consent or permission of the true owner, he is the reputed owner thereof and his ownership passes to the trustee.' It was held that the trustee had no claim to materials on site which had been paid for in interim certificate. He did, however, have a good claim to materials paid for, but retained in the contractor's yard.

Gilbert Ash (Northern) Ltd v.
Modern Engineering (Bristol) Ltd — 1973

This case involved a contractor who had deducted sums due to a nominated subcontractor for set-off, because of a breach of warranty by the subcontractor. The Gilbert Ash form of subcontract had been used, which included a set-off clause. A sentence in this clause allowed for set-off for any breach of the subcontract, however minor, and unrelated to the actual damages actually suffered. This was held to be quite outside any rights which the courts will enforce and declared to be a penalty. Another sentence did, however, allow set-off for *bona-fide* claims of the contractor, and the court held that these sums were capable of being deducted.

M.J. Gleeson (Contractors) Ltd v.
London Borough of Hillingdon — 1970

Gleeson's contracted for the erection of 300 houses and associated buildings based upon drawings and bills of quantities. The bills allowed for the completion of works in various stages, but the appendix to the conditions of contract provided for a single completion date only. It wàs held that liquidated damages could not be deducted until the date for completion shown in the appendix was exceeded. The decision was based upon the wording of the clause: 'Nothing contained in the Contract Bills shall override, modify or affect in any way whatsoever the application or intepretation of that which is contained in these conditions.' The court expressed the view that it would have been an easy matter to add words to that clause, to the effect that it was subject to conditions included in the bills. This, however, is contrary to recommended practice and could lead to confusion and uncertainty.

Gloucester County Council v.
Richardson — 1968

This contract was based upon the 1939 form of contract, which is considerably different to that in use. It illustrates the problems of warranty agreements which the new form seeks to overcome. The main contractor was instructed by the architect to accept a contract from a nominated supplier. This was for the supply of precast concrete columns, on terms and at a price agreed by the employer. After erection, cracks appeared in the units and the question of the contractor's liability arose. It was held that the contractor was not liable since he had been directed to enter into a contract which severely restricted his right of recourse against the supplier in the event of defects. It should be noted that the 1939 form did not give the contractor the right to object to nomination of a supplier or to insist upon indemnity.

Gold v
Patman & Fotheringham Ltd — 1958

This contract contained a provision whereby the contractor sought to indemnify the employer against claims in respect of damage to property arising out of the works. The indemnity only occurred where it could be shown that the contractor had been negligent in carrying out the works. He had furthermore only insured the works in his own name, and not that of the employer since this was not a requirement of the contract. (N.B. The current JCT form of contract requires a joint insurance in the names of the contractor and the employer.) During construction piling operations damaged adjoining property, but no question of negligence arose since he was carrying this out correctly within the terms of the contract. The owners of the adjoining property therefore sued the employer, and he attempted to bring an action against the contractor for failure to safeguard the employer's interest. It was held that the contractor's obligation was only to insure himself and not the employer as well.

Greaves & Co. (Contractors) Ltd v.
Baynham Meikle and Partners — 1976
A firm of consulting engineers were responsible for the design of a warehouse. The two-storey building would be used for the storage of oil drums, and forklift trucks would be used for transporting these around the building. Within a matter of a few weeks cracks occurred in the building. The engineers were sued for the costs of the remedial work that was necessary, on the basis that the design was unsuitable for the purpose intended. It was held by the Court of Appeal that because the engineers knew of the building's proposed use beforehand, they were liable for the costs of the remedial work.

Hadley v.
Baxendale — 1854
The principles for assessing damages resulting from a breach of contract were stated in this case as:

(a) that arising naturally from the breach;
(b) that which may reasonably be supported to have been in the minds of the parties at the time they entered into contract.

Howard Marine v.
Ogden and Sons — 1978
Ogden's, a firm of contractors, were one of the tenderers for the construction of a sewage works for the Northumbrian Water Authority. Surplus excavation material was to be loaded into barges, shipped downstream and dumped at sea. Howard's were a firm who owned barges that were capable of doing this work. A quotation for the hire of the barges specified the volume of material that each barge could carry, and this was 850 cubic metres. On this basis the contractor could establish the number of trips necessary and this effect upon the programme. But one fact was overlooked. Each vessel travelling on water has a safe loading line which depends upon the weight of the material. The amount carried was therefore at the most 850 cubic metres, but because the spoil was clay this in practice turned out to be considerably less. Various telephone conversations took place between Howard's and Ogden's, but misunderstandings occurred. To further complicate matters the payload figure in Lloyd's register was incorrect. This was stated as 1600 tonnes but was in actual fact only 1055 tonnes. Although Ogden's

had prudently based their calculations on a lower figure than that agreed of 850 cubic metres, the barges failed to carry even this volume. Ogden's then refused to pay for any more barges, and Howard's withdrew their transport. Howard's claimed for their outstanding hire, and Ogden's counterclaimed for misrepresentation and damages.

The moral of the story is that when making enquiries it is unsafe to rely upon telephone conversations alone. Such answers may be too casual and of little legal consequence. Either independent advice should be sought or, preferably, the salient facts should be in writing.

The principle of *Hedley Byrne* v. *Heller and Partners* (1964) came up for consideration by the Court of Appeal. This stated: 'When an enquirer consults a businessman in the course of his business and makes it clear to him that he is seeking considered advice and intends to act on it in a particular way, a duty to take care in giving such advice arises and the advisor may be liable in negligence if the advice he gives turns out to be bad. Leave to appeal to the House of Lords has been given.'

IBA v.
EMI and BICC — 1980
EMI were the main contractors for a project for the IBA. BICC were nominated subcontractors for an aerial mast. The mast collapsed because of BICC's failure to consider the effects of asymmetric ice loading on the structs. Although EMI took no part in the design process they had accepted the contractual responsibility for the adequacy of the design. It was stated that one who contracts to design and supply an article for a known purpose, must ensure that it is fit for that purpose.

Owing to the complexity of modern buildings, it is often necessary for the architect to employ specialists. Some of these may be independent consultants or subcontractors. One of the functions of the architect is to co-ordinate the design to ensure that it is compatible with the overall scheme and is reasonably fit for the purpose intended. (See *Moresk Cleaners Ltd* v. *Hicks*, (1966.)

Sir Lindsay Parkinson & Co. Ltd v.
Commissioners for Work — 1949
A construction contract was agreed on the basis that the contract price would be the cost of the works, plus a net profit not exceeding £300,000. The project was typical cost plus contract carried out at this time. Additional works were ordered which extensively increased the size of the project. The court held that the contractor was entitled to a *quantum meruit* payment for this additional work, since this work could not have been envisaged at the start of the project.

London Borough of Newham v.
Taylor Woodrow (Anglian) Ltd — 1980
This infamous case was for a contract for the erection of a 22-storey block of flats, known as Ronan Point. The building was of a prefabricated

326

concrete construction. One morning, gas caused an explosion in a flat on the 18th floor. This resulted in the collapse of the south-east corner. The local authority claimed for the cost of repairing and strengthening a number of similar blocks. The court acquitted the contractor of negligence, largely on the basis that several other local authorities had approved and accepted the design. The court held, however, that the contractor was liable for a breach of contract, on the basis that the flats should have been designed and constructed so that they would be safe and fit for their purpose. In addition, the building contract included a provision that the contractor would be responsible for any faults and repair work at his own expense. This case was again re-opened in 1984 but the final decision on liability has still to be resolved.

London County Council v.
Wilkins (Valuation Officer) — 1956
This case established that the provision of temporary accommodation on site by a contractor was rateable if erected for a sufficient period of time.

London School Board v.
Northcroft — 1889
The quantity surveyor was responsible for measuring buildings up to a value of £12,000. The employers brought an action for negligence resulting from two clerical errors in the quantity surveyor's calculations. This involved overpayments to the builder of £118 and £15, respectively. It was held that the quantity surveyor, who had employed a skilled clerk who had carried out hundreds of intricate calculations correctly, was not liable, since he had done what was reasonably necessary.

Minter v.
Welsh Health Technical Services — 1980
This case was based upon a claim for loss and expense, the equivalent of clause 26, but on the 1963 form. The amounts paid were challenged on the basis that they had not been certified and paid until long after the contractor had incurred the loss. The courts held that direct loss and/or expense were to be read as conferring a right to recover sums on the same principle as common law damages. In essence, therefore, this might include compensation for the loss of the use of capital.

Re Newman ex parte Capper — 1876
This contract included a provision of a large fixed amount of liquidated damages payable by the contractor in the event of any breach occurring. The court held that this was in effect a penalty since it could not relate with all of the varying amounts of loss which might arise. It was not, therefore, enforceable. The courts did, however, fix an appropriate amount that was upheld as being damages sustained.

North West Metropolitan Regional Hospital Board v.
T. A. Bickerton Ltd — 1976

This case placed the responsibility of renomination with the architect
rather than the contractor, after a nominated subcontractor had defaulted.
A nominated subcontractor failed to complete his work due to his
liquidation. The main contractor then requested the architect under the
terms of the contract (1963 edition) to appoint a new firm as a successor
to this nominated subcontractor. Because a new price was required, and
that this was likely to be a higher price, the employer suggested that the
contractor was responsible for completing this work in any way, but to
the approval of the architect. This may result in the contractor doing the
work himself or subletting with approval, but that any extra in cost must
be borne by the main contractor.

The 1963 edition of the form of contract is unclear on this point, but
the case was decided in the contractor's favour. It was the architect's
responsibility, therefore, to renominate in the event of default, and the
employer is therefore obliged to pay the additional cost of the new firm
employed. JCT 80 has clarified this point along the lines of this decision.

Peak Construction Ltd v.
McKinney Foundations Ltd — 1970

This case considered two separate matters concerning a project that
overran its contract period. The first problem was concerned with an
extension of time. McKinney Foundations Ltd were the nominated
subcontractors for piling work. Upon completion of this work defects
were found, but there was a prolonged delay on the part of the employer
in both obtaining an engineer's advice and deciding upon the remedial
work to be carried out. When the project overran the employer levied
liquidated damages on the main contractor. The main contractor then
attempted to recover these from the subcontractor. Furthermore, the
above was not a reasonable cause for granting an extension of time within
the terms of the contract. It was held, however, that because the delay
was due largely to the employer's default, liquidated damages could not
be deducted. This was the case if the extension of time clause did not
make provision for such a delay, or even if there was failure to extend
the time.

The second matter was concerned with the price fluctuation clause.
The court held that this clause continued to operate after the time for
completion was past. This matter has been clarified in JCT 80.

Roberts & Co. Ltd v.
Leicestershire County Council — 1961

A contractor submitted a tender which specified a completion of 18
months. The county architect, unknown to the contractor, decided that 30
months was a more appropriate contract period. Prior to the signing of

the contract, there were two meetings at which the contractor referred to his plans to complete the work according to a progress schedule in 18 months. It was held that the contractor was entitled to rectification on the grounds that the defendants were estopped by their conduct from saying that there was no mistake.

Scott v.
Avery — 1856

This case concerned an insurance policy which indicated that only arbitration proceedings were permissible in the event of a dispute occurring. It therefore sought to prohibit direct legal actions in the courts. It was held that this provision was valid. The majority of the standard forms of building contract contain arbitration provisions. This course of action is agreed to between the parties, who may consider arbitration more appropriate. If one of the parties wishes to hold to arbitration, he may apply for a stay of proceedings on the basis that the contract follows the *Scott* v. *Avery* principle. In practice, the courts in deciding whether to grant this are likely to take into consideration any hardship that may be caused.

Sutcliffe v.
Thackrah and Others — 1974

The facts of this case were that Mr Sutcliffe employed Thackrah and Others, a firm of architects, to design and supervise the construction of a house. During construction two certificates (Nos 9 and 10) were issued and duly paid by Mr Sutcliffe. Shortly afterwards the contract with the builders ended when the builders became insolvent and another firm completed the work.

It was then discovered that the two above-mentioned certificates had included defective work. Because it could not be recovered from the builders, Mr Sutcliffe sued the architects for his loss because of their negligence in issuing the certificates. The negligence was not due to a failure to detect the defective work, since one of the architects was aware of this; it was due to a failure to pass the information to the quantity surveyor who had valued it, assuming that it was in accordance with the contract.

The official referee who tried the case in arbitration, held that the architect was negligent and awarded damages to Mr Sutcliffe. The Court of Appeal reversed this decision but this was finally overruled by the House of Lords. It was held that the architect was discharging a duty under the contract between the parties, but that there was no dispute over the subject matter and so it could not be contended that he was acting in arbitration.

In order for quantity surveyors to safeguard themselves from possible repercussions in the future, they now include on their valuations words to the following effect: 'That the valuation assumes that the work is in accordance with the specification of materials and workmanship.' A quantity surveyor would clearly not include in a valuation work that was obviously defective, but the matter of quality control is more rightly the responsibility of the architect. The case of *Chambers* v. *Goldthorpe* was cited, but this was overruled by the House of Lords.

Trollope & Colls and *Holland and Hannan and Cubitts Ltd* v. *Atomic Power Construction* — 1962

The contractor tendered for work under a contract which included provisions for variations and fluctuations. After a delay of four months the contractor was requested to commence work upon the site. This request included a letter of intent to enter into a formal contract when the terms of the contract were settled. Substantial changes to the scheme had been notified to the contractor and this continued to occur until the terms of the contract were agreed 10 months later. The contractor therefore claimed that he should be paid on a *quantum meruit* basis for the work that had already been completed prior to the signing of the formal agreement. This he claimed was more equitable than on the basis of his original tender adjusted by variations, since at that time no contract was in existence.

It was held, however, that both parties had contemplated entering into a contract which would affect all the work associated with the contract. The contract was formulated in the light of the work going on at the time and it had therefore a retrospective effect.

Trollope & Colls Ltd v. *North Western Metropolitan Regional Hospital Board* — 1973

This was a very large building contract where the court of appeal reversed the decision of the trial judge; but the House of Lords confirmed the trial judge's opinion. The Hospital Board wanted the project completed in three phases, using three largely similar sets of conditions. Phase 1 was delayed by 59 weeks and the architect granted an extension of time by 47 weeks. Phase 3 was to start contractually six months after Phase 1 had received its certificate of practical completion. Phase 3 did, however, still retain its original completion date which then envisaged a 16-month contract rather than the previously accepted 30-month contract period.

In these circumstances, could the time for completion of Phase 3 be extended by the period of 47 weeks granted on Phase 1? Unexpectedly it was the contractor who suggested that it could not, but for his own advantage. The contractor professed to being able to complete in time, and they therefore called upon the Hospital Board to nominate their appropriate subcontractors. This they were unable to do. In this situation the contractors would require new prices to be agreed relevant to the prevailing date. The contractors therefore sought a declaration in the High Court that the date for completion of Phase 3 was unaffected by Phase 1 being behind schedule.

The decision was made in favour of the contractor on the basis that

330

the business efficacy of this large contract did not necessitate implying the kind of term the Board required. The House of Lords was not satisfied that the parties had overlooked the effect of delays on earlier phases, in fixing the completion date for Phase 3.

Tyrer v.
District Auditor for Monmouthshire — 1974

A firm of contractors who went into liquidation had been employed upon several contracts by a local authority. The local authority found that this firm had been overpaid on interim certificates. The district auditor established that overpayment was due to the negligence of the quantity surveyor, in accepting excessively high rates for work carried out and failing to check simple arithmetic. The auditor then surcharged the quantity surveyor for the sums that he was unable to recover from the liquidator. The quantity surveyor appealed on the grounds that he had undertaken his duties in the capacity of an arbitrator. The court, however, rejected this appeal stating that 'there was nothing to show that the appellant was in quasi-judicial position when carrying out his duties here'.

Victoria Laundry Ltd v.
Newman Ltd — 1948

This case provides an interesting contrast with the case of *Hadley* v. *Baxendale* above. The plaintiffs were launderers and dyers and required a large boiler to extend their plant and to help them win some lucrative contracts. A firm of engineers contracted to sell them such a boiler, but because of certain faults arising the delivery of the boiler was seriously delayed. The plaintiffs claimed damages. First, equivalent to the estimated loss of the increased profits the use of the boiler would have acquired for them; and second, the amount that they would have earned from dyeing contracts during the same period. The court held that the engineers were liable for the ordinary losses which they must have known from the particular circumstances. They were not liable in the second instance since this would have required special knowledge which they did not have.

Re Wilkinson ex parte Fowler — 1905

This contract allowed for the right to make direct payment to certain firms, where the main contractor defaulted or delayed in proper payment to them. The contractor became bankrupt and the employer decided to make payments out of the retentions owing to the contractor. It was held by the courts that such payments were valid against the trustee.

William Sindall v.
North West Thames Regional Health Authority — 1977

The main contractor introduced a bonus incentive scheme on a site in accordance with the principles recommended by the National Joint

Council for the Building Industry. The contract was on a fluctuations basis incorporating clause 31A. An increase in the basic rates of wages occurred and this, in a bonus scheme was a voluntary decision and not as an unavoidable consequence of following the obligatory rules or decisions, and the cost of its operation was therefore outside of the scope of clause 31A. This was in spite of the fact that once the contractor had introduced his bonus scheme on the basis of the NJCBI rules, he had to also pay the eventual increase.

Williams v.
Fitzmaurice — 1859

This involved the contractor in building a house in accordance with the drawings and specification supplied by the architect. The specification included a clause, 'that the contractor undertook to provide the whole of the materials necessary for the completion of the works and to perform all the works of every kind mentioned'. Floor boarding, although shown on the drawings, was not included in the specification. The contractor therefore refused to carry out this work unless it was paid for as extra works. It was held that the boarding was necessary and was therefore included in the contract price, even though it had been omitted from the specification.

Appendix B

Practice notes

JCT 80 Standard Form of Building Contract, Practice notes

The following practice notes have been issued by the Joint Contracts Tribunal for the *Standard Form of Building Contract*. These have been issued over a period of time since JCT 80 came into use. It is likely that additional practice notes will also be issued in the future to clarify other matters arising from the use of the contract. Some of the practice notes originated with the 1963 form, and have been adapted to suit the form that is now in general use. It should be noted, however, that the practice notes are not finally authoritative. They often deal with a practical application of the form, and contain material which will be included in future revisions to the form. Such notes, although they express only an opinion in legal terms, are considered to be based upon expert advice. They will not, however, have the same binding effect as the decisions from courts of law.

1. Sectional completion supplement.
2. Clauses 21, 22 and 30.3: Insurance provisions.
3. Clause 21.2: Insurance — liability, etc., of employer — provisional sum.
4. Clauses 5.2.2 and 5.4: Drawings — additional copies.
5. Clauses 30.3 and 16.2: Payment for off-site materials and goods.
6. Value added tax.
7. *Standard Form of Building Contract* for use with bills of approximate quantities.

8. Finance (No. 2) Act 1975 — statutory tax deduction scheme (clause 31).
9. Domestic subcontractors.
10. Nomination of subcontractors.
11. Employer/nominated subcontractor agreements (NSC/2 or NSC/2a).
12. Direct payment and final payment to nominated subcontractors.
13. Proposed nomination of a subcontractor not effected and renomination.
14. Variations and provisional sum work.
15. Nominated suppliers.
16. Extensions of time and liquidated damages.
17. Fluctuations.
18. Payment and retention.
19. Application and practice notes 9—18 to contracts in Scotland and subject to Scottish law.
20. Deciding on the appropriate form of JCT main contract.
21. The employer's position under the 1980 edition of the *Standard Form of Building Contract* compared to the 1963 edition.
22. The amendments to the Insurance and related liability provision 1986, and guide thereto.
23. Contract sum analysis.

Index